Paul's Gospel of Divine Self-Sacrifice

In this book, Paul K. Moser explains how self-sacrificial righteousness of a reparative kind is at the heart of Paul's gospel of God. He also shows how divine self-sacrifice authenticates that gospel via human reciprocity toward God in reconciliation. A basis for this reciprocity lies in a teaching of ancient Judaism that humans are to reciprocate toward God for the sake of an interpersonal relationship that is righteous and reconciled through voluntary self-sacrifice to God. Moser demonstrates that Paul's gospel calls for faith, including trust, in God as reciprocity in human self-sacrifice toward God. Although widely neglected by interpreters, this theme brings moral and evidential depth to Paul's good news of reparative redemption from God. Moser's study thus enables a new understanding of some of the controversial matters regarding Paul's message in a way that highlights the coherence and profundity of his message.

PAUL K. MOSER is Professor of Philosophy at Loyola University Chicago. He is the author of many books, most recently, *The Divine Goodness of Jesus* (2021), *Understanding Religious Experience* (2020), and *The God Relationship* (2017).

Paul's Gospel of Divine Self-Sacrifice

Righteous Reconciliation in Reciprocity

PAUL K. MOSER
Loyola University Chicago

CAMBRIDGE
UNIVERSITY PRESS

Shaftesbury Road, Cambridge CB2 8EA, United Kingdom

One Liberty Plaza, 20th Floor, New York, NY 10006, USA

477 Williamstown Road, Port Melbourne, VIC 3207, Australia

314–321, 3rd Floor, Plot 3, Splendor Forum, Jasola District Centre, New Delhi – 110025, India

103 Penang Road, #05–06/07, Visioncrest Commercial, Singapore 238467

Cambridge University Press is part of Cambridge University Press & Assessment, a department of the University of Cambridge.

We share the University's mission to contribute to society through the pursuit of education, learning and research at the highest international levels of excellence.

www.cambridge.org
Information on this title: www.cambridge.org/9781009249157

DOI: 10.1017/9781009249171

© Cambridge University Press & Assessment 2022

This publication is in copyright. Subject to statutory exception and to the provisions of relevant collective licensing agreements, no reproduction of any part may take place without the written permission of Cambridge University Press & Assessment.

First published 2022
First paperback edition 2025

A catalogue record for this publication is available from the British Library

ISBN   978-1-009-24918-8   Hardback
ISBN   978-1-009-24915-7   Paperback

Cambridge University Press & Assessment has no responsibility for the persistence or accuracy of URLs for external or third-party internet websites referred to in this publication and does not guarantee that any content on such websites is, or will remain, accurate or appropriate.

God who did not withhold his own Son, but gave him up for all of us, will he not with him also give us everything else?

Romans 8:32

Our paschal lamb, Christ, has been sacrificed.

1 Corinthians 5:7

Present your bodies as a living sacrifice, holy and acceptable to God, which is your spiritual worship.

Romans 12:1

Contents

	Preface	*page* ix
1	Gospel of Righteous Self-Sacrifice	1
	Gospel Summary	2
	A Righteous God	7
	Remedy in Reparative Sacrifice	11
	Human Reciprocity in Sacrifice	19
	Righteous Agitation in History	32
	Thy Kingdom Come	40
2	Faith Grounded in Self-Sacrifice	42
	Paul on What Counts	43
	Faith and Divine *Agapē*	50
	Agapē and the Law of God	59
	Access to God	67
	Dying into Faith	73
3	Incarnational Ethics of Self-Sacrifice	80
	Upholding the Law	81
	Law Incarnate	86
	End of Law	92
	Lawgiver First	98
	Desiderata	103
4	Hope and Fear toward Divine Self-Sacrifice	105
	Toward Grounded Hope	106
	Down Payment for Hope	113
	Variable Hope	117
	Hope and Fear	121

	Motivational Fear	126
	Fearing God	131
	Fear, Judgment, and Love	139
5	**Responsible Agency toward Divine Self-Sacrifice**	**151**
	Divine Purpose	151
	Grace for Voluntary Faith	155
	Divine Regret	164
	Voluntary Credit in Election	167
	Spirited Life for Co-sacrifice	180
6	**Assessing God's Gambit in Self-Sacrifice**	**184**
	God's Gambit in Redemption	184
	Redemptive Interpersonal Knowing	186
	Agapē in Knowing	190
	Righteousness in Spiritual Wisdom	197
	Traditional Natural Theology Omitted	204
	Scandal of Self-Sacrifice	208
	Resurrection through Self-Sacrifice	220
	Select Bibliography	230
	Index	235

Preface

Paul of Tarsus, a Jewish missionary for Jesus as God's Son, offered "good news" to all people, non-Jews and Jews alike. Whatever else he was, he was a man with a message of good news. We cannot adequately understand his good news, however, without sufficient understanding of the moral character of his God behind this good news. In addition, we cannot adequately understand the moral character of his God without due understanding of his God's distinctive character of self-sacrificial righteousness.

This book explains, motivates, and grounds Paul's good news in relation to divine self-sacrifice for humans and human reciprocity toward God in self-sacrifice. It thereby honors the Jewish background to his good news while correcting interpreters' widespread neglect of reciprocal self-sacrifice between God and humans in Paul's thought. In order to capture Paul's understanding of redemption, the book uses an undervalued idea of reparative, or repairing, self-sacrifice, aimed at a reconciled relationship in righteousness. It thus restores a central feature of Paul's thought that has not been adequately developed by scholarly and non-scholarly commentators on Paul.

Divine righteousness, in Paul's perspective, is goal-directed and active, not static or abstract. It actively agitates among humans, through an undeserved divine gift of self-sacrifice and other good interruptions in experience and conscience, to bring reconciliation with God to them. Such self-sacrifice aims, for a reparative purpose, at human reciprocity in sacrifice to God. It seeks to build a righteous community on this basis.

This book explains how reparative self-sacrificial righteousness is at the heart of Paul's gospel of God. It also explains how such sacrifice authenticates that gospel via human reciprocity toward God in reconciliation. We see the beginning of this reciprocity in the following divine command from ancient Judaism: "I am the Lord who brought you up from the land of Egypt, to be your God; you shall be holy, for I am holy" (Lev. 11:45, NRSV). According to this tradition, shared by Paul, humans are to reciprocate toward God for the sake of an interpersonal relationship that is righteous and reconciled through their voluntary self-sacrifice to God.

A key theme of this book is that Paul's gospel in his undisputed letters calls for faith, including trust, in God as reciprocity in human self-sacrifice toward God. Although widely neglected by Paul's interpreters, this theme has roots in the Jewish scriptures. It also brings important moral and motivational depth to Paul's good news of reparative redemption from God. The book's main topics under this theme are as follows: Gospel of Righteous Self-Sacrifice (Chapter 1); Faith Grounded in Self-Sacrifice (Chapter 2); Incarnational Ethics of Self-Sacrifice (Chapter 3); Hope and Fear toward Divine Self-Sacrifice (Chapter 4); Responsible Agency toward Divine Self-Sacrifice (Chapter 5); and Assessing God's Gambit in Self-Sacrifice (Chapter 6).

The expected reciprocity toward divine self-sacrifice is not just human imitation of God or Christ. It depends on humans' experience of God's redemptive action toward them and on their cooperative reliance on that experience for reciprocating divine self-sacrifice. Righteous self-sacrifice by humans thus includes willing obedience in response to God, that is, giving themselves, including their will, to God in response, against any contrary will. The relevant sacrifice, then, is no matter of mere ritual, external practice, physical suffering, or bodily death.

The book identifies Jesus in Gethsemane as a model of righteous self-sacrifice to God, in keeping with Paul's focus on such self-giving obedience to God in the willing death of Jesus (Phil. 2:8). Paul drew his notion of reparative self-sacrifice from his experience and his understanding of God's self-giving love in "the Son of God, who loved me and gave himself for me [παραδόντος ἑαυτὸν ὑπὲρ ἐμοῦ]" (Gal. 2:20, NRSV). The book illuminates this notion from Paul's understanding of divine self-sacrifice in the Jewish scriptures.

The self-sacrificing power of God, according to Paul, reflects and enacts divine righteousness. This righteousness, complete with distinctive "weapons" for what is good, is powerful toward introducing and sustaining divine goodness in the world, including the redemption of humans. This book explains how such righteousness contributes, in Paul's thought, to the reparative redemption of humans in divine–human reconciliation through self-sacrifice. It identifies how faith and hope in God, according to Paul, depend on a distinctive kind of reciprocated self-sacrifice. Paul finds a practical pattern in "dying with Christ" into obedient life with God. Such dying includes a responsive repentance in turning from an anti-God will to God in cooperative trust and obedience. The book explains how this theme informs Paul's ethics, individual and social, and his distinctive approach to the law of God.

The book finds two main themes underlying Paul's gospel of righteousness: (i) a theme from the book of Isaiah that portrays divine righteousness to include "salvation" and "deliverance" by God for humans (Isa. 46:13; 51:5, 6, 8; 61:8), as well as divine vindication of this righteousness (Isa. 41:2; 61:3, 7; cf. Psalm 24:5) and (ii) a theme, captured in this book's opening quotations, indicating that redemption by God includes divine self-sacrifice and an expected response in kind from humans. The book also suggests, on the basis of Romans 3:25, that Paul understood divine righteousness itself to include self-sacrifice for the sake of redeemed life with God. The role of divine self-sacrifice coupled with human reciprocity in Paul's gospel has been inadequately explained by contemporary interpreters. This book corrects that omission by giving due attention to reparative atonement in Paul, courtesy of his Jewish heritage. It thus lets Paul be Paul.

What of the "good news" in Paul's gospel of righteousness? The book explains how God's giving up his beloved Son to death in self-sacrifice is, according to Paul, God's righteous way to disable the powers of sin and death and thereby to offer all people reconciled life with God, in God's kingdom family. Such life survives the powers of sin and death that hinder divine–human reconciliation. (Paul thinks of sin as stemming from human obstacles to reconciliation to God, particularly from lack of trust and obedience toward God.) People still die on earth, according to Paul, but they can die under the reparative power of the divine self-sacrifice in Christ.

God vindicates Christ and God's people, Paul holds, with a powerful gift of resurrected life that survives sin and death. As a result, people can live under the power of the good news of God, without domination from sin and death. That is, they can live with God in the righteous freedom of reconciliation intended by God, with a benefit of lasting resurrected life. Paul's focus on righteous self-sacrifice, then, is for the sake of resurrection life with God, including in present life with God's family of faith.

The book explains how Paul's good news avoids being a fairy tale, courtesy of its evidential grounding in human experience of God. This experience, being morally robust, is distinctive in being sensitive to the will and values of a person. It arises from the self-presentation of God's moral character of righteous *agapē* to humans, including in conscience. It also seeks human cooperation in righteous self-sacrifice, for the sake of bringing about God's will. The absence of such cooperation thus would make divine self-presentation pointless relative to that goal. This consideration accounts for how the evidence for Paul's good news can be hidden, or veiled, at times from some people but experienced by others. It thus bears on the reality of diverse human responses to his good news.

The book's approach to Paul's gospel, as the center of his thought, enables us to see its evidential and moral resilience. It saves Paul from fideism and dogmatism, and it highlights the evidential and moral depth of his good news. The book thus recommends that we give Paul's message due attention in the light of divine righteousness and its use of reparative self-sacrifice for the sake of divine–human reconciliation. The result promises to be an illuminating interaction with Paul's good news for any people in need of such news.

This book has benefited from comments and suggestions from many people. For constructive help, I thank Fred Aquino, Simon Babbs, David Bukenhofer, Tom Carson, Todd Long, Chad Meister, Aeva Munro, Ben Nasmith, Clinton Neptune, and Aaron Simmons. I also thank students in my classes at Loyola University, Chicago, and various anonymous referees. For excellent help at Cambridge University Press, as usual, I thank Beatrice Rehl, publisher. I also thank Dr. Trent Hancock for his careful copyediting of the book.

Parts of the book make use of revised materials from some of my recent essays: "Paul the Apostle," in *The Oxford Handbook of the Epistemology of Theology*, eds. William Abraham and Fred Aquino (Oxford University Press, 2017); "Christian Philosophy and Christ Crucified: Fragmentary Theory in Scandalous Power," in *Christian Philosophy: Conceptions, Continuations, and Challenges*, ed. J. Aaron Simmons (Oxford University Press, 2019); "God as Righteous Agitator: Grounding Biblical Theology," *Biblical Theology Bulletin* 51 (2021); "Grounded Hope in God: Epiphany and Promise," *Theology Today* 79 (2022); "The Fear of the Lord: The Beginning of Reconciliation," *Irish Theological Quarterly* 87 (2022).

I Gospel of Righteous Self-Sacrifice

> I am not ashamed of the gospel; it is the power of God for salvation to everyone who has faith, to the Jew first and also to the Greek.
>
> Romans 1:16

The apostle Paul was a former Pharisee working in the wake of Jesus as God's Messiah. He was, by his self-avowed divine calling, a Jewish–Christian missionary and apostle announcing good news, a gospel (εὐαγγέλιον), from God for the salvation of all people into God's "family of faith" (Gal. 3:26, 6:10). His undisputed letters reveal that the noun "εὐαγγέλιον" is one of his favorite words, used forty-eight times, while the verb "to announce the gospel" (εὐαγγελίζεσθαι) is used nineteen times.[1]

Our attention to Paul's use of "gospel" will clarify what he thought of himself, his mission, and more importantly, God. It also will lead us to see the key role of divine righteousness and self-sacrifice in his gospel, including self-sacrifice for its recipients. We begin with a summary of Paul's gospel in his Epistle to the Romans.

---

[1] Paul's undisputed letters providing the focus of this book are 1 Thessalonians, 1 and 2 Corinthians, Galatians, Romans, and Philippians. I thus do not give primary attention to Ephesians, Colossians, 2 Thessalonians, or the Pastoral letters. In the latter group, Colossians has a serious chance of originating with Paul, but I do not push that controversial idea. Out of due caution, I also avoid using Acts as a primary source for Paul's history or theology. For a careful presentation of the relevant evidence, see Werner Georg Kümmel, *Introduction to the New Testament*, rev. ed., trans. H. C. Kee (Nashville, TN: Abingdon Press, 1975), pp. 255–366; and Raymond E. Brown, *An Introduction to the New Testament*, ABRL (New York: Doubleday, 1997), Part III. On some of the conflicts between Acts and Paul's letters, see Jürgen Becker, *Paul: Apostle to the Gentiles*, trans. O. C. Dean Jr. (Louisville, KY: Westminster, 1993), pp. 12–16.

GOSPEL SUMMARY

Paul's introduction to his Epistle to the Romans summarizes his role for "the gospel":

> Paul, a servant of Jesus Christ, called to be an apostle, set apart for the gospel [εὐαγγέλιον] of God, which he promised beforehand through his prophets in the holy scriptures, the gospel concerning his Son, who was descended from David according to the flesh and was declared to be Son of God with power according to the spirit of holiness by resurrection from the dead, Jesus Christ our Lord, through whom we have received grace and apostleship to bring about the obedience of faith among all the Gentiles for the sake of his name.
> (Rom. 1:1–5, NRSV here and in subsequent Biblical translations, unless otherwise noted)

Paul's talk of "the gospel of God," for which he is "set apart," connotes the gospel from God. This is indicated by his mention of God having promised it through the prophets in the Jewish scriptures (see also Gal. 1:1, 12, 3:8). God, in Paul's perspective, set him apart as an apostle to preach the gospel and to build churches on its basis, particularly among the Gentiles.[2]

In an earlier letter, Paul mentions his having received the gospel and his handing it on to others:

> I handed on to you as of first importance what I in turn had received: that Christ died for our sins in accordance with the

---

[2] I thus find it misleading for Luke Timothy Johnson to suggest that "the 'Paul' of the canonical letters is ... a pastor and moral teacher. His primary concern is with the formation of character among his readers." See Johnson, *The Canonical Paul, Vol. 2: Interpreting Paul* (Grand Rapids, MI: Eerdmans, 2021), p. 6. Paul's gospel, we shall see, calls for something beyond mere "formation of character" as the primary concern. It calls for a distinctive relation of faith in God on the basis of his gospel. J. Christiaan Beker claims that "Paul is essentially an *interpreter* of the gospel." See Beker, *The Triumph of God: The Essence of Paul's Thought* (Minneapolis, MN: Fortress Press. 1990), p. 118. I suspect that Paul would prefer a self-description that includes his obedient preaching of the gospel.

scriptures, and that he was buried, and that he was raised on the third day in accordance with the scriptures, and that he appeared to Cephas, then to the twelve. Then he appeared to more than five hundred brothers and sisters at one time, most of whom are still alive, though some have died. Then he appeared to James, then to all the apostles. Last of all, as to one untimely born, he appeared also to me. For I am the least of the apostles, unfit to be called an apostle, because I persecuted the church of God. Whether then it was I or they, so we proclaim [κηρύσσομεν] and so you have come to believe.

(1 Cor. 15:3–9, 11)

Paul has in mind the proclaiming of "the gospel" (1 Cor. 15:1–2), and he acknowledges that he "had received" it. A natural question is: Received it from whom?

Paul reports to the Galatian Christians that his initial preaching of his gospel did not result from his conferring with other humans. "When God, who had set me apart before I was born and called me through his grace, was pleased to reveal his Son to me, so that I might proclaim him among the Gentiles, I did not confer with any human being, nor did I go up to Jerusalem to those who were already apostles before me" (Gal. 1:15–17). God, according to Paul's report, is the source of his preaching the gospel, through his revealing Christ to him. Three years after his initial preaching, however, he went up to Jerusalem: "Then after three years I did go up to Jerusalem to visit Cephas and stayed with him fifteen days; but I did not see any other apostle except James the Lord's brother" (Gal. 1:18–19). He does not specify, however, what he learned from Peter or James.

Paul continues his autobiographical remarks: "Then after fourteen years I went up again to Jerusalem with Barnabas, taking Titus along with me. I went up in response to a revelation. Then I laid before them (though only in a private meeting with the acknowledged leaders) the gospel that I proclaim among the Gentiles, in order to make sure that I was not running, or had not run, in vain" (Gal. 2:1–2). This remark calls for a distinction between Paul's source for his gospel and the endorsement of his gospel by the leaders in Jerusalem. He adds: "When James and Cephas and John, who were acknowledged pillars, recognized the grace that had been given to me, they gave to Barnabas and me the right hand of fellowship, agreeing that we should go to the Gentiles and they to the circumcised" (Gal. 2:9). Paul does not say that the leaders in Jerusalem are the source of his gospel, but he did seek and get their endorsement of his gospel and his Gentile mission. Perhaps he received historical information about the ministry of Jesus from them, but as suggested, he does not say.

Paul received his gospel from God, by his account, although he refrains from explaining in detail how this occurred. He states, as noted, that "God was pleased to reveal his Son to me, so that I might proclaim him among the Gentiles" (Gal. 1:15–16). He also remarks: "I did not receive [the gospel] from a human source, nor was I taught it, but I received it through a revelation of Jesus Christ" (Gal. 1:12; cf. 1 Cor. 1:17; Acts 9:5–6). In a different context, Paul reports: "Last of all, as to one untimely born, [Christ] appeared [ὤφθη] also to me" (1 Cor. 15:8). As a result, he asks a rhetorical question: "Have I not seen [ἑόρακα] Jesus our Lord?" (1 Cor. 9:1). Paul does not confirm all of the details of his divine calling reported in Acts 9, but he does concur with its representing him as "an instrument ... chosen to bring [God's] name before Gentiles and kings and before the people of Israel" (Acts 9:15; cf. Rom. 11:13).

Paul does not specify in his letters the exact information he received for his gospel through "a revelation of Jesus Christ." As far as our evidence indicates, doing so would not have served his purposes in writing to various churches. In addition, he could have discussed any relevant details during his visits with the churches. It can be misleading, however, to think of this revelation as prompting his "conversion" to the God served by Jesus.[3] That God, according to Jesus and Paul, is the God of the Jewish scriptures, and Paul was

---

[3] I thus recommend due caution regarding the language of "conversion" found in, for instance, Alan F. Segal, *Paul the Convert* (New Haven, CT: Yale University Press, 1990), especially chs. 2 and 3.

committed to that God at the time of his calling to preach the gospel, whatever the details of that calling, particularly regarding Jesus.

Paul's calling through "a revelation of Jesus Christ" gave him, at least by his assessment, a corrected, more profound understanding of God. It convinced him that the God of the Jewish scriptures aimed to redeem people, Gentiles as well as Jews, in accordance with the life-giving ministry of Jesus. That was a dramatic change from his earlier zealous role as a Pharisee who "persecuted the church of God" (Gal. 1:13; 1 Cor. 15:9; cf. Gal. 1:23; Phil. 3:6). His earlier support for such persecution assumed that Jesus was neither Lord nor Messiah but at best an imposter. Perhaps one may talk of Paul's "conversion" to Jesus as Lord and Messiah from God, but he puts the emphasis on his calling, through a revelation of Christ, to be an apostle who preaches the gospel from God.

Paul affirms, as suggested in Romans 1, that the gospel from God was active before the arrival of Christ, in the life of Abraham. He says: "The scripture, foreseeing that God would justify the Gentiles by faith, declared the gospel beforehand to Abraham, saying, 'All the Gentiles shall be blessed in you'" (Gal. 3:8; cf. Gen. 12:3; Rom. 4:13). This gospel is inherently universal in its intended scope, going to Gentiles as well as Jews. Paul, as suggested, saw a seminal mission for himself as an "apostle to the Gentiles" in taking God's good news to them (Gal. 1:15–16; 1 Cor. 1:17; Rom. 1:14–16, 11:13). As indicated, he found this mission foreshadowed in the Jewish scriptures.

Paul saw the gospel at work not only in relation to Abraham but also in connection with the book of Isaiah. He remarks: "How are they to proclaim him [the Lord] unless they are sent? As it is written, 'How beautiful are the feet of those who bring good news!' But not all have obeyed the good news; for Isaiah says, 'Lord, who has believed our message?'" (Rom. 10:15–16; cf. Isa. 53:1). The book of Isaiah relates the good news to salvation from God, as does Paul: "How beautiful upon the mountains are the feet of the messenger who announces peace, who brings good news, who announces salvation, who says to Zion, 'Your God reigns'" (Isa. 52:7; cf. Rom. 1:16). So, Paul thought of his "gospel of God" as having its ultimate source in God, particularly in God's effort of salvation for humans. He saw this gospel and this effort at work in the Jewish scriptures.[4]

The Gospels of Mark and Matthew portray Jesus as preaching good news from God, regarding God's arriving kingdom (Mark 1:15; Matt. 4:23), and the Gospel of Luke represents Jesus as applying the following passage from the book of Isaiah (61:1) to himself:

> The Spirit of the Lord is upon me,
> because he has anointed me
> to bring good news [εὐαγγελίσασθαι] to the poor.
> He has sent me to proclaim release to the captives
> and recovery of sight to the blind,
> to let the oppressed go free,
> to proclaim the year of the Lord's favor.
>
> *(Luke 4:18–19)*

Paul introduced his gospel in the wake of Jesus, but he does not cite any historical saying from Jesus to authorize his gospel. Instead, as suggested, he invokes God as its source, and he finds support in some of the Jewish scriptures.

Paul's gospel of God is, by his understanding throughout his letters, the "gospel of Christ" (1 Thess. 3:2; Gal. 1:7; Phil. 1:27; 1 Cor. 9:12; 2 Cor. 2:12, 9:13, 10:14; Rom. 1:3, 15:19). He sometimes uses "the word [ὁ λόγος] (of God)" synonymously with "the gospel" (1 Thess. 1:6, 2:13; 1 Cor. 1:17), and this use typically brings his focus to what God has done and is doing through Christ for human salvation. This divine effort, according to Paul, gets its importance from God's role in the death and resurrection of Christ on behalf of humans. So, Paul refers to the God of his gospel as the God "who raised Jesus our Lord from the dead, who was handed over to death for our trespasses and was raised for our justification" (Rom. 4:24–25).

---

[4] Given such passages as Romans 1:16, 3:29–31, and Phil. 2:9–11, John G. Gager misrepresents Paul in claiming that he limits the focus of his gospel of God's work in Christ to Gentiles. See Gager, *Reinventing Paul* (New York: Oxford University Press, 2000).

Paul offers his gospel as irreducible to mere information about God, because he holds that it includes divine power: "I am not ashamed of the gospel; it is the power of God for salvation to everyone who has faith, to the Jew first and also to the Greek" (Rom. 1:16). He makes a related claim about the gospel in an earlier letter: "Christ did not send me to baptize but to proclaim the gospel, and not with eloquent wisdom, so that the cross of Christ might not be emptied of its power. For the message [ὁ λόγος] about the cross is foolishness to those who are perishing, but to us who are being saved it is the power of God" (1 Cor. 1:17–18). How could Paul's missionary good news be "the power of God for salvation"? We need to clarify that matter in the light of divine righteousness.

A RIGHTEOUS GOD

According to Paul, "in [the gospel] the righteousness [δικαιοσύνη] of God is revealed [ἀποκαλύπτεται] through faith for faith; as it is written, 'The one who is righteous [δίκαιος] will live by faith'" (Rom. 1:17, citing Hab. 2:4; cf. Gal. 3:11). We should let Paul's remarks and the material he cites clarify, at least at the start, his understanding of "the righteousness of God" and of how it "is revealed" (present tense) through faith. This interpretive strategy is more reliable than drawing from linguistic usage prior to Paul that may not bear on his understanding. The New English Bible makes an important suggestion in translating Paul's talk of righteousness in Romans 1:17 in terms of "God's way of righting wrong." We shall see that this captures part of Paul's thinking about divine righteousness.

Paul's citation of the prophet Habakkuk is important. The original context of the passage relates the relevant kind of righteousness to God's moral character of being "pure," in contrast with "evil" and "wrongdoing." Habakkuk proclaims to God:

> Your eyes are too pure [καθαρὸς, LXX] to behold evil [πονηρά, LXX], and you cannot look on wrongdoing;
> why do you look on the treacherous,

and are silent when the wicked swallow
those more righteous than they?

(Hab. 1:13)

This is a statement about God's purity as righteous moral character, particularly God's being too morally pure to condone any evil or wrongdoing and thus any corresponding unrighteousness.

Habakkuk identifies a clash between God as morally pure or righteous and humans who are unrighteous or morally treacherous. Paul would have been aware of this contrast in the original context of Habakkuk 2:4. Sam K. Williams approaches what Paul has in mind: "Although, on the basis of Rom 1:16-17, we cannot say exactly what Paul 'means' by *dikaiosynē theou*, I think we can say that he intends for this phrase to bring to mind that aspect of God's nature which we might point to with such additional expressions as God's steadfast adherence to what is right and fitting, his constancy, his trustworthiness, and his readiness to save."[5] Paul has in mind the righteous character of God and not merely God's acting in a righteous way.

The factor of God's moral character is explicit not only in Habakkuk but also in Romans 3 with its emphasis on the self-manifestation of the righteousness of God (δικαιοσύνη θεοῦ) (see Rom. 3:21, 25, 26). Paul assumes that the manifestation arises from God's righteous character, as in Habakkuk. Apart from having a righteous character, God would not be in a position to self-manifest righteousness with integrity.

Paul thinks of God's faithfulness as an important factor in divine righteousness. He writes:

---

[5] Sam K. Williams, "The 'Righteousness of God' in Romans," *Journal of Biblical Literature* 99 (1980), 263. Ernst Käsemann, in emphasizing God's saving *activity*, neglects the previous quotation from Habakkuk 1:13 (in the context of Paul's quotation from Habakkuk); he thus gives inadequate attention to the role of God's righteous *character* for Paul. See his "'The Righteousness of God' in Paul," in *New Testament Questions of Today*, trans. W. J. Montague (London: SCM Press, 1969), pp. 168–82.

> What if some were unfaithful? Will their faithlessness nullify the faithfulness of God? By no means! Although everyone is a liar, let God be proved true, as it is written, "So that you [God] may be justified [δικαιωθῇς] in your words, and prevail in your judging."
>
> *(Rom. 3:3–4, citing Psalm 51:4)*

Paul's appeal to God's being "justified" in God's words assumes that God has a moral character of righteousness and faithfulness. His talk of the faithfulness of God suggests divine loyalty to God's promises and moral character of righteousness. So, Paul affirms the "righteousness of God" (θεοῦ δικαιοσύνην) in the next verse (Rom. 3:5).

It is inadvisable to understand God's faithfulness and righteousness just in terms of God's loyalty to divine covenants. Divine covenants can be variable and transitory in ways that God's character of faithful righteousness is not.[6] God's righteous moral character, according to Paul, includes "the riches of [God's] kindness and forbearance and patience," and it aims to lead people to turn to God in faithful obedience (Rom. 2:4–5).

Paul, as suggested, cites the last clause of the following remark from Habakkuk: "Look at the proud! Their spirit is not right in them, but the righteous [δίκαιος, LXX] live by their faith" (Hab. 2:4). Living by faith in God, according to Paul, is the fitting response to God's good news, just as it was the fitting response for Abraham to God and the divine promise to bless all nations (Rom. 4:16–17). Faith accommodates, via trust and cooperation, God's freely offered remedy for what Paul deems the human predicament of ongoing harm by two powers: sin and death. The remedy includes not only divine forgiveness but also divine power for moral improvement, in relation to God, for cooperative humans.

---

[6] For discussion of the relation between divine righteousness and covenants in ancient Israel, see Ernest W. Nicholson, *God and His People: Covenant and Theology in the Old Testament* (Oxford: Oxford University Press, 1986), pp. 201–17; and Michael F. Bird, *The Saving Righteousness of God* (Milton Keynes: Paternoster, 2006), pp. 35–39. It would be a mistake to assume that divine righteousness in the Hebrew Bible functions only in the context of a covenant.

Sin, according to Paul, arises from a human deficiency regarding trust in God: "Whatever does not proceed from faith is sin" (Rom. 14:23). This deficiency occurs in people who "did not honor [God] as God or give thanks to him" (Rom. 1:21). So, it is not just a matter of performing wrong actions, even though sins as wrong actions typically accompany a broader human state of sin. Paul identifies sin as an obstruction to righteousness by God's standard for every human, affirming that "all [humans], both Jews and Greeks, are under the power of sin" (Rom. 3:9). He remarks: "All who have sinned apart from the [Mosaic] law will also perish apart from the law, and all who have sinned under the law will be judged by the law" (Rom. 2:12).

Paul adds that, owing to sin, "no human will be justified in God's sight by deeds prescribed by the law" (Rom. 3:20). A debilitating problem here is that "all have sinned and fall short of the glory of God" (Rom. 3:23; cf. Rom. 11:32), and this problem cannot be reduced to relations between human social groups, such as Jews and Gentiles. God is in the mix for a redemptive purpose, by Paul's lights.

Even if some people do not "see fit to acknowledge God," according to Paul, they still can be responsible for sin by God's standard for righteousness (Rom. 1:28–32). By that standard, Paul would affirm that the following applies even to those people: "The wages of sin is death" (Rom. 6:23; cf. Rom. 5:12, 6:21, 7:13). He has in mind sin not as an isolated act of wrongdoing but as having "presented your members as slaves to impurity and to greater and greater iniquity" (Rom. 6:19). The "impurity" in question has the defect of not being willingly guided by God's righteousness. Paul thus talks of "when you were slaves of sin, you were free in regard to righteousness" (Rom. 6:20), as divine righteousness was not then an accepted guide for the people in question. Paul's good news aims to attract people to God's righteousness as an ongoing guide, and that prospect calls for a remedy for sin.

REMEDY IN REPARATIVE SACRIFICE

The remedy for the human predicament of sin, in Paul's gospel, comes from God. It arises from a divine gift of self-sacrifice, intended for human redemption through righteous mercy found in Christ. The gift, undeserved by humans, aims to repair the problem of sin that alienates humans from God and divine righteousness. Paul sums this up: "They [all who have sinned] are now justified by his grace as a gift [δωρεὰν τῇ αὐτοῦ χάριτι], through the redemption [ἀπολυτρώσεως] that is in Christ Jesus, whom God put forward as a sacrifice of atonement [ἱλαστήριον] by his blood, effective through faith. He did this to show his righteousness, because in his divine forbearance he had passed over the sins previously committed" (Rom. 3:24–25). The undeserved gift of a remedy is thus in divine self-sacrifice as a costly offering aimed at repairing humans by their righteous redemption through Christ.

Paul thinks of Jesus as having an active role of self-sacrifice in the divine self-giving for human redemption. This is clear from his understanding of Jesus's remarks at the Last Supper: "I received from the Lord what I also handed on to you, that the Lord Jesus on the night when he was betrayed took a loaf of bread, and when he had given thanks, he broke it and said, 'This is my body that is for you. Do this in remembrance of me'. In the same way he took the cup also, after supper, saying, 'This cup is the new covenant in my blood. Do this, as often as you drink it, in remembrance of me'" (1 Cor. 11:23–25).[7] Paul sees an active intentional role for Jesus in giving himself in death "for you." According to Paul, Jesus "loved me and gave himself for me"

---

[7] On this passage and its historical setting, see Joseph A. Fitzmyer, *First Corinthians*, AYB (New Haven, CT: Yale University Press, 2008), pp. 435–48. On historical evidence regarding the origin of understanding the death of Jesus as sacrificial, see James D. G. Dunn, "When Did the Understanding of Jesus' Death as an Atoning Sacrifice First Emerge?," in *Israel's God and Rebecca's Children*, eds. D. B. Capes et al. (Waco, TX: Baylor University Press, 2007), pp. 169–81. I suspect the historical origin is with Jesus, particularly at the Last Supper.

(Gal. 2:20), on behalf of God's redemptive intervention. This is an active intentional role for Jesus in self-sacrifice for God.

Reparative self-sacrifice aimed at redemption by God does not guarantee its being cooperatively received by humans or even seriously considered by them. It does, however, provide a unique offering aimed at attracting humans to cooperate in being led by God in righteousness. As Paul says: "All who are led by the Spirit of God are children of God" (Rom. 8:14). He has in mind being led in a righteous relationship with God as a faithful child of God, after the model of Jesus yielding to God as Abba.[8] The idea of divine leading in righteousness for God's people has a distinguished history, including that of Psalm 23: "He leads me in paths of righteousness for his name's sake" (Psalm 23:3, RSV).

The reparative intention of the cross of Christ is at the center of Paul's thought, even though it is neglected by some commentators. Peter T. Forsyth points us in the right direction in proposing that the death of Christ is motivated by "solidary reparation" whereby Christ self-identifies with humans for the sake of "robbing sin of its power to prevent communion with God."[9] He rightly seeks an account that portrays Christ's death as having intended "moral results on the soul."[10] I prefer talk of a "reparative sacrifice," however, because it fits better with Paul's thinking in Romans, and it enables us to focus, along with Paul, on how the divine self-sacrifice seeks to repair the human predicament through uncoerced divine leading in righteousness. Reparative self-sacrifice by God, in Paul's thought, is required by divine self-giving *agapē* toward humans, and such *agapē* is integral to divine righteousness.

Paul confirms a theme of reparative sacrifice in his following remark: "For our sake he [God] made him [Christ] to be sin who knew

---

[8] For an attempt to clarify this model, see Paul K. Moser, *The Divine Goodness of Jesus: Impact and Response* (Cambridge: Cambridge University Press, 2021), ch. 3.
[9] Peter T. Forsyth, *The Work of Christ* (London: Hodder and Stoughton, 1910), p. 164; cf. pp. 223, 225–26.
[10] Forsyth, *The Work of Christ*, p.182.

no sin, so that in him we might become the righteousness of God" (2 Cor. 5:21). God thus put forth Christ at the cross to deal with sin, for the sake of enabling human righteousness in relation to God. Indifference to righteousness, then, will obscure the center of Paul's gospel. Divine righteousness aims to repair the human predicament of its failure in righteousness and its resulting failure in suitably relating to God. It thus seeks to satisfy the divine requirement of righteousness among humans, including in their relating to God. In this regard, the self-giving death of Christ intends to be a reparative sacrifice, but Paul does not say that it satisfies a divine requirement of punishment.

The NRSV and NIV translation of "ἱλαστήριον" as "sacrifice of atonement" in Romans 3:25 is commendable and better than its competitors. Avoiding an occupational hazard in translation and exegesis, it does not over-interpret Paul, beyond our evidence, with talk of "the mercy seat" from Exodus 25:17 and Leviticus 16:2.[11] Similarly, it does not suggest that Christ had to "propitiate" or absorb divine anger with his death, particularly as if God and Christ had diverging motives toward the cross or even as if God had to "self-propitiate."[12] If Paul had wanted to refer to the mercy seat (say, with use of the definite article, as does Hebrews 9:5) or to Christ's propitiating God (say, with an explicit connection), he could have done so clearly. Over-interpreting here would detract from Paul's purpose in referring to Christ as a sacrifice of atonement for righteous redemption. We need to clarify that purpose, with special attention to Paul's remarks in their context, rather than in relation to sweeping claims about the meaning of Greek or corresponding Hebrew terms.

---

[11] A number of recent commentators over-interpret in this way, including Joseph A. Fitzmyer, *Romans*, AB (New York: Doubleday, 1993), p. 350; Morna D. Hooker, *Not Ashamed of the Gospel* (Carlisle: Paternoster, 1994); pp. 43–44; and Arland J. Hultgren, *Paul's Letter to the Romans* (Grand Rapids, MI: Eerdmans, 2011), pp. 157, 662–75.

[12] For a proposal of divine "self-propitiation," see Frances Young, *Sacrifice and the Death of Christ* (Philadelphia: Westminster Press, 1975), pp. 93–95. See also Young, *The Use of Sacrificial Ideas in Greek Christian Writers from the New Testament to John Chrysostom*, PMS (Cambridge, MA: Philadelphia Patristic Foundation, 1979), pp. 204–11.

Paul holds that God judges and inflicts wrath toward human sin (Rom. 3:5–6), adding that the ultimate aim, stemming from righteousness, is to show mercy to all people (Rom. 11:32). He does not portray God, however, as judging or inflicting wrath toward Christ on the cross, even given Galatians 3:13 and Romans 8:3. He holds that Christ, through his justifying death, saves people from divine wrath (Rom. 5:9; 1 Thess. 5:9–10), but it does not follow that this wrath was redirected to Christ on the cross. Some commentators read such a view of divine wrath and propitiation into Romans 3:25, but the needed evidence is not there regarding Paul's intended meaning.[13]

As Vincent Taylor notes: "Romans 3:25 in no way suggests that Christ died to appease the wrath of God; it does not teach a doctrine of vicarious punishment .... The main question with which Paul is concerned is how God can be recognized as righteous and at the same time as one who declares righteous believers in Christ."[14] Paul does not say that God had left the sins committed beforehand "unpunished," as the NIV and the original NASB translations over-interpret Paul's language. We thus shall refrain from over-interpreting Paul here in a way that goes beyond our actual evidence for his intentions.

God could prove divine righteousness after passing over past sins, we shall see, without putting the focus on divine punishment. Instead of relying on a notion of divine propitiation or self-propitiation, Paul suggests a kind of divine self-vindication whereby God satisfies the divine standard of righteousness in redemption. He reports that God, through the redemption of humans in Christ, aims

---

[13] In support of reading divine wrath and propitiation in to Romans 3:25, see Leon Morris, *The Cross in the New Testament* (Grand Rapids, MI: Eerdmans, 1965), pp. 225–26; C. E. B. Cranfield, *A Critical and Exegetical Commentary on the Epistle to the Romans*, ICC (Edinburgh: T&T Clark, 1975), vol. 1, pp. 214–16; Thomas Schreiner, *Romans*, BECNT (Grand Rapids, MI: Baker Academic, 1998), pp. 191–92; and I. Howard Marshall, *Aspects of Atonement* (Milton Keynes: Paternoster, 2007), pp. 47–48.

[14] Vincent Taylor, "A Great Text Reconsidered [Romans 3:25]," in Taylor, *New Testament Essays* (London: Epworth Press, 1970), p. 137.

"to prove at the present time that he himself is righteous" (Rom. 3:26; cf. Rom. 3:4, 8:33).[15]

Paul is clear about two features of the sacrificial death of Christ. First, it is "for us" (1 Thess. 5:9–10; Gal. 3:13; 2 Cor. 5:14; Rom. 5:6, 8, 8:32). Second, it is "for our sins" (Gal. 1:3–4; 1 Cor. 15:3; Rom. 4:25). These provisions for us, in Paul's thinking, could not have been provided by us, given our inadequacies before God. It does not follow, however, that Christ died instead of, or in place of, humans, according to Paul.[16] He could have expressed such an idea of substitution clearly with his use of prepositions (such as "ἀντί"), but he does not. In addition, the followers of Christ still die a physical death, and they still die to sin, in Paul's perspective; so, there is no idea of substitution there, strictly speaking. Even if the death of Christ saves people from their sins and even from perishing irreversibly, this does not entail that the saving depends on substitution in Christ's death. At most it entails that his death figured as a central means in this saving. We shall try to clarify this means without over-interpreting or otherwise misrepresenting Paul.

A notion of Christ's representative death to be shared, or participated in, by other humans helps to clarify Paul's perspective, and it can include a sacrificial component. He says of Christ: "We are convinced that one has died for all; therefore, all have died" (2 Cor. 5:14; cf. Rom. 6:10–11; Phil. 3:10). This kind of representative death does not depend on vicarious punishment by God, that is, on God's punishing Christ, directly or indirectly, instead of humans. Similarly, it does not rely on a notion of Christ's death as something that humans deserved to undergo but were spared by Christ's death. In addition, it

---

[15] For a classic wide-ranging treatment of divine self-vindication, see Peter T. Forsyth, *The Justification of God* (London: Duckworth, 1916).

[16] Here I dissent from the interpretations of Paul on substitutionary atonement in, for example, Marshall, *Aspects of Atonement*, ch. 2; and Simon Gathercole, *Defending Substitution: An Essay on Atonement in Paul*, ASBT (Grand Rapids, MI: Baker Academic, 2015).

does not entail that Christ died in the place of humans. Paul does not speak in such terms, in contrast with many later theologians.

We get some clarification from the following remark by Paul: "You know the generous act of our Lord Jesus Christ, that though he was rich, yet for your sakes he became poor, so that by his poverty you might become rich" (2 Cor. 8:9; cf. 2 Cor. 5:21). Morna D. Hooker has defended a notion of interchange here that does not rely on substitution or vicarious punishment:

> Galatians 3:13 and 2 Corinthians 5:21 are both statements of what some of us have described – for lack of a more adequate term – as an "interchange" between Christ and the believer. Christ is identified with our condition, in order that we may be identified with him, and so share in what he is. What Paul understood by this was expressed brilliantly by Irenaeus, in the classic summary: "Christ became what we are, in order that we might become what he is."[17]

The death of Christ, according to Paul, stands for others in some sense, and I have suggested a reparative sacrificial component compatible with interchange. Even given ideas of representation, sacrifice, and interchange, however, we need to explain how we are to be motivated to yield to the divine righteousness found in Christ's death. Paul, we shall see, has a definite view on this matter.

An important part of the suggested representative sense is Christ's obedient, self-giving death as a practical model for relating obediently to God, even in suffering and dying, with the emphasis on shared obedience to God (Phil 2:5–8, 3:10). Markus Barth points in the right direction: "The sacrifice of Christ is not an alternative to complete obedience to God and total love for humans. It is their very sum

---

[17] Morna D. Hooker, "On Becoming the Righteousness of God: Another Look at 2 Cor. 5:21," *Novum Testamentum* 50 (2008), 361. See also Hooker, "Interchange and Atonement," in Hooker, *From Adam to Christ* (Cambridge: Cambridge University Press, 1990), p. 26.

and substance."[18] Assuming that sum and substance, Paul highlights the importance of dying with Christ, even over time, that is: "Always carrying in the body the death of Jesus, so that the life of Jesus may also be made visible in our bodies" (2 Cor. 4:10; cf. Phil. 3:10). Paul gives more attention to the practical and ethical-theological importance of Christ's death than to its metaphysical nature. (Chapter 2 returns to the importance for Paul of dying and rising with Christ in connection with divine sacrifice and reciprocal human sacrifice.)

Joseph A. Fitzmyer expresses a misleading concern about Paul on divine sacrifice: "Paul never uses *thyma* [sacrifice] for the Christ-event in any of his uncontested letters; he never says that Christ was sacrificed for our sake (contrast Ephesians 5:2, where *thysia* is so used)... [Such talk] is at best a reformulation of an implication of *hilastērion*, because Christ's 'blood' is here [Romans 3:25] implied to be substitute for the sacrificial blood of the animals in the Day of Atonement rite."[19] Talk of sacrifice attributed to Paul is indeed a clear implication of his mention of *hilastērion* and the blood of Christ in Romans 3:25, as well as his undeniable use of sacrificial ideas in other contexts (such as 1 Cor. 5:7, 6:20, 11:25; 2 Cor. 5:21; and Rom. 5:9, 8:32; cf. Gal. 2:20, 3:13). Contrary to Fitzmyer's suggestion, however, Paul uses a passive verbal form for "sacrifice" regarding Christ in his uncontested letters: τὸ πάσχα ἡμῶν ἐτύθη Χριστός (1 Cor. 5:7). So, we can proceed on firm ground with the idea of Christ's death as a sacrifice in Paul's thinking, even though its exact relations to the various kinds of sacrifices in the Jewish scriptures are left unclear.

Given his concern for righteous redemption (Rom. 3:24–6), Paul offers an important snapshot of his understanding of "redemption": "The creation itself will be set free from its bondage to decay and will

---

[18] Markus Barth, *Justification*, trans. A. M. Woodruff (Grand Rapids, MI: Eerdmans, 1971), p. 45.
[19] Joseph A. Fitzmyer, *Romans*, AB (New York: Doubleday, 1993), p. 122. For some support for my correction of Fitzmyer here, see James D. G. Dunn, *The Theology of Paul the Apostle* (Grand Rapids, MI: Eerdmans, 1998), pp. 212–23.

obtain the freedom of the glory of the children of God ... and not only the creation, but we ourselves, who have the first fruits of the Spirit, groan inwardly while we wait for adoption, the redemption [ἀπολύτρωσιν] of our bodies" (Rom. 8:21, 23). This snapshot of Paul on redemption, as deliverance from bondage into a right relationship with God, occurs in a context of his explicit concern for righteousness, in particular his focus on righteousness by the divine law and the Spirit of God (Rom. 8:4, 10).

God's righteousness, in Paul's view, seeks full redemption for humans, that is, the setting free from bondage to decay, including sin and death, as the avenue to realizing (adoption in to) "the glory of the children of God." This divine effort of redemption, according to Paul, arises paradigmatically in God's work in Christ, including in his self-giving, sacrificial death for others: "The Lord Jesus Christ gave himself for our sins to set us free from the present evil age, according to the will of our God and Father" (Gal. 1:3–4). Here again "setting free" arises in righteous redemption; it brings deliverance from what obstructs a righteous relationship with God.

Paul identifies something God has done through Christ to bring righteous redemption to undeserving humans under sin. God is the one "who justifies the ungodly," that is, people unrighteous on their own before God (Rom. 4:5; cf. Rom. 5:6–7). From the standpoint of humans, this is God's "objective" contribution to their redemption. It does not depend on human cooperation or any kind of human response. It therefore is God's "grace as a gift," owing nothing to human credit or merit. Paul thus speaks of "the free gift of righteousness [τῆς δωρεᾶς τῆς δικαιοσύνης]" (Rom. 5:17).

The undeserved gift of righteous redemption is costly and even sacrificial for God, "who did not withhold his own Son, but gave him up for all of us" (Rom. 8:32; cf. Rom. 5:8). This is God's reparative sacrifice, in Paul's thinking, because God is offering "his own Son" in death for human redemption. Paul thus announces, in the wake of God's sacrifice in Christ, that "you were bought with a price; therefore, glorify God in your body" (1 Cor. 6:20; cf. 2 Cor. 5:15; Rom. 14:9).

In connection with the binding of Isaac, Jon D. Levenson has remarked: "Both the Jewish and the Christian systems of sacrifice come to be seen as founded upon a father's willingness to surrender his beloved son and the son's unstinting acceptance of the sacrificial role he has been assigned in the great drama of redemption .... The Christian doctrine is incomprehensible apart from the history of Jewish biblical interpretation."[20] Even so, we shall identify Paul's distinctive understanding of the redemptive drama.

HUMAN RECIPROCITY IN SACRIFICE

The grace of divine self-sacrifice aimed at redemption, in Paul's thought, comes with a divine expectation of human reciprocity. It yields a human responsibility by way of a human response in kind. The divine "setting free" of humans from decay, through Christ's sacrifice, arises from its revealing divine power in redemptive righteousness and making it available to humans. Humans, however, must appropriate, or cooperatively receive, this power for it to come to fruition in their redemption, even though the prior divine action is crucial as a source for the power. Available divine power for redemption, then, may or may not reach its intended goal in actual human cooperation with redemption. A "subjective" (or, better, "person-relative") contribution from humans in a response of faith in God would depend on God's objective contribution, but it would exceed it in providing a cooperative response. It would supply a person-relative appropriation of God's objective provision of redemption.

We do well to distinguish "objective" and "subjective" factors in Paul's understanding of redemption, including being "reconciled," being "saved," and being "justified."[21] This calls for a distinction

---

[20] Jon D. Levenson, *The Death and Resurrection of the Beloved Son* (New Haven, CT: Yale University Press, 1993), pp. 174–75.

[21] Vincent Taylor, at least at times, overlooks the subjective, or human, side of reconciliation in Paul (such as in 2 Corinthians 5:20). See Taylor, *The Atonement in New Testament Teaching*, 3rd ed. (London: Epworth Press, 1958), pp. 83, 95. Even so, he recognizes the importance of subjective and objective contributions in the larger context of Paul on atonement; see Taylor, *The Cross of Christ* (London:

between the conditions for an undeserved divine gift and the conditions for human reception of that gift. On the objective side, Paul comments: "If while we were enemies, we were reconciled to God through the death of his Son, much more surely, having been reconciled, will we be saved by his life" (Rom. 5:10). As suggested, this is just one side – the objective side – of Paul's gospel, courtesy of God's antecedent provision of redemption through a gift of grace in Christ.

Regarding the role of sacrifice in redemption, a traditional Christian view restricts this role to God's objective side. I. Howard Marshall thus claims:

> God takes the initiative, God himself bears the sin, and gives his Son in his sacrificial death as the way or means by which sinners can come to him. The sinner no longer needs to bring an offering to God, for Christ has already made that offering in the heavenly sanctuary. The conferral of forgiveness costs the sinner nothing, but it costs God everything.[22]

This one-sided, cessationist view of human sacrifice in redemption is typical among commentators on Paul, but it misrepresents Paul, who endorsed a kind of reciprocity in human sacrifice to God.

Paul wrote to the Roman Christians: "I appeal to you therefore, brothers and sisters, by the mercies of God, to present [παραστῆσαι] your bodies as a living sacrifice [θυσίαν ζῶσαν], holy and acceptable to God, which is your spiritual worship [τὴν λογικὴν λατρείαν]" (Rom. 12:1). Paul takes such self-sacrifice to God to be required for a response of "reasonable service" to God, and he regards it as ongoing. Leander

---

Macmillan, 1956), pp. 88–89. On the subjective, appropriation side of divine–human reconciliation, in terms of human reciprocity, see C. F. D. Moule, "The Sacrifice of Christ," in Moule, *Forgiveness and Reconciliation* (London: SPCK, 1998), pp. 154–56.

[22] I. Howard Marshall, *Aspects of the Atonement*, pp. 57–58. He is echoing Hebrews 10:18: "Where there is forgiveness of these [sins], there is no longer any offering for sin." Paul's view, we shall see, is more complicated.

Keck rightly points to the widely neglected reciprocity endorsed by Paul: "This self-offering is the beneficiaries' *response* to God's own self-giving."[23] He correctly notes that "this *latreia* is honoring God as God."[24] It is to be motivated, in Paul's perspective, by "the mercies of God" extended to Gentiles as well as Jews in redemption (cf. Rom. 11:32, 12:1).

Markus Barth has sounded, in passing, the proper note for Paul: "The manifestation of God's righteousness ... aims at reciprocity: humans are to show such righteousness and truth as correspond to God's."[25] In a similar vein, C. F. D. Moule has remarked about a response of Christian sacrifice to God: "If 'sacrifice' is a spontaneous and inevitable term for the costly offering of Christian adoration, thanksgiving and obedience, then perhaps it must be retained (as it undeniably is in the New Testament) – but let it be rid of all evil connotations of bribery or propitiation."[26] Moule rightly notes the reciprocal activity involved here, in addition to its costly character. We shall clarify in detail what such reciprocal sacrifice entails for Paul and his gospel.

---

[23] Keck, *Romans*, ANTC (Nashville, TN: Abingdon Press, 2005), p. 291. Similarly, see Young, *Sacrifice and the Death of Christ*, pp. 96–97. Neither Keck nor Young develops the case for the role of human reciprocity of divine self-sacrifice in Paul's thought. The same is true of C. F. D. Moule, who mentions reciprocity in passing regarding atonement in the New Testament. See Moule, "The Sacrifice of Christ," in Moule, *Forgiveness and Reconciliation*, pp. 154, 156; cf. Young, *Construing the Cross* (London: SPCK, 2016), p. 40. For three wide-ranging cases for the importance of mutuality of self-sacrifice in Christian thought, see Ian Bradley, *The Power of Sacrifice* (London: Darton, Longman, and Todd, 1995); Erin Lothes Biviano, *The Paradox of Christian Sacrifice* (New York: Crossroad, 2007); and Robert J. Daly, *Sacrifice Unveiled* (London: T&T Clark, 2009).

[24] Keck, *Romans*, p. 293.   [25] Markus Barth, *Justification*, p. 17.

[26] C. F. D. Moule, "The Sacrifice of the People of God," in Moule, *Essays in New Testament Interpretation* (Cambridge: Cambridge University Press, 1982), p. 295. See also Moule, "Sanctuary and Sacrifice in the Church of the New Testament," *Journal of Theological Studies* 1 (1950), 29–41; and Moule, *Christ Alive and at Large*, eds. Robert Morgan and Patrick Moule (London: Canterbury Press, 2010), pp. 182–86.

According to Paul, God sends Jesus to atone with self-sacrifice for human sin and thereby to enable divine-human reconciliation in righteousness. Our human sacrificial response in reciprocity, however, does not atone for human sin or offer divine reconciliation for humans. Instead, in Paul's thought, it is the way for humans to receive atonement and reconciliation from God, through our reciprocal gift to God as our sharing in Christ's obedient self-sacrifice to God (Phil. 2:5–8, 3:10; 2 Cor. 4:7–11). God's part in the sacrificial process is costly self-giving for the covering of human sin with reconciliation. Our part is the costly receiving of this reconciliation in self-giving to God. The sacrificial process of redemption is thus bimodal in Paul's perspective.

Paul refers the Christians at Rome to his "priestly service of the gospel [ἱερουργοῦντα τὸ εὐαγγέλιον]" that seeks the offering of its recipients to God (Rom. 15:16). This reference is important for understanding Paul, as it directly connects his ministry of the gospel with the reciprocal self-sacrifice of its recipients. He speaks of his goal that "the offering of the Gentiles [ἡ προσφορὰ τῶν ἐθνῶν] may be acceptable, sanctified by the Holy Spirit." One might propose that this offering is limited to Paul's work in preaching the gospel, but this reading is unduly narrow. Paul easily could have talked of "my offering of the Gentiles," but he does not. Romans 12:1 suggests that Paul has a broader role for self-sacrificial offering to God, a role that includes self-sacrifice by the recipients of his gospel, including the kind of self-giving love shown by Jesus in service to God (cf. Rom. 12:9–11). Even if one limits Romans 15:16 to Paul's offering, Paul himself shows a concern for a wider source for self-sacrifice in Romans 12:1.

Paul refers the Christians at Philippi to his "being poured out as a libation over the sacrifice and the offering of your faith [τῇ θυσίᾳ καὶ λειτουργίᾳ τῆς πίστεως ὑμῶν]." This reference suggests that a response to God in faith includes human sacrifice (Phil. 2:17). It is significant for understanding Paul, because it directly relates his understanding of faith in God, as a response to the gospel, to self-sacrifice to God. Paul could have spoken of "my sacrifice and offering" of your faith, but he does not, and, in any case, Romans 12:1 shows that he did not limit a role for self-sacrifice to himself.[27]

Gordon Fee finds it unclear how faith could be offered up as a sacrifice,[28] but the idea fits well with Paul's talk in Romans 12:1 of presenting yourselves as a living sacrifice acceptable to God.[29] A person's faith in God, on a natural reading of Paul, is to be part of such a sacrificial self-offering to God. Paul himself is part of a sacrificial offering as a libation poured over it, in his ministry of the gospel to the Philippians. Given Romans 12:1, however, we should not limit the source of sacrificial offering to Paul; it applies, in Paul's perspective, to all people who receive the gospel in faith.

Ernst Käsemann misses the significance of reciprocity in divine and human self-sacrifice in his comment on Romans 12:1, but he does acknowledge the importance of Paul's talk of sacrifice. He writes:

> Paul deliberately and in no way fortuitously employs cultic language and, in particular, the language of sacrifice. But in reality it is precisely this which demonstrates the radical nature of the shift which has taken place here. So far from there being any room left for cultic thinking, the use of cultic terminology becomes itself the means of making clear, through a paradox, the extent of the upheaval. In the eschatological age ... there is nothing holy in the cultic sense except the community of the holy people and their self-abandonment in the service of the Lord to whom the world and all its dominions belong .... The total Christian community with all

---

[27] It is thus ill-advised for Fitzmyer to recommend "my sacrifice and offering" for Philippians 2:17 and to have this guide his reading of Romans 15:16. See his *Romans*, p. 712.

[28] Gordon Fee, *Paul's Letter to the Philippians*, NICNT (Grand Rapids, MI: Eerdmans, 1995), p. 255.

[29] Fitzmyer, *Romans*, p. 639, rightly notes that by "your bodies" Paul means "yourselves," and this is confirmed by Paul's elaboration in Romans 12:2, as long as the selves are not divorced from embodied selves. Similarly, see Keck, *Romans*, p. 291; and Dunn, *Romans 9–16*, WBC (Dallas, TX: Word Books, 1988), p. 709. The REB translates with "offer your very selves."

its members is the bearer of this worship and not only sacred functions but also cultically privileged persons lose their right to exist.³⁰

Käsemann finds "paradox" where Paul does not. If we understand Paul as linking human self-sacrifice to divine righteousness, as a reciprocal response to it, we can avoid paradox here and retain distinctive moral content.

Käsemann proposes eschatological content that is not moral, but the distinction is dubious when facing a God of perfect righteousness. Paul thinks in terms of self-giving obedience to God's righteous will – a will that is "good and acceptable and perfect [ἀγαθὸν καὶ εὐάρεστον καὶ τέλειον]"– and therefore moral content is indispensable. He thus offers an approach to self-sacrifice that is morally more robust than what Käsemann has in mind.³¹ Paul's subsequent remarks in Romans 12 bear this out, in their straightforward attention to the moral goodness, including the unselfish love, that he expects of self-sacrifice to God (see Rom. 12:9–21).

Paul is explicit about a reciprocal role for human self-sacrifice to God in his Epistle to the Philippians: "Let the same mind be in you that was in Christ Jesus .... Being found in human form, he humbled himself and became obedient to the point of death – even death on a cross" (Phil. 2:5, 8). Paul, we have seen, regards Christ's death on the cross to be a self-sacrifice to, and on behalf of, God (Rom. 3:24–25; 1 Cor. 11:23–25), and he regards humble, self-giving obedience to God as central to Christ's role in his cross (cf. Rom. 5:19). Given that perspective, Paul thinks of such obedience as central to human self-sacrifice to, and on behalf of, God. With that role for obedience in self-sacrifice

---

³⁰ Ernst Käsemann, "Worship and Everyday Life: A Note on Romans 12," in Käsemann, *New Testament Questions of Today*, trans. W.J. Montague (London: SCM Press, 1969), pp. 192, 191. Cf. Ernst Käsemann, *Commentary on Romans*, trans. G. W. Bromiley (Grand Rapids, MI: Eerdmans, 1980), pp. 326–29.

³¹ For critical discussion of Käsemann on Romans 12, see David Peterson, "Worship and Ethics in Romans 12," *Tyndale Bulletin* 44 (1993), 271–88.

to God, we can acknowledge a central place for such sacrifice in Paul's thought.³²

Recipients of the gospel as people of faith, according to Paul, have their own self-sacrifice to make to God. This includes a sacrificial offering of their faith to God as a way to honor God as God. Suffering for such faith under persecution also can highlight a sacrificial role for faith, by making the costly nature of the sacrifice transparent. Paul's notion of self-sacrifice to God in Romans 12 coheres with his idea of a sacrifice of faith to God in Philippians 2. Both contexts assume a response to God that reciprocates the kind of costly divine self-giving central to Paul's understanding of redemption. Indeed, the previous remarks by Paul make it hard to imagine how he could have been more explicit about a role for self-sacrifice to God on the human side. We thus shall give a central role to Paul's sacrificial view in our explanation of his position on redemption.³³

A direct parallel to Romans 12:1 arises in Romans 6 in connection with righteousness and obedience. Paul commands the Roman Christians: "Present yourselves [παραστήσατε ἑαυτοὺς] to God as those who have been brought from death to life, and present your members to God as instruments of righteousness" (Rom. 6:13). For clarification, he asks: "Do you not know that if you present yourselves to anyone as obedient slaves, you are slaves of the one whom you obey, either of sin, which leads to death, or of obedience, which leads to righteousness?"

---

[32] We then can correct any misleading inference from Vincent Taylor's remark that "it cannot be said that Paul makes a pronounced use of sacrificial ideas." See *The Cross of Christ*, p. 33. If Paul has focused reciprocated sacrifice in terms of self-giving obedience to God, as I have suggested, a sacrificial idea is central to his thinking about redemption.

[33] It is noteworthy that the Deutero-Pauline Epistle to the Ephesians is explicit in its sacrificial understanding of Christ's death in terms of love: "Live in love, as Christ loved us and gave himself up for us, a fragrant offering and sacrifice [θυσίαν] to God" (Eph. 5:2; cf. Gal. 2:20). The evidence we have presented suggests that Paul would have concurred with this sacrificial understanding of redemption.

We have evidence here that Paul understands "presenting yourselves to God" in terms of obedience for the sake of righteousness. This consideration bears directly on what Paul has in mind in Romans 12:1.

God does not settle for just the objective side of redemption, according to Paul, because human sin as alienation from God includes internal, subjective factors. The divine righteousness antithetical to sin thus must have internal, motivational efficacy. This need emerges in Paul's previous quotation from Habakkuk: "Their spirit is not right in them, but the righteous live by their faith" (Hab. 2:4; cf. Rom. 1:17; Gal. 3:11). In the same vein, Paul remarks: "A person is a Jew who is one inwardly, and real circumcision is a matter of the heart – it is spiritual and not literal" (Rom. 2:29; cf. Rom. 7:6). A key issue becomes: How can the spirit or heart of humans, Jew or Gentile, become right in them? Paul's short answer: Their spirit or heart can become right in them through a right(eous), reconciled relationship with God. This answer prompts the question of how such a relationship can arise. It does not arise, in Paul's perspective, just from human willing or believing, but humans nonetheless have a vital role to play in its reception.

Paul gives credit to God for prompting and attracting humans with divine goodness that can be cooperatively received in their experience. He asks: "Do you despise the riches of his kindness and forbearance and patience? Do you not realize that God's kindness [χρηστὸν] is meant to lead [ἄγει] you to repentance?" (Rom. 2:4). Paul also speaks of "God's kindness toward you, provided [ἐὰν] you continue [ἐπιμένῃς] in his kindness" (Rom. 11:22; cf. Gal. 1:6). Paul's conditional indicates that human reception of divine goodness and kindness is voluntary and not mechanical or coerced (see also Rom. 11:23). Paul has in mind God's "kindness" included in divine goodness as righteousness seeking the redemption of humans through voluntary repentance. Its role in goodness as righteousness takes it beyond mere tolerance and accommodation to a moral challenge toward what is "good" in relating to God. Paul thus moves directly to a divine expectation of voluntary human actions that are "good" (ἀγαθόν) (Rom. 2:7, 10; cf. Rom. 15:2).

The goodness in humans and their actions, according to Paul, is to come as a voluntary response to divine goodness as righteousness. Paul makes the connection between divine righteousness and divine goodness clear when he uses "δικαία" and "ἀγαθή" interchangeably in connection with God's law (Rom. 7:12). He also portrays God as working all things "for good" (εἰς ἀγαθόν) for those responding voluntarily with love toward God (Rom. 8:28), and he calls God's will "good and perfect [ἀγαθὸν καὶ τέλειον]" (Rom. 12:2). Divine righteousness in Paul's perspective, then, is an inherently moral power, centered on moral goodness as a basis for divine redemptive action, including reparative sacrifice. In addition, it respects the voluntary character of a human response, without condoning human unrighteousness.

God's moral goodness includes not just kindness but also love, including the high point of such love in divine self-sacrifice: "God proves his love [ἀγάπην] for us in that while we still were sinners Christ died for us" (Rom. 5:8). Such love intends to bring about what is genuinely good for its recipients. This is divine righteous love that seeks a cooperative human response, for the sake of human appropriation of divine goodness in relating to God. It includes divine willing of what is righteous for humans, and it does so in action that goes beyond mere talk. Talk can be cheap, but redemptive love that self-sacrifices in action comes with a price. Paul holds that, at God's command, Jesus paid the ultimate price with his life for others. Jesus as the filial center of God's righteous love is thus at the center of Paul's gospel of divine self-sacrifice for righteous redemption.

Paul names the importance of divine righteous love (ἀγάπη) as a central motivation of redemption in Christ, including the divine sacrifice of Christ "given up for us" (Gal. 2:20; Rom. 8:32–39). This love extends even to people who are "enemies" of the divine redemption in Christ (Rom. 11:28; cf. Rom. 10:21), and this theme echoes the outreach of Jesus to "sinners" in his ministry.[34] The love in question, as suggested, includes divine kindness (χρηστὸν) toward humans aimed at eliciting their repentance (Rom. 2:4, 11:22).

A neglected theme from Paul is that the redemption in Christ aims to elicit, and thus to be received with, a human motive in the same kind of love (Rom. 8:28–30). This calls for a voluntary human response to receive divine righteousness, through faith, with what Paul calls "the heart," the volitional center of a human (Rom. 10:10; cf. Rom. 11:22). He seeks a human response motivated "by our Lord Jesus Christ and by the love of the Spirit" (Rom. 15:30; cf. 2 Cor. 5:14–15). We have noted that Paul expects a kind of human self-sacrifice by way of an elicited response, in reciprocity to God's self-giving redemption. (Chapter 2 returns to the role of divine love in redemption, including in a human response to God, and Chapter 5 returns to the role of a voluntary human response.)

Humans fall short of divine goodness as impeccable righteousness, according to Paul, and therefore God "reckons (or credits) righteousness" to them through voluntary faith, in keeping with needed forgiveness. Paul appeals to the Jewish scriptures: "God reckons righteousness apart from works: 'Blessed are those whose iniquities are forgiven, and whose sins are covered; blessed is the one against whom the Lord will not reckon sin'" (Rom. 4:7–8, citing Psalm 32:1–2; cf. Gal. 3:6–8; Psalm 85:2). In crediting righteousness to humans, God forgives them and refrains from crediting sin to them as requiring divine judgment of them. God credits this righteousness through human faith, in order to accommodate ungodly people as candidates for justification as divine approval. Otherwise, no mere human would qualify, according to Paul. Divine reckoning through voluntary faith is God's way to justify the ungodly, the undeserving, and it honors their responsible agency by avoiding mechanical coercion.

---

[34] On this parallel between Jesus and Paul, see James D. G. Dunn, *Jesus, Paul, and the Gospels* (Grand Rapids, MI: Eerdmans, 2011), pp. 98–106.

The divine crediting of righteousness does not entail fictional righteousness, according to Paul, because it begins with the receiving of transformative divine righteousness in a human life. Such a beginning, illustrated by Paul with Abraham's voluntary trust in God, awaits completion in full human restoration, including bodily resurrection (Rom. 4:3, 20–21, 8:21, 23), but it is a real start toward that end. It is a genuine beginning of righteousness in humans, in virtue of their new cooperative relation with God, despite their being ungodly.[35] Paul thus identifies God's aim that "in him [Christ] we might become the righteousness of God" (2 Cor. 5:21), and he expects the righteousness required by the divine law to be fulfilled in God's people (Rom. 8:3–4). (Chapter 5 returns to the topic of Paul on credited righteousness.)

Paul, as indicated, thinks of divine righteousness as forgiving and covering sin (Rom. 4:7). He acknowledges a divine prerogative in how forgiving as covering sin proceeds toward the redemptive renewal of humans (Rom. 9:14–16). That prerogative, according to Paul, leads to God's sending Jesus to die on the cross as a sacrifice of atonement for Gentiles as well as Jews. Paul makes a striking statement on this matter: "Christ redeemed us from the curse of the law by becoming a curse for us – for it is written, 'Cursed is everyone who hangs on a tree' – in order that in Christ Jesus the blessing of Abraham might come to the Gentiles, so that we might receive the promise of the Spirit through faith" (Gal. 3:13–14). Paul here cites Deuteronomy 21:23, but he omits its mention of being cursed "by God." He does not say that God cursed Christ on the cross nor does he ask his audience to infer that. He puts the focus on "the curse of the law," not a curse by God.

---

[35] We should qualify Vincent Taylor's interpretation that, according to Paul, "God puts the believing person right with himself because, through faith in the Crucified, he has righteous desires and a righteous will." See *The Cross of Christ*, p. 39. Given faith in God, one can have an intention, or a resolve, to receive divine righteousness, while still having many unrighteous desires and a morally imperfect will. This accounts for many of Paul's corrective injunctions to Christian churches.

We should interpret Paul in keeping with his statements that "in Christ God was reconciling the world to himself, not counting their trespasses against them" (2 Cor. 5:19), and that (thereby) "God proves his love for us in that while we still were sinners Christ died for us" (Rom. 5:8). These statements assume a shared motivation by God and Christ for the cross in divine forgiveness and love. This motivation includes God's sending Christ as a righteous sacrifice to cover and condemn sin (Rom. 8:3–4). There is no need or assumption in Paul, however, of God's cursing, condemning, or otherwise punishing Christ, "the Lord of glory" who did not deserve his crucifixion (1 Cor. 2:8).

We might try to express Paul's thinking about sin and Christ's death with a direct analogue to his idea of God's "reckoning" or "crediting" certain responsive behavior as righteousness. Analogously, Christ's willing death in the world of human sin and its wages can be credited by God as the cursing or judging of Christ as a sacrificial sin-bearer, as one who was "made sin" and "cursed" in order "to deal with sin" (Rom. 8:3). (The NIV translates with "sending his own Son … to be a sin offering.") Paul says that "the death he died, he died to sin, once for all" (Rom. 6:10). God can reckon his death as his being that of a sacrificial sin-bearer on God's behalf for the redemption of humans, even undergoing judgment for their benefit as a result of the world's sin. It does not follow, however, that Christ sinned or that God cursed, condemned, punished, or judged him. So, Paul refrains, in Galatians 3:13 and Romans 8:3, from saying that God cursed, condemned, punished, or judged Christ.

As in the case of Romans 3:25, we must be cautious not to overinterpret Paul in his talk of Christ being "made sin," as though he had a detailed account in mind. Sharing this concern, Victor Paul Furnish has suggested that the context of 2 Corinthians 5:21 does not include the idea of a sin-offering: "It is more likely that Paul is thinking in a general way of Christ's identification with sinful humanity."[36] It thus

---

[36] Victor Paul Furnish, *II Corinthians*, AB (New York: Doubleday, 1984), p. 340.

seems unnecessary to invoke Isaiah 53:6, for instance, as a basis for Paul's comment. Even so, Paul is somehow implicating God in his talk of Christ's being "made sin" and "becoming a curse for us." This takes us beyond Furnish's idea of "a general way of Christ's identification with sinful humanity" to a role for God. Paul's notion of what God "credits" can give God a key role while it fittingly omits a need or a claim of the divine cursing, condemning, punishing, or judging of Christ.

We can preserve a central role for divine sacrifice in Paul's thinking, while letting go of details found in the sacrificial traditions of the Jewish scriptures. Vincent Taylor has offered a sound perspective: "In [Christ's] self-offering there are elements only faintly represented in the Old Testament rites, and aspects not found in them at all. It is the *basic pattern* in these sacrifices which serves as a vehicle for the New Testament doctrine [of sacrifice] – the *idea of a representative offering with which the worshipper identifies himself, so that it becomes the means of his approach when in penitence he 'draws near' to God.*"[37] Romans 12:1 and Philippians 2:5, 8 suggest that for Paul the offering of oneself in obedience to God replaces any need for the animal sacrifices of the Jewish tradition.

We can proceed with a general representative-offering approach to divine and human self-sacrifice in Paul. This approach allows that he thinks of the sacrifice of Christ as comparable to the Passover lamb of Exodus 12 without elaborating on details.[38] Paul thinks of the divine sacrifice through Christ, in keeping with the Passover

---

[37] Vincent Taylor, *The Cross of Christ* (London: Macmillan, 1956), p. 91. Similarly, see W. D. Davies, *Paul and Rabbinic Judaism*, 2nd ed. (London: SPCK, 1955), pp. 253, 259. On the various kinds of sacrifice in the Jewish scriptures and various Christian responses, see Frances M. Young, *Sacrifice and the Death of Christ*, pp. 21–30, 47–63; Young, *The Use of Sacrificial Ideas in Greek Christian Writers from the New Testament to John Chrysostom*, chs. 2, 6; and Everett Ferguson, "Spiritual Sacrifice in Early Christianity and its Environment," in *Aufstieg und Niedergang der römischen Welt*, II 23:2 (1979), pp. 1152–89.

[38] For consideration of the Passover lamb in terms of a sacrifice, see Exodus 12:11, 27; Deuteronomy 16:2, 5; and Leviticus 23:5. See also Young, *The Use of Sacrificial Ideas in Greek Christian Writers*, pp. 45–46.

(cf. Deut. 6:21), as life-giving for humans, but he also regards it as inviting a voluntary human response in faithful obedience that is self-sacrificial to God. We turn to some illuminating background for Paul's understanding of divine righteousness.

RIGHTEOUS AGITATION IN HISTORY

Paul offers his gospel not as an innovator but as one building from biblical history, where, as suggested, he finds a basis for his good news (Rom. 1:1–3; Gal. 3:8; cf. Gen. 12:3). From a broad perspective, the biblical history important to Paul is largely a record of God's agitating for righteousness that includes the spiritual and moral benefit of people, often against their own plans and purposes. We can capture a large part of that history with the Pauline idea that in the patriarchs, Israel, Christ, and the early church, God was actively intervening to "reconcile the world to himself," in righteous redemption. The relevant idea of divine agitator is broader than that of God as a holy "warrior."[39] Warfare is not the only means of divine agitation for righteous redemption. Access to God often comes with divine agitation because God typically intends such access to be redemptive toward divine-human reconciliation in a context of human waywardness. Paul's approach to God and divine righteousness, we shall see, assumes as much.

The Oxford English Dictionary, 3rd ed., characterizes an agitator as follows: "A person who instigates unrest; a person who carries out agitation. The arousing of concern in order to bring about action." Paul himself has offered an important summary of divine agitation for righteousness: "The creation was subjected to futility, not of its own will but by the will of the one who subjected it, in hope that the creation itself will be set free from its bondage to decay and will

---

[39] On the idea of God as a holy warrior, see Gerhard Von Rad, *Holy War in Ancient Israel*, trans. M. J. Dawn (Grand Rapids, MI: Eerdmans, 1958 [1991]); G. Ernest Wright, "God the Warrior," in Wright, *The Old Testament and Theology* (New York: Harper, 1969), pp. 121–50; and Patrick D. Miller, *The Divine Warrior in Early Israel*, HSM (Cambridge, MA: Harvard University Press, 1973).

obtain the freedom of the glory of the children of God" (Rom 8:20–21). God, according to Paul, subjected the created world to decay, frustration, and failure in order to attract people to receive a righteous filial relationship with God, as liberated children of God: "the freedom of the glory of the children of God." This is a divine trademark at the center of biblical theology (if we may use that loaded idea), including Paul's theology of divine redemption.

Paul thinks of righteousness as characteristic of the Spirit and the life of God: "The Spirit is life because of righteousness [τὸ πνεῦμα ζωὴ διὰ δικαιοσύνην]" (Rom. 8:10). As a result, he thinks of divine redemption as a life of righteousness with God, and, as suggested, he follows Habakkuk regarding faith in God as central to such a life (Gal. 3:11: "Ὁ δίκαιος ἐκ πίστεως ζήσεται"; cf. Rom 1:17). Such faith enables a human to receive "the gift of righteousness" as an undeserved gift of "grace through redemption" (Rom. 3:24, 5:17). In receiving this gift, according to Paul, people become the temple of God as the dwelling place of the Spirit of God (1 Cor. 3:16; 2 Cor. 6:16).[40] We shall see, in Chapter 3, how this bears on the role of sacrifice in Paul's thought about righteous redemption.

Paul portrays the Spirit of God as giving humans the power of faithful obedience to kill evil deeds as a way to righteous life with God: "If you live according to the flesh, you will die; but if by the Spirit you put to death the deeds of the body, you will live" (Rom. 8:13; cf. Rom. 6:12–14; Col. 3:5–6). He has in mind evil deeds associated with the human body, what he calls "deeds of the flesh." God's Spirit, in Paul's perspective, seeks to kill such deeds in order to attract people to reconciled, righteous life with God. The divine killing of human evil, for the sake of righteousness, is neglected in many presentations of divine action in history. As a result, God's key role as righteous agitator for human good is likewise widely neglected.

---

[40] In a related metaphor, Paul suggests that God's people become a letter written by the Spirit of God (2 Cor. 3:2–3). Chapter 6 returns to the topic of personifying evidence of God in humans.

We shall consider some biblical history that counters that deficiency and fits with Paul's approach to divine agitation for righteousness.

We find evidence of God's modus operandi for righteous agitation, both individual and social, in biblical history. A seminal case of divine agitation for human good occurs in the life of Abraham. Paul, as noted, takes this case to include the preaching of the gospel to Abraham: "The scripture, foreseeing that God would justify the Gentiles by faith, declared the gospel beforehand to Abraham, saying, 'All the Gentiles shall be blessed in you'" (Gal. 3:8; cf. Rom. 4:16–17).

The narrative involving Abraham in Genesis includes:

> The word of the Lord came to Abram in a vision, "Do not be afraid, Abram, I am your shield; your reward shall be very great."... He brought him outside and said, "Look toward heaven and count the stars, if you are able to count them." Then he said to him, "So shall your descendants be." And he believed the Lord; and the Lord reckoned it to him as righteousness [δικαιοσύνην, LXX].
>
> *(Gen. 15:1, 5–6)*

The divine promise to Abraham identifies the good news of God's goal but not the means to that goal. The unidentified means includes, as we know, some disturbing surprises for Abraham and his kin.

The good news did not come easy for Abraham, because it was accompanied by divine challenges of various sorts. God called him to social dislocation, for instance, including giving up his homeland, for the higher good promised to him:

> Now the Lord said to Abram, "Go from your country and your kindred and your father's house to the land that I will show you. I will make of you a great nation, and I will bless you, and make your name great, so that you will be a blessing. I will bless those who bless you, and the one who curses you I will curse; and in you all the families of the earth shall be blessed."
>
> *(Gen. 12:1–3)*

Abraham was left without an explanation of much of God's plan for blessing "all the families of the earth." Paul reports, however: "No distrust made him waver concerning the promise of God, but he grew strong in his faith as he gave glory to God, being fully convinced that God was able to do what he had promised" (Rom. 4:20–21). Such faith, according to Paul, is the way to receive divine righteousness as well as God's promise of redemption (Rom. 4:13). (Chapter 2 returns to this topic, in relation to a role for righteous *agapē*.)

God tested Abraham for his faith in God and thereby for his receptivity to righteousness. Indeed, the divine testing of Abraham with the commanded sacrifice of Isaac was divine agitation to the extreme, complete with the appearance of child abuse. It began as follows: "God tested Abraham. He said to him, 'Abraham!' And he said, 'Here I am.' He said, 'Take your son, your only son Isaac, whom you love, and go to the land of Moriah, and offer him there as a burnt offering on one of the mountains that I shall show you'" (Gen. 22:1–2). Abraham proceeded to obey, if with hesitation. (Perhaps we have a foreshadowing of Gethsemane.)

A twofold question arises: Did God intend to have Abraham sacrifice Isaac, and did Abraham believe that God intended to have him sacrifice Isaac? Our literary evidence includes this verse: "Abraham said to his young men, 'Stay here with the donkey; the boy and I will go over there; we will worship, and then we will come back to you'" (Gen. 22:5). This expectation of their returning fits with Abraham's reply to a question from Isaac about the lamb to be offered: "God himself will provide the lamb for a burnt offering, my son" (Gen. 22:8). Our evidence also includes this last-minute report from the angel of the Lord: "Do not lay your hand on the boy or do anything to him; for now I know that you fear God, since you have not withheld your son, your only son, from me" (Gen. 22:12). Our evidence thus indicates that God did not intend to have Abraham sacrifice Isaac and that Abraham did not believe that God intended to have him do so.

God's disturbing command, according to Genesis 22, sought to agitate Abraham in order to reveal and build Abraham's trust and obedience toward God. Viewed from the outside, God's command to sacrifice Isaac can be taken at face value, and the relevance of Abraham's trust in God can be neglected. His trust in God, however, led him to expect God to find a way to spare Isaac, even though he did not know how God would do so. Perhaps Abraham knew that he was being tested by God, but he did not know the exact means the test would use in advance of God's final intervention. God emerges as an agitator for trust in God, but God cannot be blamed for condoning child sacrifice or abuse. God was after the growth of righteousness in Abraham, if with severe means.[41]

The divine agitation of Abraham has a successor in the nation of Israel during and after the Exodus:

> Has any god ever attempted to go and take a nation for himself from the midst of another nation, by trials, by signs and wonders, by war, by a mighty hand and an outstretched arm, and by terrifying displays of power, as the Lord your God did for you in Egypt before your very eyes? To you it was shown so that you would acknowledge that the Lord is God; there is no other besides him. From heaven he made you hear his voice to discipline you.
>
> *(Deut. 4:32–36)*

The divine desire to have Israel "acknowledge that the Lord is God" did not seek just intellectual affirmation of God's existence. It sought to have Israel trust and obey God in a righteous relationship. The talk of "discipline" of Israel suggests trustful obedience, learned under agitation from God. Such agitation for discipline may or may not include divine judgment, and that judgment need not include the termination of human life. It seeks a righteous divine–human relationship, with or without divine judgment.[42]

The divine agitation of humans can be severe, as indicated in the "Song of Moses": "See now that I, even I, am he; there is no god

---

[41] For related discussion, see Terence E. Fretheim, "God, Abraham, and the Abuse of Isaac," *Word & World* 15 (1995), 49–57; and Jon D. Levenson, *Inheriting Abraham* (Princeton, NJ: Princeton University Press, 2012), pp. 66–111.

[42] For relevant discussion of divine judgment, see Terence E. Fretheim, *God and World in the Old Testament* (Nashville, TN: Abingdon Press 2005), pp. 157–98; and Stephen H. Travis, *Christ and the Judgement of God* (Peabody, MA: Hendrickson, 2008). Chapter 4 takes up the topic of Paul on divine judgment.

besides me. I kill and I make alive; I wound and I heal; and no one can deliver from my hand" (Deut. 32:39). This is not the god of deism, of course, given the divine role for corrective intervention in human lives, whether by killing, making alive, wounding, or healing. The divine action toward ancient Israel often agitated for the sake of improving their relationship with God in righteousness, including their improved trust and obedience toward God. It thus reflected the divine precedent toward Abraham.

God did not give Moses and Aaron the privilege of entering the promised land, owing to their inadequate trust and obedience toward God: "Both of you broke faith with me among the Israelites at the waters of Meribath-kadesh in the wilderness of Zin, by failing to maintain my holiness among the Israelites. Although you may view the land from a distance, you shall not enter it – the land that I am giving to the Israelites" (Deut. 32:51–52). There is judgment in this divine response, but divine judgment can include righteous agitation for moral good among humans. It thus can be redemptive when humans are suitably responsive.

The book of Isaiah offers illuminating background to Paul's understanding of divine righteousness. It fits with Paul's portrayal of divine righteousness aimed at redemption as salvation: "I bring near My righteousness [צִדְקָתִי; δικαιοσύνην, LXX], it is not far off; And My salvation will not delay" (Isa 46:13, NASB). Similarly: "My righteousness [צִדְקִי; δικαιοσύνη, LXX] is near, My salvation has gone forth" (Isa. 51:5, NASB). Divine righteousness, according to the book of Isaiah, is active and not static; it seeks the redemption of responsive people, even if judgment is included. Paul shares this general approach to God's redemption in righteousness (Rom. 11:26–32).

Against its background concern for human redemption, the book of Isaiah affirms God's role in human woes as well as human goods: "I am the Lord, and there is no other. I form light and create darkness. I make weal and create woe. I the Lord do all these things" (Isa. 45:6–7). Similarly, the book of Lamentations affirms God's active role in causing grief for humans: "The Lord will not reject forever.

Although he causes grief, he will have compassion according to the abundance of his steadfast love; for he does not willingly afflict or grieve anyone" (Lam. 3:31–33). A divine motive for causing human grief or woe (not to be confused with evil), according to the book of Jeremiah, is morally significant: "Thus says the Lord of hosts: I will now refine and test them, for what else can I do with my sinful people?" (Jer. 9:7). The divine "refining and testing" aim for righteousness in relation to God, through a relationship of trust and obedience toward God. We shall see that, in keeping with Paul's general approach, faithful obedience is God's approved way for humans to receive reconciliation with God in righteousness.

The claim of Lamentations that God does not "willingly afflict or grieve anyone" indicates that such agitation is not God's first choice. God does afflict or grieve people intentionally but only when needed to "refine and test them." This is a matter of God's agitating for human righteousness as a redemptive relationship, and not God's creating evil in human lives. The prophet Hosea likewise endorses this approach to divine agitation: "Come, let us return to the Lord; for it is he who has torn, and he will heal us; he has struck down, and he will bind us up" (Hosea 6:1). The agitation is for the moral refining of God's people toward a righteous relationship with God, who is the ultimate personal standard of righteousness.

The prophet Malachi connects God's coming to humans with the divine refining of them as a means to righteousness: "[The Lord] is like a refiner's fire and like fullers' soap; he will sit as a refiner and purifier of silver, and he will purify the descendants of Levi and refine them like gold and silver, until they present offerings [θυσίαν, LXX] to the Lord in righteousness [δικαιοσύνῃ, LXX]" (Mal. 3:2–3; cf. Zech. 13:8–9; Ps. 66:10–12). So, the divine agitation of humans through refining aims at their righteousness in relation to God, including their presenting righteous offerings, or sacrifices, to God. We cannot adequately understand divine action toward humans, including in

Paul's perspective, apart from such agitation for righteousness. In neglecting that kind of agitation, we would neglect the moral intentions at the heart of God's righteous character and redemption.

Divine announcements of creating woe and grief for humans often come in the context of denouncing idolatry and affirming that God stands in sharp contrast to false gods. The false gods do not sustain the kind of righteous relationship sought by God. In particular, they do not agitate to "refine" people toward righteousness in their relationship with God and others. Instead, they are blind to the unrighteousness despised and challenged by God. From a moral point of view, God is agitating and disturbing for the sake of righteousness in ways that false gods are not. Divine agitation with woe and grief, then, is not an end in itself. It aims for the realization and advancement of divine righteousness among humans, by means of a relationship of trust and obedience toward God.

Divine agitation for righteousness stems from God's righteous character as worthy of worship and trust (for righteousness), but human expectations for God often overlook this connection. It seems more convenient for us to portray God as being accommodating toward us without agitation for righteousness. Opting for convenience, however, can lead to a false god, a god of our own preference for convenience. A dominant theme of the biblical writings, including Paul's theology, is that God opts for righteousness over human convenience and pursues such righteousness above all else.

God agitates for righteousness among humans by seeking for them as a shepherd searches for scattered sheep (Ezek. 34:11–14; cf. Jer. 23:3). This seeking aims to bring them into a needed righteous relationship with their shepherd. The book of Isaiah, as suggested, concurs with this central biblical theme that divine righteousness aims to redeem wayward people: "Zion shall be redeemed by justice, and those in her who repent, by righteousness [בִּצְדָקָה]" (Isa. 1:27). Paul would concur (Rom. 11:25–27), and he would extend the theme to Gentiles as well (Rom. 11:11–12), the focus of his ministry.

THY KINGDOM COME

In its version of the Lord's Prayer, Matthew's Gospel connects the response of Jesus in Gethsemane with God's aim to build a kingdom of righteousness: "Thy kingdom come, Thy will be done, on earth as it is in heaven" (Matt. 6:10, RSV; cf. Matt. 6:33). We may read this verse as: "Thy kingdom come, *that is,* Thy will be done, on earth as it is in heaven." The Gethsemane response of Jesus to divine agitation for righteousness focuses the way that God's kingdom comes to earth. It signals how divine righteousness comes to cooperative humans, for the sake of building God's kingdom of righteousness.

The manifestation of the suffering and death of Jesus in his disciples through divine agitation aims to build God's kingdom. It does so by morally attracting and refining its members as what Paul considers "the liberated children of God" and "the temple of God." To that end, God's kingdom manifests and recommends the unique moral character of God, thereby portraying its distinctive moral power and benefit for all suitably inclined people. In Luke's Gospel, Jesus's parable of the sower refers to the latter people as "the ones who, when they hear the word, hold it fast in an honest and good heart, and bear fruit with patient endurance" (Luke 8:15; cf. Mark 4:21). A good heart, in Paul's thought, is formed in cooperative response to the divine righteousness offered to it (Rom. 10:6–10), often through divine agitation.

As a cooperative response to the divine good on offer in experience, trust in God has a basis in God's self-manifested character of perfect righteousness. That basis underlies not just faith but also grounded hope in God. Paul thus states that "hope [in God] does not disappoint us, because God's love has been poured into our hearts through the Holy Spirit that has been given to us" (Rom. 5:5). Paul has in mind the evidential basis of hope in God, and he finds that basis in God's self-presentation of divine righteousness in the moral center, the "heart," of receptive humans. As a result, hope in God is not a disappointment or any kind of wishful thinking. Such hope, when grounded in divine righteousness, can help to sustain a person in life's hardships, including in divine agitation (2 Cor. 1:8–10, 4:7–9). It can enable one to receive life's agitations and frustrations without despair, courtesy of the divine righteousness at work toward redemption now begun but to be completed in the fullness of time.[43]

If we overlook the ongoing role of God as agitator for righteousness, we neglect a central feature of God's redemptive effort, including in the mission of Jesus and in the message of Paul. In addition, we then may fail to understand God adequately for a suitably grounded commitment to God. We have seen that God's role as righteous agitator permeates the biblical writings, in both testaments. Despite its being widely neglected, we do well to give it a central place in Paul's theology as well as in biblical theology generally. The result will be a more resilient and compelling approach to Paul's theology and to biblical theology in general. The result also can include seeing new evidence for God's reality and presence in the agitations of human life toward righteousness. Paul, as we shall see, would emphasize the latter prospect. We turn now to the role of divine sacrificial love as a basis, motivational and evidential, for Paul's gospel of divine self-sacrifice.

---

[43] On the "now, but not yet fully" feature of God's kingdom, see Moser, *The Divine Goodness of Jesus*, ch. 7. On the formation of community in Paul's thinking and in biblical theology more generally, see J. Paul Sampley, *Pauline Partnership in Christ* (Philadelphia: Fortress Press, 1980); Robert J. Banks, *Paul's Idea of Community*, 3rd ed. (Grand Rapids, MI: Baker Academic, 2020); and Paul D. Hanson, *The People Called* (Louisville, KY: Westminster Press, 2001). Chapters 2 and 4 return to the topic of grounded faith and hope in Paul's thinking.

2 Faith Grounded in Self-Sacrifice

> The only thing that counts is faith made effective through love.
>
> Galatians 5:6

Paul's gospel, as Chapter 1 showed, is grounded in a message of divine righteousness aimed at human redemption through reconciliation with God. It gives a central role to divine sacrificial love and human faith in God, but we need to clarify the relation between those two factors. This chapter takes up that task. Paul mentions *agapē* and faith together at several places in his undisputed letters. At one point, he offers a critically important but disputed connection between the two: "In Christ Jesus neither circumcision nor uncircumcision counts for anything; the only thing that counts is faith working [or made effective] through love" (Gal. 5:6). This verse has divided interpreters for centuries but, I suggest, without due cause once we clarify Paul's thinking in its literary context, particularly in relation to the widely neglected relevance of Galatians 5:16, 22.

This chapter contends that Paul understood faith in God to have a formative basis in divine *agapē* and that this basis secures rather than threatens a foundational role for divine grace. The case benefits from a neglected appreciation of a bimodal, combined middle and passive voice of a participle for Paul. The result is Paul's view of a divinely intended ground and expression of faith in divine *agapē*. The chapter explains, with aid from some of Paul's other undisputed letters, how this approach figures in an illuminating understanding of Paul on the fulfillment-expression of the law of God in divine *agapē*. In doing so, the chapter offers an underappreciated basis for the importance of such *agapē* in faith and in pursuing the law, according to Paul.

PAUL ON WHAT COUNTS

Paul's letter to the Galatians was prompted by intense controversy over how faith, *agapē*, and God's law are related and how the controversy implicated the apostle Peter and James the brother of Jesus (Gal. 2:11–15). In his summary response, Paul remarks: "In Christ Jesus neither circumcision nor uncircumcision counts for anything; the only thing that counts is faith made effective through love" (Gal. 5:6, using "made effective" from the NRSV margin). Paul's summary touches on faith, *agapē*, and the law, but elaboration is needed with help from the larger context of his remark. We need to ask: "Made effective" by whom?

Regarding the phrase "faith made effective through love" (πίστις δι' ἀγάπης ἐνεργουμένη) in Galatians 5:6, Victor Paul Furnish remarks:

> The participle ἐνεργουμένη may be taken as either middle ("working," RSV) or passive ("inspired," NEB margin) .... There is much to be said for the latter. It has become evident that for Paul faith's obedience is an obedience in love but an obedience which has the *character* of love because its ground is God's own love by which the sinner has been claimed by and thus reconciled to God. The translation of Galatians 5:6b as "faith rendered active through love" is appropriately suggestive: faith is a response to the event of grace and in that sense constituted by it; but as *obedience* to the Lord faith has its own work ... as the "labor of love" (1 Thess. 1:3).[1]

---

[1] Victor Paul Furnish, *Theology and Ethics in Paul* (Nashville, TN: Abingdon Press, 1968), pp. 201–2. Cf. Charles B. Cousar, *Galatians*, Interpretation (Louisville, KY: John Knox, 1982), pp. 117–18. In a later work, Furnish offers "faith enacted in love"; see his *II Corinthians*, AB (New York: Doubleday, 1984), p. 328. His use of the passive voice here, as in his earlier treatment, allows for divine love having an active role in the enacting of human faith in love.

Furnish points in the right direction, but he does not present the evidence we need from Paul's letters to justify going in the direction of suggested duality in (active and passive) modes of "through love." We shall uncover the needed evidence for the important but widely neglected truth that, in Paul's perspective, the "ground [of faith in God] is God's own love," thereby adding support for the relevant duality.

The dominant view among modern commentators, favoring the translation "faith working through love," goes against the direction recommended by Furnish and the present chapter.[2] Commenting on Galatians 5:6, Michael J. Gorman states: "Faith is the presupposition of love, not the other way around (i.e., love does not give rise to faith) .... The text suggests that faith inaugurates the life of love because it is a power, a force that operates on an in individuals and communities."[3] If we take this language at face value, Gorman denies that Paul is suggesting that divine love grounds faith in God. This chapter opposes that view, based on evidence from Paul himself, while acknowledging that faith is nonetheless to express divine love. It thus supports the view that, in Paul's thought, being loved by God and loving others are to be held together.

James D. G. Dunn says of the phrase "faith working through love" that it "is almost a single concept, faith-through-love, love-energized faith," but he rejects "faith energized by God's love (Duncan 157–58) ... in view of the elaboration of the thought in

---

[2] See, for instance, Ernest De Witt Burton, *A Critical and Exegetical Commentary on the Epistle to the Galatians*, ICC (New York: Charles Scribner's Sons, 1920), p. 281; F. F. Bruce, *Commentary on Galatians*, NIGNTC (Grand Rapids, MI: Eerdmans, 1982), pp. 232–33; Joseph A. Fitzmyer, "The Letter to the Galatians," in the *New Jerome Biblical Commentary*, eds. Raymond S. Brown, et al. (Englewood Cliffs, NJ: Prentice-Hall, 1990), p. 780; Richard Longenecker, *Galatians*, WBC (Waco, TX: Word, 1990), pp. 229–30; J. Louis Martyn, *Galatians*, AB (New York: Doubleday, 1997), p. 474; Sam K. Williams, *Galatians*, ANTC (Nashville, TN: Abingdon Press, 1997), p. 138; and John M. G. Barclay, *Paul and the Gift* (Grand Rapids, MI: Eerdmans, 2015), p. 100.

[3] Michael J. Gorman, *Cruciformity* (Grand Rapids, MI: Eerdmans, 2001), pp. 130–31.

[Galatians] 5:13–14."⁴ He thinks of it instead as "faith coming to expression in and through love (Burton 280)." A key issue concerns the source of the love "through" which faith arises.

Three points are noteworthy. First, George Duncan opts for the passive rather than the middle voice. He proposes: "a faith that is quickened into life by a sense of God's love."⁵ Paul himself invokes *agapē* rather than "a sense of" *agapē,* and we do well not to collapse that distinction. Second, "the elaboration of the thought in 5:13–14" does not conflict with the suggested passive feature from the NRSV margin: "faith made effective through love." Faith made effective through divine love can reflect that love as its source and thus extend such love to others, as represented in the love commands from the Torah and Jesus. Third, Dunn's remarks ignore a role for divine *agapē* in Paul's understanding here of the relation between faith and *agapē.* It is misleading for Dunn not to consider the important role for divine *agapē.* We shall correct that omission.

In later work, Dunn offers a broader approach to Galatians 5:6 that can accommodate the translations suggested by George Duncan and the NRSV and NEB margins. He remarks: "It is precisely faith as complete reliance on and openness to God's grace which (inevitably) comes to expression in love."⁶ The acknowledged reliance of faith on divine grace entails the reliance of faith on divine love, given the inclusion of such love in grace, according to Paul's understanding (see Rom. 8:32–39 and Rom. 5:1–5, where Paul mentions grace and love working together). So, Dunn's remark evidently commits him, at least, to the gist of Duncan's suggested translation that faith is "quickened" by divine love.

---

⁴ James D. G. Dunn, "Neither Circumcision nor Uncircumcision, but …," in Dunn, *The New Perspective on Paul,* rev. ed. (Grand Rapids, MI: Eerdmans, 2008), p. 331. Cf. Dunn, *Commentary on the Epistle to the Galatians* (London: Black, 1993), p. 262.

⁵ George Duncan, *Epistle of Paul to the Galatians,* MNTC (New York: Harper, 1934), p. 158.

⁶ James D. G. Dunn, *The Theology of Paul the Apostle* (Grand Rapids, MI: Eerdmans, 1998), p. 638.

Evidence in support of Duncan's translation arises from Paul's following remark in the immediate context of Galatians 5:6: "The fruit of the Spirit is love [ἀγάπη], joy, peace, patience, kindness, generosity, faith [πίστις], gentleness, and self-control .... If we live by the Spirit, let us also be guided by the Spirit" (Gal. 5:22-23, 25; replacing "faithfulness" in the NRSV with "faith"). Paul thinks of love and faith as originating from the Spirit of God, even if they depend also (in part) on human receptivity and cooperation toward them. J. Louis Martyn thus comments on faith (πίστις) according to Paul in Galatians 5:23: "Faith is a mark of the fruit that the Spirit is bearing in the daily life of the community of Christ."[7] Paul does not suggest that divine love is a fruit of human faith, of course, even if human faith can provide an opportunity for receiving and expressing such love.

We find a widely neglected suggestion in Galatians 5:16 for interpreting (and translating) Galatians 5:6: "I say, walk by the Spirit [πνεύματι περιπατεῖτε], and you will not carry out the desire of the flesh" (Gal. 5:16-18, NASB). Paul's injunction to "walk by the Spirit" anticipates his reference to the Spirit who empowers people with the fruit of divine love and in their faith in God (Gal. 5:22), thus countering "the desire of the flesh." Walking by the Spirit, then, is walking by the power and fruit of God's Spirit. It captures what Paul has in mind with a basis of "faith made effective through love," the love and faith empowered by God's Spirit. So, his talk of "by the Spirit" is important as an indicator of a passive component, from a human perspective, in "faith made effective through love." That component depends on divine love as a ground, although humans can resist that ground, thereby grieving God's Spirit. That ground is to come to fruition in an expression of divine love toward others.

We should interpret (and translate) Galatians 5:6 in the light of Galatians 5:22-23. The participle ἐνεργουμένη merits at least a passive component, given that, according to Galatians 5:22-23, the relevant love is a fruit of God's Spirit (while divine love, as just noted, is not a

---

[7] Martyn, *Galatians*, p. 499.

fruit of human faith, in Paul's thought). Paul's use of this participle in Galatians 5:6 suggests a semantic duality of passive as well as middle features. This goes against the familiar exclusive interpretation of passive and middle forms in New Testament commentaries and Greek grammars. The NRSV translation "made effective" (from the margin) serves well as long as we allow for the effectiveness to be bimodal, made by God (allowing for a passive sense) as well as by humans (allowing for a middle sense).

In his work on passive and middle voices in classical and koine Greek, Carl W. Conrad has suggested the relevant kind of semantic duality in the voice of the imperatives in Romans 12:2: μὴ συσχηματίζεσθε τῷ αἰῶνι τούτῳ, ἀλλὰ μεταμορφοῦσθε τῇ ἀνακαινώσει τοῦ νοός. He explains:

> This exhortation follows upon Paul's urging that Roman believers "offer up your σώματα as a θυσίαν ζῶσαν . . ." Clearly the will and initiative to this "living sacrifice" lies in the believers – else Paul would not be exhorting them. The imperatives that follow in verse 2, "μὴ συσχηματίζεσθε" and "μεταμορφοῦσθε," should be understood as having *middle* sense – even if the transformation indicated by "μεταμορφοῦσθε" is one that God is to execute. It is the Roman believers who are not to adapt *themselves* to the pattern of this world-age, and they are to deliberately, consciously permit God to transform them in a renovation of their mind-set (ἀνακαινώσει τοῦ νοός). Here too, then, it is possible to recognize that the "middle-passive" form is not really *passive* in sense and that the Greek-speaking Paul had no need to choose between a *middle* or *passive* sense. For my part I would suggest that verse 2 be Englished as a sort of "permissive passive": "Don't let this world mold you but allow yourselves to be transformed in the process of reconstruction of your mind-set . . . ."[8]

---

[8] Carl W. Conrad, "New Observations on Voice in the Ancient Greek Verb," https://cpb-usw2.wpmucdn.com/sites.wustl.edu/dist/8/2865/files/2020/10/newobsancgrkvc.pdf.

The lesson for our purpose is that "Paul had no need to choose between a *middle* or *passive* sense" in all cases. In other words, he can use semantic duality with some of his passive or middle forms, combining features of the passive and the middle. The best semantic fit for a particular context should be the basis for ascribing such semantic duality, in keeping with interpretation and translation in general. Given its literary context, Galatians 5:6, like Romans 12:2, merits careful consideration as having a participle with such semantic duality. We shall clarify the relevant evidence.

We have noted the relevance of Galatians 5:22–23 to a passive feature for "ἐνεργουμένη" in Galatians 5:6. We also should note Paul's emphasis, in the same context, on "being led [ἄγεσθε] by the Spirit," in Galatians 5:18. Paul would say that being thus led is central to "the only thing that counts" (Gal. 5:6, NRSV; cf. Rom. 8:14). Indeed, in Galatians 5:5 he credits the Spirit as a source of faith and hope, thus suggesting that they have a passive component. Likewise, he would acknowledge a passive component in his direct parallel to Galatians 5:6: "Neither circumcision nor uncircumcision is anything; but a new creation is everything." God, according to Paul, brings the relevant new creation, even if humans must be receptive or cooperative toward it (cf. Rom. 4:17, 20–21). So, we should make room for a passive component in "the only thing that counts" in Galatians 5:6, that is, in faith "made effective" through divine love.

The context of Galatians 5:6 indicates Paul's concern for an active as well as a passive component in "faith ἐνεργουμένη in relation to love" and in "new creation." He thus remarks that "there is no law against such things" as love and faith (Gal. 5:23), thus suggesting that humans can be responsible for them. In addition, he relates love and faith to the Galatians' "living" (ζῶμεν) and "walking" (στοιχῶμεν) by the Spirit (Gal. 5:25), and he uses injunctions to encourage love and faith among the Galatians. For instance, he advises: "Through love become slaves to (δουλεύετε) one another. For the whole law is summed up in a single commandment, 'You shall love your neighbor as yourself'" (Gal. 5:13–14). He also speaks of "sowing [σπείρων] to the Spirit," in the present context (Gal. 6:8). So, Paul has in mind active as well as passive features in "the only thing that counts" and in "new creation." Contrary to Dunn's previous suggestion, the active features suggested by Galatians 5:13–14 do not count against Paul's intended role for passive features, too. We should avoid, then, a false disjunction of "either–or" here.

Hans Dieter Betz rightly looks to the wider context of Galatians 5:6 to clarify Paul's understanding. He translates with the middle voice, but then adds: "When the Christian 'believes in Jesus Christ', he believes that the Son of God died on the cross because he 'loved me and gave himself up for me.' When the Christian receives the Spirit of the Son of God (4:6), he also receives the divine power of love which enabled Christ to do what he did. Love is named first in the list (5:22–23) called 'the fruit of the Spirit.'"[9] Such attention to the larger context is necessary for responsible interpretation of Paul, especially when an interpretation cannot be settled on grammatical grounds alone.

Further confirmation of an active divine role in the basis of faith comes from Paul's probing questions about the Spirit of God and faith for the Galatian Christians: "Did you receive the Spirit by doing the works of the law or by believing what you heard? ... Did you experience so much for nothing? – if it really was for nothing. Well then, does God supply [ἐπιχορηγῶν] you with the Spirit and work miracles among you by your doing the works of the law, or by your believing what you heard?" (Gal. 3:2, 4–5). Paul thus speaks of receiving "the promise of the Spirit through faith [διὰ τῆς πίστεως]" (Gal. 3:14). Faith, then, is the human attitude that receives God's active Spirit. Paul thus brings together the Spirit and faith in the context of Galatians 5:6: "Through the Spirit, by faith, we eagerly wait for the hope of righteousness" (Gal. 5:5). In the absence of God's

---

[9] Hans Dieter Betz, *Galatians*, Hermeneia (Minneapolis, MN: Fortress Press, 1979), p. 263.

active Spirit, faith in God would lose the exercise of its receptive, responsive function and thus its received ground.

The Spirit has real features experienced and sometimes received in human lives, according to Paul. Luke Timothy Johnson has commented accordingly on Galatians 5:6: "The Holy Spirit working within [the Galatians] enables them to live with a power that makes external markings irrelevant."[10] The Spirit includes, as noted, definite "fruit" (Gal. 5:22–23), particularly divine love that grounds receptive faith in God. Paul makes the latter idea explicit in Romans 5:1–5 (quoted just below), where Paul's thinking on faith (and the law) is arguably more developed than in his letter to the Galatians.[11] We turn then to Paul's related comments on the topic of faith's connection with (divine) *agapē*, to clarify his proposed ground for faith.

FAITH AND DIVINE *AGAPĒ*

The context of Galatians 5:6 requires us to consider Paul's autobiographical remark at Galatians 2:20: "It is no longer I who live, but it is Christ who lives in me. And the life I now live in the flesh I live by faith in the Son of God [ἐν πίστει ζῶ τῇ τοῦ υἱοῦ τοῦ θεοῦ], who loved me and gave himself for me."[12] This remark reveals Paul's understanding, at least in part, of the relation between faith and divine *agapē* in

---

[10] Luke Timothy Johnson, *The Canonical Paul, Vol. 1: Constructing Paul* (Grand Rapids, MI: Eerdmans, 2021), p. 212. See also David John Lull, *The Spirit in Galatia: Paul's Interpretation of Pneuma as Divine Power* (Chico, CA: Scholars Press, 1980).

[11] For relevant discussion, see Thomas H. Tobin, *Paul's Rhetoric in Contexts* (Peabody, MA: Hendrickson, 2004), pp. 47–78. Cf. E. P. Sanders, *Paul, the Law, and the Jewish People* (Minneapolis, MN: Fortress Press, 1983), pp. 100–101; and Dunn, *The Theology of Paul the Apostle*, pp. 729–33.

[12] We need not digress to the controversy over the status of the genitive "πίστεως Ἰησοῦ Χριστοῦ", as represented in Galatians 2:16. The latter verse shows that Paul is concerned at least with general human faith: ἡμεῖς εἰς Χριστὸν Ἰησοῦν ἐπιστεύσαμεν. Galatians 2:20 is referring to Paul's own faith in Christ (dative) as representative for his audience. For discussion of the general controversy, see Arland J. Hultgren, "*Pistis Christou*: Faith in or of Christ?," in Hultgren, *Paul's Letter to the Romans* (Grand Rapids, MI: Eerdmans, 2011), pp. 623–61. For a plausible approach, allowing Paul to refer to the faith of Jesus in Romans 3, in parallel to the faith of Abraham in Romans 4, see Luke Timothy Johnson, *The Canonical Paul, Vol. 2: Interpreting Paul* (Grand Rapids, MI: Eerdmans, 2021), pp. 13–26.

Christ. Paul's faith is a response, of acceptance and cooperation, toward the one from God who loved him with self-sacrificial *agapē*. It is thus a response to divine sacrificial *agapē* as a ground or basis that can counteract disappointment or hopelessness about faith. Furnish thus remarks: "Paul understands faith itself to originate in God's love met in the cross. This is apparent when he writes about his (and every believer's) living by 'faith in the Son of God who loved me and gave himself [=died] for me'."[13] We shall see that this is half of the story for Paul.

Paul is well-known for his overlapping comments on faith in God and hope in God (cf. Gal. 5:5). This extends to some of his undisputed writings other than Galatians. In one noteworthy comment in his letter to the Romans, Paul moves directly from faith to hope:

> Since we are justified by faith, we have peace with God through our Lord Jesus Christ, through whom we have obtained access to this grace in which we stand; and we boast in our hope of sharing the glory of God. And not only that, but we also boast in our sufferings, knowing that suffering produces endurance, and endurance produces character, and character produces hope, and hope does not disappoint [καταισχύνει] us, because God's love has been poured into our hearts through the Holy Spirit that has been given to us.
> *(Rom. 5:1–5)*

Faith in God through Christ, in Paul's thinking, gives humans "access" to divine "grace," and that grace includes a self-presentation of divine *agapē* through God's Spirit.

We may think of divine grace as a redemptive power that includes divine righteous *agapē* in action through sacrificial gift-giving. Divine *agapē*, as Chapter 1 suggested, is integral to divine righteousness, because such righteousness is self-giving for the good, including the redemption, of people, and *agapē* supplies that

---

[13] Furnish, *II Corinthians*, p. 326.

self-giving. In addition, faith leads to hope in God and divine righteousness (Gal. 5:5), given a divine promise of eventual human sharing in the fullness of God's goodness (or "glory"). Such hope has its ground in a reality that blocks our being "disappointed" or left hopeless. Paul identifies this grounding reality: "God's love has been poured into our hearts through the Holy Spirit that has been given to us."

In Romans 5:1–5, Paul has in mind a divinely provided ground for hope and faith in God. Its role as a ground is indicated by its preventing ultimate disappointment or hopelessness regarding God's reality or goodness. The divine *agapē* in question, according to Paul, has a self-manifestation through the historical life of Jesus: "God proves his love for us in that while we still were sinners Christ died for us" (Rom. 5:8). In addition, and this is the second part of Paul's account, it has a contemporary manifestation in (receptive) human experience.

Gordon Fee comments:

> God's love [according to Paul] has been demonstrated historically in its most lavish and expansive expression through Christ's death for his enemies (Rom. 5:6-8, thus the basis for "peace with God" and "access" to his gracious presence). But neither is such love merely an objective historical event. God's love, played out to the full in Christ, is an experienced reality in the "heart" of the believer by the presence of the Spirit. *This* is what the Spirit has so richly "shed abroad in our hearts."[14]

This presented *agapē* is a divine self-manifestation of God's gracious moral character toward humans, and it can influence human moral experience in a powerful way. It figures in the kind of divine power of God's Spirit that Paul relates to faith: "My speech and my

---

[14] Gordon Fee, *God's Empowering Presence: The Holy Spirit in the Letters of Paul* (Peabody, MA: Hendrickson, 1994), p. 496. Cf. Ernst Käsemann, *Commentary on Romans*, pp. 135–36.

proclamation were not with plausible words of wisdom, but with a demonstration of the Spirit and of power, so that your faith might rest not on [μὴ ᾖ ἐν] human wisdom but on [ἐν] the power of God" (1 Cor. 2:4–5). Paul expects faith in God to be (grounded) in the power of God, particularly the self-sacrificial love characteristic of God.

Paul thinks of divine *agapē* as not only experienced but also motivating, or leading, toward a goal for a person and thus a basis for hope in God. He remarks: "The love of Christ urges us on," assuming that this is God's love from Christ (2 Cor. 5:14; cf. Rom. 8:31–35). Such divine motivating guidance for cooperative people figures, as noted, in his understanding of being a child of God: "All who are led by the Spirit of God are children of God" (Rom. 8:14; cf. Gal. 5:18). God's powerful character of *agapē*, then, anchors hope and faith in God, according to Paul.

The ground of hope and faith in divine *agapē* is a matter of (uncoercive) causal influence and evidence for them. The NEB translates with: "such a hope is no mockery." That is, it is no "fantasy" (REB), from the standpoint of fact and the standpoint of available evidence. Leander Keck touches on both standpoints in connection with Romans 5:5: "What is hoped for is real, and its reality will be evident; otherwise, its illusory character would disgrace those who hope .... Paul avers that the experience of God's love generates the assurance that the hoped-for glory is real, since God's love does not deceive."[15] He notes further, in connection with Romans 5:8, that "by using the present tense Paul says that God demonstrates that love [manifested in Christ] now, in the heart – the core of the self and the seat of the will."[16] Paul has in mind people with the receptivity of faith toward God in Christ. This is confirmed by his opening remark on faith in Romans 5.

Returning to the immediate context of Galatians 5:6, we have seen that Paul puts *agapē* first in his list of what God's Spirit yields:

---

[15] Leander Keck, *Romans*, ANTC (Nashville, TN: Abingdon Press, 2005), p. 138.
[16] Keck, *Romans*, p. 139.

"the fruit of the Spirit is love ..." (Gal. 5:22). Paul thinks of *agapē* as stemming from God, as we have seen in Romans 5:5, and his list confirms this. Martyn captures this consideration regarding Galatians 5:22: "Paul does not speak of a romantic emotion between two persons, but rather of the kind of love that was defined by Christ when he gave his life 'for us.' Thus, the love that is now a communal characteristic of daily life in the church as community is the love that has its ultimate source and pattern in God (Gal. 5:6, 13, 14; 2:20)."[17] I share Martyn's position that Galatians 2:20 and 5:6 should be read to support the view that, according to Paul, *agapē* "has its ultimate source and pattern in God." I have argued, on the basis of relevant evidence, that it is also, in Paul's thinking, an evidential ground for faith (and hope) in God.

Even if one favors the middle voice in translating Galatians 5:6, as does Martyn among others, my suggestion that divine *agapē* grounds faith for Paul should hold. The reason is straightforward: Faith that expresses itself or "works" through *agapē*, in Paul's perspective, depends on *agapē*, including enemy-love, which is not a purely human product. It has, as Martyn notes, its ultimate ground or source in God's character of *agapē*. So, if we understand Paul's broader position on *agapē*, translation by the middle voice in Galatians 5:6 will not undermine his view on the relation between faith and divine *agapē*.

I have recommended a combination of the passive and middle voices, because this explicitly captures Paul's central position, suggested elsewhere in Galatians and in Romans, on the grounding role of divine *agapē* in faith in God. It also accommodates his relevant imperatives on love and faith. Omitting or obscuring Paul's central position leads to a misrepresentation of him on the relation between love and faith.

It is doubtful that Paul is directly responsible for the substance of the Epistle to the Ephesians, even though its substance is Pauline in

---

[17] Martyn, *Galatians*, p. 498.

various ways. Without digressing to that long-standing controversy, we should note one passage that reflects the substance of Paul's own theology: "I pray that ... Christ may dwell in your hearts through faith [διὰ τῆς πίστεως], as you are being rooted and grounded [ἐρριζωμένοι καὶ τεθεμελιωμένοι] in love [ἀγάπῃ]. I pray that you may have the power to ... know the love of Christ that surpasses knowledge, so that you may be filled with all the fullness of God" (Eph. 3:17–19). The author captures Paul's view that faith in God through Christ is "rooted and grounded" in divine *agapē*, the *agapē* from Christ that goes beyond mere knowledge.

The "power to know" divine *agapē*, according to the author of Ephesians, comes from God (to whom he prays), and therefore this power is not just human power. In addition, the knowing in question is experiential, and not just theoretical, given that it leaves one "filled with all the fullness of God," that is, the fullness of God's character of righteous *agapē*. This experienced divine *agapē*, according to the prayer, will leave one's faith in God "rooted and grounded" in that divine character of *agapē*. We have in Ephesians, then, an affirmation of Paul's own view of the grounding relation between divine *agapē* and faith found in Galatians and Romans. This does not settle the interpretation or the translation of Galatians 5:6, of course, but it indicates that an early influential interpreter of Paul would agree with a key feature of the understanding of Paul proposed here.

Faith in God, according to Paul, is not just intellectual assent to intellectual information about God or Christ. It includes trust in God, and such trust has God, and not just information about God, as its object.[18] As Paul says, "Abraham believed God" (Gal. 3:6; cf. Rom. 4:3). He adds, in his letter to the Romans: "To one who without works trusts [πιστεύοντι ἐπὶ] him who justifies the ungodly, such faith

---

[18] It is misleading, then, for Martin Buber to downplay this feature of Paul's view of faith in God. See Buber, *Two Types of Faith*, trans. N. P. Goldhawk (New York: Macmillan, 1951), pp. 97–98.

[πίστις] is reckoned as righteousness" (Rom. 4:5; cf. Rom. 4:17, 24; Gal. 3:6; 2 Cor. 1:9).

Faith requires trusting in God, according to Paul, and this includes an acquaintance with God that goes beyond intellectual information about God. This acquaintance, according to Romans 5:5, includes a meeting with God's moral character of righteous *agapē*, and that character is irreducible to intellectual information about God. Paul also thinks of receiving grace through faith as requiring "obedience from the heart," beyond mere intellectual assent (Rom. 6:17).

Paul explains the divine motive for promoting faith in God: "The scripture, foreseeing that God would justify the Gentiles by faith, declared the gospel beforehand to Abraham, saying, 'All the Gentiles shall be blessed in you.' For this reason, those who believe are blessed with Abraham who believed" (Gal. 3:8–9; cf. Rom. 4:16). According to Paul, God wants the divine promise of redemption for all people of Abraham's faith to depend on grace and thereby be well-grounded for all of them. As a result, Gentiles will not end up as second-class citizens in God's society. The key issue now concerns Paul's understanding of the guarantee or ground for faith in God.

We have noted, in connection with Galatians 2:20 and Romans 5:5, a role for divine *agapē* in human experience as a ground for faith. Paul elaborates on his perspective in an important claim about divine activity: "It is God who is at work in [ἐνεργῶν ἐν] you, enabling you both to will and to work for his good pleasure [εὐδοκίας]" (Phil 2: 13; cf. 1 Cor. 12:6). In enabling people "to will" for God's good pleasure, God would work in human experience to attract them to will in agreement with God's good pleasure and will. This would include God's presenting the divine good will in human experience in a way that engages and challenges a human will toward cooperation with God's will (cf. Rom. 12:2). Divine *agapē* would be part of this good will, because it would include divine willing of what is good, all things considered, for people, and it thus would have normative value. In addition, such willing would emerge as a causal influence in human experience for the sake of attracting people to divine righteousness.

Paul's understanding of divine *agapē* as a causal influence in grounding faith does not support a relation of causal determination of faith by God. It allows for human rejection of an offered ground for faith in divine *agapē*. So, God does not do the decision-making, acting, believing, or trusting for humans. Paul thus takes rejection of God's offer to be a live option in Galatians: "I live by faith in the Son of God, who loved me and gave himself for me. I do not nullify [ἀθετῶ] the grace of God" (Gal 2:20–21; cf. Gal. 4:9, 5:4).

Choosing to reject faith grounded in divine *agapē*, according to Paul, would be a way to nullify, or set aside, the grace of God. This consideration is important, because neither faith nor its ground in divine *agapē* is causally forced on a person. God, in Paul's thinking, takes the risk of human rejection or refusal of divine *agapē* and faith in God. He thus portrays God to plead for the return of people who have turned away (Rom. 10:21; cf. Isa. 65:2).

Paul assumes that humans can decide to reject (their cooperatively receiving) divine goodness, including the *agapē* that grounds faith. He thus asks: "Do you despise the riches of [God's] kindness and forbearance and patience? Do you not realize that God's kindness is meant to lead you to repentance [μετάνοιάν]?" (Rom 2:4; cf. Rom. 1:18, 10:21). It is misleading, then, for Furnish to say that "Paul understands man's response to be an expression of God's power to redeem and transform, not of man's power to comply and perform."[19]

Paul does not hold that only God's power, and not human power, lies behind a human response to God regarding faith or

---

[19] Furnish, *Theology and Ethics in Paul*, p. 238; cf. p. 239. A similarly misleading approach to Paul on divine power is found in C. E. B. Cranfield, *A Critical and Exegetical Commentary on the Epistle to the Romans*, ICC (Edinburgh: T&T Clark, 1975), vol. 1, p. 90; and Käsemann, *Commentary on Romans*, p. 226. For critical discussion, see Chapter 5. An additional misleading approach to faith in God can be found in Gustaf Aulén, *The Drama and the Symbols*, trans. S. Linton (London: SPCK, 1970), pp. 137–39.

obedience grounded in divine *agapē*. Otherwise, he would put at risk human responsibility in responding to divine *agapē* with faith, along with the human freedom allowed by such *agapē*.[20] Paul's many injunctions to obedience, faith, and love assume human responsibility to God.

Paul's understanding of faith grounded in divine *agapē* fits with his view that "hearing" is an avenue of faith in God: "Faith comes from what is heard, and what is heard comes through the word of Christ" (Rom. 10:17). The "word of Christ" is, according to Paul, the good news of what God has done in Christ (Rom. 10:6–9, 15–16). This good news focuses on, and is anchored in, divine *agapē* toward humans. Paul thus announces, as noted: "God proves his love for us in that while we still were sinners Christ died for us" (Rom. 5:8).

Divine love, in Paul's thinking, anchors the good news of divine reconciliation and forgiveness toward humans (Rom. 5:10–11; 2 Cor. 5:19). So, Paul's good news presents the divine *agapē* that anchors faith in God. This good news, according to Paul, is thus "the power of God for salvation to everyone who has faith" (Rom. 1:16). That power includes divine *agapē*, to be received by voluntary faith in God.

In his Corinthian correspondence, Paul understands his good news in relation to the power of divine creation. He says of this good news: "We do not proclaim ourselves; we proclaim Jesus Christ as Lord .... For it is the God who said, 'Let light shine out of darkness,' who has shone in our hearts to give the light of the knowledge of the glory of God in the face of Jesus Christ" (2 Cor. 4:5–6). Paul announces this good news "so that grace, as it extends to more and more people, may increase thanksgiving, to the glory of God" (2 Cor. 4:15).

As suggested, Paul understands the grace of the good news to include divine *agapē*. He makes this explicit with his remark that

---

[20] On the role of human responsibility in Paul's thought, see Leander Keck, "The Accountable Self," in Keck, *Christ's First Theologian* (Waco, TX: Baylor University Press, 2015), pp. 133–45. Chapter 5 returns to the topic of human agency in relation to Paul's gospel.

"the love of [= from] Christ urges us on, because we are convinced that one has died for all; therefore, all have died" (2 Cor. 5:14). So, we may understand "the light of the knowledge of the glory of God in the face of Jesus Christ" in parallel with Romans 5:5, and thus to include divine *agapē* presented as a ground in human experience for faith in God. We thus find additional confirmation for our reading of Paul on a ground of faith from divine *agapē*.

We should ask, briefly, how much of Paul's notion of divine goodness or righteousness is included in his conception of divine *agapē*. At times Paul appears to have divine *agapē* include divine righteousness, given his appeal to the self-giving of Christ as a benchmark.[21] He seems to suggest, in at least two passages, that *agapē* requires what is good and right and thus cannot be unrighteous (contrary to a common use of the term "love"). Thus: "Love does no wrong to a neighbor" (Rom. 13:10). In addition, "[love] does not rejoice in wrongdoing" (1 Cor. 13:6). The latter remarks invite the question of the exact relation of divine *agapē*, in Paul's perspective, to divine goodness more generally and thus to the law of God. Without digressing to that broader topic, we now can talk of righteous divine *agapē* to ensure the moral robustness of Paul's talk of *agapē* and to distinguish it from a loyal partnership in evil. We shall clarify briefly Paul's understanding of the relation of *agapē* to the law of God.

AGAPĒ AND THE LAW OF GOD

I have argued that divine *agapē*, in Paul's thought, is a ground for faith in God, while it also is to be expressed through such faith. I also have suggested that his notion of divine *agapē* is morally robust, requiring righteous actions. This position raises the question of how the relevant *agapē* is related to the law of God, given the bearing of the law on righteous actions.

---

[21] For a broader discussion of the topic, bearing on the relevant views of Karl Barth and Anders Nygren, see N. H. G. Robinson, *The Groundwork of Christian Ethics* (London: Collins, 1971), pp. 291–307. Robinson plausibly takes exception to the positions on the law of God and divine determinism suggested by Barth and Nygren.

E. P. Sanders has commented on Galatians 5:14 and 6:2 in a way that clarifies our present topic: "The reader of Galatians can understand Paul as saying 'you are not under *the* law, but nevertheless you are under *a* law, the law of Christ, which commands love of the neighbor' *or* 'you are not under the law, but nevertheless you should fulfill it, not by being circumcised but by loving your neighbor: that is real fulfillment.' I think that the latter is by far the more likely meaning, especially since the law which is to be fulfilled is Leviticus 19:18."[22] Sanders adds that "Paul's ethics are grounded on the Spirit and on love of the neighbor."[23] That claim seems defensible as far as it goes, but how exactly does Paul relate divine *agapē* to the fulfilled law? We should consider that the relation involves what we have identified regarding Paul on faith: Divine *agapē* is a ground and a fulfillment-expression for obeying the law as fulfilled, that is, "the law of Christ." The topic is complex, but we can identify some contours.

In his letter to the Romans, Paul calls the law of God "the law of faith" (Rom. 3:27), and he claims that his view of faith in God upholds the law of God rather than abolishes it (Rom. 3:31; cf. Rom. 7:12–13, 22). He also claims, in his Corinthian correspondence, that "circumcision is nothing, and uncircumcision is nothing; but obeying the commandments of God is everything" (1 Cor. 7:19). This position is contrary to antinomianism. Paul thus understands opposition to God in terms of not submitting to God's law: "The mind that is set on the flesh is hostile to God; it does not submit to God's law – indeed it cannot" (Rom. 8:7). In addition, Paul holds that the law is summed up or fulfilled (πεπλήρωται) by love of neighbor (Gal. 5:14; cf. Rom.13:8, using "πεπλήρωκεν"), and that this does not remove the law but makes its fulfillment "the law of Christ [τὸν νόμον τοῦ Χριστοῦ]" (Gal. 6:2; cf. 1 Cor. 9:21). These views call for comment on the relation between

---

[22] Sanders, *Paul, the Law, and the Jewish People*, p. 98.
[23] Sanders, *Paul, the Law, and the Jewish People*, p. 103.

agapē and the law, given Paul's view that divine *agapē* grounds faith in God.

Paul remarks that "the law was our disciplinarian until Christ came, so that we might be justified by faith. But now that faith has come, we are no longer subject to a disciplinarian" (Gal. 3:24–25). It would be premature, given our previous evidence, to infer that Paul abandons the law of God altogether. Instead, he suggests that the law as fulfilled continues as the "law of Christ." The law as fulfilled, in Paul's perspective, centers on divine *agapē* and Christ. We need to see how this centering proceeds.

C. F. D. Moule remarks of Paul:

> It seems to have come home to him that only when one is "put right" with God by the response of faith to the antecedent grace of God does it become possible to fulfil the real demands of the law, when these are formulated in terms of its "spirit" rather than its "letter".... A trustful response to love is the only means of getting anywhere near to meeting the demands of love. Thus, Paul's ... "yes" to faith turns out to be, in fact, his "yes" to the "law of love" (all the deeds required by love – see Rom. 13:8, Gal. 5:14), a "yes" made possible only because it is the result of faith .... It is because of Paul's understanding of Jesus Christ – because he has found in him the revelation and embodiment and mediation of the love of God – that faith in Jesus Christ is for him thenceforward the way to God.[24]

Moule means faith as "the way to God" even in relation to the law of God. He is a rare commentator who sees the relation, in Paul's thinking, between faith as a response to divine *agapē* and the law of God. The key is to appreciate Paul's focus on fulfilling the law in terms of

---

[24] C. F. D. Moule, "Jesus, Judaism, and Paul," in *Tradition and Interpretation in the New Testament*, eds. Gerald Hawthorne and Otto Betz (Tübingen: Mohr Siebeck, 1987), p. 49. See also Furnish, *Theology and Ethics in Paul*, pp. 191–94, 199–203; and Furnish, *The Love Command in the New Testament* (Nashville, TN: Abingdon Press, 1972), pp. 95–102.

its purpose of realizing righteous *agapē* from God in and among its hearers. We thus see that Paul is no antinomian but is an advocate of the law of God properly pursued, relative to God's main redemptive purpose.

Paul endorses faith, grounded in divine *agapē*, as crucial to how the law of God is to be pursued: "Gentiles, who did not pursue righteousness, attained righteousness, even the righteousness which is by faith; but Israel, pursuing [διώκων] a law of righteousness, did not arrive at *that* law. Why? Because *they did* not *pursue it* by faith, but as though *it were* by works" (Rom. 9:30–32, NASB, with italics indicating additions). Faith is thus the way to pursue the law, in Paul's understanding, and therefore it does not reject the law. Instead, it responds cooperatively to the "righteous requirement of the law" (Rom. 8:4) that seeks fulfillment of the law in righteous *agapē* in and among its hearers.

Paul, we have seen, takes the *agapē* in question to have a divine basis in God's Spirit and unique character (Gal. 5:22; Rom. 5:5) and to be received by faith as cooperative trust in God. Such faith, on that divine ground, will then reflect divine *agapē* in humans as they cooperate with it (Gal. 5:6). God does not cooperate for them, because they are responsible agents before God and not simply extensions of God's will. Assuming responsible agency among humans, Paul holds that "whatever does not proceed from faith is sin," that is, is displeasing to God (Rom. 14:23). Whatever does not proceed from faith, according to Paul, does not pursue the opportunity of receiving and extending God's power of divine righteous *agapē*. In that case, God's law is not fulfilled relative to its divine purpose.

We can clarify our interpretation of Paul by identifying Paul's position on "works of the law" that contrast with faith. Paul's sharp contrast entails his following position: "We have come to believe in Christ Jesus, so that we might be justified by faith in Christ, and not by doing the works of the law, because no one will be justified by the works of the law" (Gal. 2:16; cf. Rom. 3:28). Paul adds: "The law does not rest on faith; on the contrary, 'Whoever does the works of the law will live by them'" (Gal. 3:12; cf. Rom. 10:5; Lev. 18:5). He means: "Will live by the works of the law, *and not by faith.*" We need to account for this contrast to understand Paul on faith and its ground in divine *agapē*.

"Works of the law," in Paul's sense of the phrase, do not pursue the law by faith, at least according to his understanding in Romans. They thus do not properly accommodate the divine grace and *agapē* motivating the law as fulfilled through faith (from the standpoint of God's purpose). They conflict, then, with faith grounded in divine *agapē*, that is, faith that cooperatively receives and expresses divine righteous *agapē* as an unearned gift from God intended for all people, Gentiles as well as Jews. Paul's sharp contrast is straightforward: "If it is by grace, it is no longer on the basis of works, otherwise grace would no longer be grace" (Rom. 11:6). We have noted this corollary already: "For this reason it depends on faith, in order that the promise may rest on grace" (Rom. 4:16). Faith is the divinely approved mode of approaching God to receive divine grace and *agapē*, but "works of the law," including in the special sense indicated by Romans 4:4, are not part of that mode. Hence, Paul draws his sharp contrast, making room for unearned divine grace and *agapē*, while acknowledging God as setting the standard for relating to God through the law.

If we separate faith from its ground in divine *agapē*, we separate it also from the aim of the biblical love commands. Paul countered this problem in his Corinthian correspondence and elsewhere (e.g., 1 Cor. 13:1–8). The "works of the law," contrasted with faith in God by Paul, include an exclusive use of national identity-markers for Israel, but they are not limited to that use.[25] Paul thought of some members of Israel, himself included, as having misunderstood the underlying divine purpose of the law and thus as having misunderstood how to "pursue" the law, with faith grounded in the grace of divine *agapē*

---

[25] Dunn acknowledges this in his later work, such as "The New Perspective," in Dunn, *The New Perspective on Paul*, rev. ed., pp. 21–36. For relevant discussion, see Barclay, *Paul and the Gift*, pp. 159–66.

(Rom. 9:31–32; Phil. 3:9). He did not characterize Judaism as inherently or altogether legalistic, however, as seeking to earn divine approval by obeying the law.[26] In fact, he found the basis for his message of grace and faith in the Jewish scriptures, as his letters to the Galatians (3:8–9) and the Romans (4:3–10) illustrate.

Paul was aware of human tendencies to disregard the needed gift of divine grace that comes through faith, and he made this clear in his comments on Abraham. He remarks: "To one who works, wages are not reckoned as a gift but as something due [ὀφείλημα]" (Rom. 4:4), while noting: "If Abraham was justified by works, he has something to boast about, but not before God" (Rom. 4:2). So, we may think of "works" here as disregarding the human need of divine grace as an unearned gift through faith in God. Paul portrays God to treat such works, apart from faith, as God's owing something to humans on account of their earning or merit. By that misguided standard, humans fall short of God's expectation for righteousness under divine grace.

Paul denies that God owes overall approval to people obeying the law. Instead that approval comes, in the righteousness of a right relationship, by receiving it as an undeserved divine gift through faith in God (Rom. 3:24, 5:17, 6:23; cf. Gal. 2:16, 21). This, in Paul's perspective, is difficult but good news for anyone pursuing the law to make God indebted to one, without faith in divine grace.

The national identity-markers of Israel, in circumcision, food laws, and the Sabbath, attracted Paul's critical attention on various occasions, including in his letters to the Galatians and the Romans. He does not claim, however, that they always figured in an effort to "earn" divine approval, even if at times they figured in an effort to be

---

[26] We need this reminder when reading many Christian interpreters of Paul on the law, including Moule, "Jesus, Judaism, and Paul." Paul does oppose at some places an aim to earn divine approval in "legalism," as Moule argues, but I suggest that Paul's concern about "works of the law" is broader. For further support, see Sanders, *Paul, the Law, and the Jewish People*, pp. 154–60; and Dunn, "The New Perspective," pp. 3–17. Cf. Moule, "Obligation in the Ethic of Paul," in Moule, *Essays in New Testament Interpretation* (Cambridge: Cambridge University Press, 1982), pp. 263–75.

"justified by works of the law" (Gal. 2:16). Instead, he regards any exclusive use of the identity-markers to be incompatible with God's seeking, in grace through human faith in Christ, to attract the Gentiles and thereby to fulfill the promise of redemption to Abraham (Gal. 3:13–14, 5:2–4; Rom. 3:28–30, 4:16–17). Paul has no objection, however, to national identity-markers of the law when they are not used exclusively (1 Cor. 9:20–22; cf. Acts 16:3), or, more generally, when they do not run afoul of divine grace and *agapē* for all concerned, Gentiles as well as Jews.

God's righteous *agapē*, according to Paul, is not exclusive in the way the "false brothers" (Gal. 2:4) were in their understanding and pursuit of the law. He thinks of such "brothers" as "perverting the gospel of Christ" (Gal. 1:7), particularly in curbing its extension to people outside Judaism, as promised to Abraham. Such curbing goes against the inclusive divine *agapē* through which the law of God, in Paul's perspective, should be understood and pursued in its fulfillment through faith. The "law of faith," being representative of God's gracious character, is antithetical to such curbing.

We now can see the importance of divine *agapē* as a ground and fulfillment-expression for pursuing the law through faith rather than through "works of the law." Divine righteous *agapē* calls for the law as the expression of God's character of righteous *agapē* toward all concerned, Gentiles as well as Jews, and the human pursuit of the law should represent that righteous *agapē*. Because faith in God is the approved human mode of cooperatively receiving such *agapē*, it must figure in the pursuit of the law for its fulfillment. It must include trust in God in a way that accommodates God's *agapē* toward all people, even those outside any community pursuing the Mosaic law.

"Works of the law" that are exclusive toward any group within the scope of divine *agapē* will conflict with the grace of divine *agapē* (see 1 Cor. 8:9–13; Rom. 14:15–20). Legalism as an effort to earn divine approval, then, is not the only way to run afoul of divine *agapē* as a ground and fulfillment-expression for pursuing the law. National or ethnic exclusiveness is another way. It can do harm to people excluded from available benefits from God, social and otherwise. In its exclusion, it runs afoul of both divine *agapē* and the law such *agapē* fulfills in its human reception through faith.

Faith in God as ultimate contrasts, in an important respect, with obedience to the law as ultimate. The ultimacy of faith in God allows for God as lawgiver to have ultimate authority and thus to update the law, at least in its approved interpretation, for the good of others. Paul saw Gentiles receive the Spirit of God by faith, apart from "works of the law." He thus asked the Galatian Christians, as noted: "Did you receive the Spirit by doing the works of the law or by believing what you heard? Are you so foolish? Having started with the Spirit, are you now ending with the flesh?" (Gal. 3:2–3).

Pursuing "the works of the law," rather than "the law of faith," is part of "the flesh," according to Paul, because it runs afoul of the spirit of divine *agapē* central to the law's fulfillment (cf. Rom. 8:7). This led Paul to oppose any absolute requirement of the national identity-markers in the law. The law's fulfillment in *agapē* determines how the law is to be pursued, and faith in the lawgiver gives priority to the divine purpose of fulfilling the law in *agapē* for all concerned, Gentiles as well as Jews. In this regard, and in contrast to "works of the law," Paul "died to the law" (in its unfulfilled form) in order to live to God and divine *agapē* grounding faith in God (Gal. 2:19, Rom. 7:4). His approach to the law thus calls for facing God in faith and not just a law from God.

The prospect of God's updating the law, at least in its approved interpretation at a time, raises a serious problem, as Paul's letter to the Galatians indicates.[27] Advocates of a previous understanding of the law and its divine purpose can take exception to the proposed update and teach the law accordingly. This is what Paul faced in the teachers he deemed to be "false brothers." How is one to resolve such a conflict?

---

[27] For relevant discussion, see Sanders, *Paul, the Law, and the Jewish People*, pp. 100–105.

Paul's answer is straightforward. The criterion for divine updating comes from God's original purpose behind the law: to fulfill it in divine *agapē* extended to all hearers of the good news begun with Abraham and confirmed in Jesus Christ. Paul remarks, as noted: "The scripture, foreseeing that God would justify the Gentiles by faith, declared the gospel beforehand to Abraham, saying, 'All the Gentiles shall be blessed in you'" (Gal. 3:8; cf. Rom. 1:2, 3:21–22, 30). So, the divine updating has a definite redemptive ground for all concerned and therefore is not arbitrary. Paul confirms this understanding with his straightforward question: "Is God the God of Jews only? Is he not the God of Gentiles also?" (Rom. 3:29; cf. Gal. 3:28–29). The answer is clear to Paul, and this answer guides his understanding of the law of God and its approved pursuit through faith grounded and expressed in divine *agapē* for all concerned, Gentiles as well as Jews. We need to clarify how such faith, in Paul's thought, figures in human access to God.

ACCESS TO GOD

The righteousness sought by God, according to Paul, goes beyond mere obedient actions to a relational, interpersonal reality: reconciliation of humans to God through a volitional relationship of faith and obedience, "from the heart," toward God (Rom. 6:17, 10:10). A common human lament is that faith in God is misplaced when some people have no access to God even if they want it. We should take this lament seriously in order to understand how faith relates to divine righteousness. In the perspective of Paul, as suggested, humans need a means of access to God, and God alone has the authority to determine what this means is.

Humans lack the authority to decide the proper means of access to God, and this should be no surprise. We humans are not in a position, morally or cognitively, to advise a perfectly righteous God on the suitable means of access to that God. God's perfect moral character, in contrast, is an ideal basis for the manner of human access to God. As perfectly righteous, God would specify the manner of access for the good of all concerned, regardless of ethnic or national origin.

Anticipating Paul, the book of Isaiah connects righteousness with faith or trust in God: "Open the gates, so that the righteous nation that keeps faith may enter in. Those of steadfast mind you keep in peace – in peace because they trust in you. Trust in the Lord forever, for in the Lord God you have an everlasting rock" (Isa. 26:2–4). The prophet Habakkuk, as indicated, draws the same kind of connection: "The righteous live by their faith" (Hab. 2:4; cf. Rom. 1:17). He contrasts this kind of trust in God with the inadequacy of idols: "What use is an idol once its maker has shaped it – a cast image, a teacher of lies? For its maker trusts in what has been made, though the product is only an idol that cannot speak!" (Hab. 2:18; cf. Isa. 44:8–11). Trust in God, according to the books of Habakkuk and Isaiah, is a needed alternative to the failure of idols. Such trust, in contrast with trust in idols, is central to redemptive access to reconciliation with the living, agitating God.

Paul, as indicated, attributes a unique role to Jesus in righteous reconciliation and access to God. His summary of the good news from God is as follows: "In Christ God was reconciling the world to himself, not counting their trespasses against them, and entrusting the message of reconciliation to us" (2 Cor. 5:19). This reconciliation comes by grace, as an undeserved gift, and it includes peace: "We have peace with God through our Lord Jesus Christ, through whom we have obtained access [προσαγωγὴν] to this grace in which we stand" (Rom. 5:1–2). The Deutero-Pauline Epistle to the Ephesians sounds a similar note: "Through him [Christ], both of us [Jews and Gentiles] have access [προσαγωγὴν] in one Spirit to the Father" (Eph. 2:18). Paul would have agreed with this summary statement in Ephesians.

Jesus serves as the unique means of access to God, according to Paul, because he "became for us wisdom from God, and righteousness and sanctification and redemption" (1 Cor. 1:30). He could do so, because, as Paul says, he existed "in the form of God" [ἐν μορφῇ θεοῦ]

(Phil. 2:6). Similarly, in Paul's perspective, he exists as the "Son of God" (Gal. 2:20) who is the "image of God" [εἰκὼν τοῦ θεοῦ] (2 Cor. 4:4; cf. Col. 1:15), thus representing God without defect. In perfectly representing God, Jesus can bring the righteousness of God to wayward humans and thereby lead them to God in a reconciled relationship in that righteousness. His relation to God, Paul holds, gives him a unique status in this regard.

Jesus can provide access to God and lead people to God in righteousness, according to Paul, because he "became a life-giving Spirit" through his resurrection by God (1 Cor. 15:45). Without his resurrection, Jesus would fail to accomplish the goal of his sacrificial death in leading people lastingly to God in filial righteousness. If Jesus is still dead, he is inactive and therefore cannot intentionally lead anyone to God. Paul thus remarks that Christ "was handed over to death for our trespasses and was raised for our justification" (Rom. 4:25). In the same vein, he states: "If Christ has not been raised, then our proclamation has been in vain and your faith has been in vain" (1 Cor. 15:14).

A dead Lord, in Paul's thinking, is no Lord at all; only a living, active Lord can lead people to God lastingly in a righteous relationship. So, Paul's talk of the crucified Christ should not be separated from his commitment to the risen Christ. He tells the Corinthian Christians: "I decided to know nothing among you except Jesus Christ, and him crucified" (1 Cor. 2:2). Jesus Christ here is, in Paul's perspective, the Christ now risen. Paul thus knows of no "theology of the cross" apart from a theology of the resurrection of Christ.[28]

Paul holds that in his resurrection status, Jesus represents and agitates for divine righteousness among humans, for the sake of divine–human reconciliation. Paul also claims that the risen Jesus, "at the right hand of God, intercedes for us" (Rom. 8:34). The kind of

---

[28] For a case for the centrality of resurrection in Paul's letter to the Romans, see J. R. Daniel Kirk, *Unlocking Romans: Resurrection and the Justification of God* (Grand Rapids, MI: Eerdmans, 2008).

righteousness sought by Jesus emerged in his earthly ministry as he called people to turn from their own ways to receive God's kingdom of righteousness (Matt. 6:33). Paul identifies this "kingdom" with "righteousness and peace and joy" in the Spirit of God (Rom. 14:17), the same Spirit he identifies with "the Spirit of Christ" (Rom. 8:9). He reveals the fourfold focus of his apostolic calling when he refers to his ministry as "the ministry of righteousness" (2 Cor. 3:9), "the ministry of reconciliation" (2 Cor. 5:18), "the ministry of the Spirit" (2 Cor. 3:8), and "the priestly service of the gospel" as a sacrificial offering of its recipients to God (Rom. 15:16; cf. Phil. 2:17).

The Spirit of Christ, in Paul's understanding, provides for an interpersonal relationship with God, beyond mere moral demands. As personal, this Spirit gives divine righteousness an inherently personal character, and that character is exemplified in Jesus Christ, including in his cross and resurrection.[29] This Spirit enables people to "live with" the crucified and risen Christ by the power of God (1 Thess. 5:10; 2 Cor. 13:4; Rom. 6:8; cf. Rom. 14:7–9). As a result, Paul characterizes a life with God as dying-and-rising with Christ (Rom. 6:1–14). He takes the relevant "living with Christ" to include the present as well as the future.

The role of the Spirit of Christ in reconciliation precludes confusion with an amorphous or a generic god, including any god of deism. There is nothing amorphous or generic about the character or mission of Jesus as represented in the New Testament gospels and epistles. Luke's Gospel notes that Jesus was alleged to be an agitator among the Jews for his mission (Luke 23:2; cf. Acts 24:5). For instance, his enacted judgment on certain established temple practices earned him a reputation as an agitator for a divine cause, if not for divine judgment (Mark 11:15–19; Matt. 21:12–13; Luke 19:45–48; John

---

[29] For relevant discussion, see H. Wheeler Robinson, *The Christian Experience of the Holy Spirit* (London: Nisbet, 1928); and James D. G. Dunn, *Jesus and the Spirit* (London: SCM Press, 1975).

2:13–17). Jesus himself would have identified God's righteousness as his standard in disturbing certain temple practices.[30]

Divine forgiveness of humans, as a merciful release from condemnation, is central to divine righteousness and reconciliation, but it is not the full story. God's righteousness, we have noted for Paul's thinking, is redemptive and therefore reparative or corrective, at least in intent. The divine righteous love that motivates and agitates for the reception of divine forgiveness and reconciliation aims to convict people to turn to cooperation with God, away from their anti-God tendencies alienating them from God (Rom. 2:4).

The intended conviction is not just thinking, talking, or anything simply intellectual. It brings, in Paul's perspective, a powerful motivational challenge in human experience that calls for a voluntary response, whether in rejection, cooperation, or indifference. This challenge includes a manifestation of divine goodness, or righteousness, anchored in divine love toward a person. It may be difficult corrective love, but it is love nonetheless, aimed at divine-human reconciliation in righteousness. In addition, it is among our best evidence for God's reality and presence, in Paul's thinking (Rom. 5:5; 2 Cor. 5:14). (Chapter 6 returns to the latter topic, in assessing Paul's gospel of divine self-sacrifice.)

Paul gives his readers a sense of conviction by God as follows: "Woe to me if I do not proclaim the gospel! If I do this of my own will, I have a reward; but if not of my own will, I am entrusted with a commission" (1 Cor. 9:16–17). Paul means *"just* of my own will," because he has in mind co-willing, that is, willing by God and himself. He considers himself and other followers of Jesus to be "co-workers" with God (1 Cor. 3:9, NIV). He thus acknowledges a crucial role for his

---

[30] For discussion, see E. P. Sanders, *The Historical Figure of Jesus* (London: Penguin, 1993), pp. 252–62; and Simon Joseph, *Jesus and the Temple*, SNTSMS (Cambridge: Cambridge University Press, 2016). On Paul's use of the temple metaphor, see Lucien Cerfaux, *The Christian in the Theology of St Paul*, trans. Lilian Soiron (New York: Herder, 1967), pp. 278–81; and Dunn, *The Theology of Paul the Apostle*, pp. 545–46, 721–22.

own will when he says: "Woe to me if I do not proclaim the gospel!" The threat of a "woe" suggests a responsible voluntary role for Paul's will; such a threat would make no sense if God unilaterally coerced Paul to proclaim the gospel. So, a human can reject the relevant divine conviction, and divine judgment may result from the rejection.[31] (Chapter 4 returns to the topic of Paul on divine judgment.)

Paul's approach to divine conviction bears on his following remark about divine action in human lives: "Work out your own salvation with fear and trembling; for it is God who is at work in you, enabling you both to will and to work for his good pleasure" (Phil. 2:12–13). God's "work" in this regard does not coerce a human will but motivates it while allowing for human rejection of the motivation. As a result, humans are accountable for their voluntary response, and in this regard they differ from rocks, plants, and machines. They thus are not at the mercy of divine conviction, as if their own will did not matter. Paul therefore issues many injunctions for humans to conform their will to God's will, including: "We entreat you on behalf of Christ, be reconciled to God" (2 Cor. 5:20). (Chapter 5 draws out the importance of a voluntary human response to divine righteousness.)

God's "work in" a human comes to fruition with the cooperation of that human's will with God's will. Because such cooperation does not always come easy, it is sometimes encouraged by a search-and-kill mission by God toward the opposing attitudes and actions. Theologians often neglect this mission, but it merits special attention in our understanding of the biblical God. Paul thus speaks of "God who searches the heart" (Rom. 8:27; cf. 1 Thess. 2:4), echoing Psalm 139: "Search me, O God, and know my heart; test me and know my thoughts. See if there is any wicked way in me, and lead me in the way

---

[31] Vincent Taylor has commented, with regard to the role of receiving righteousness, that "to bestow righteousness [non-voluntarily] is a contradiction in terms." Taylor, *The Atonement in New Testament Teaching*, 3rd ed. (London: Epworth Press, 1958), p. 76. Chapter 5 returns to the topic of an uncoerced response to God, in Paul's thought.

everlasting" (Ps. 139:23–24; cf. Jer. 17:10). The "way everlasting" is the way of divine righteousness, and Paul finds its earthly culmination in the divine self-sacrifice in Christ.

DYING INTO FAITH

The divine searching of humans, for the sake of eliciting faith and obedience toward God, goes beyond the mere revealing of information to them. It includes in its goal the delivering of people to a difficult but redemptive kind of "death." Paul reports:

> We have this treasure in clay jars, so that it may be made clear that this extraordinary power belongs to God and does not come from us. We are afflicted in every way, but not crushed; perplexed, but not driven to despair; persecuted, but not forsaken; struck down, but not destroyed; always carrying in the body the death of Jesus, so that the life of Jesus may also be made visible in our bodies. For while we live, we are always being given up [παραδιδόμεθα] to death for Jesus's sake, so that [ἵνα] the life of Jesus may be made visible in our mortal flesh.
> *(2 Cor. 4:7–11; cf. 2 Cor. 1:9, 6:9)*

An immediate question is: Given up to death by whom?

Because "being given up to death" is "for Jesus's sake," it is not just a result of enemy forces. Instead, we have the divine passive here: God is giving up God's children to death for Jesus's sake. They are to die with Christ, in accordance with God's will, for the sake of manifesting God's righteous power, the same redemptive sacrificial power manifested in the life and death of Jesus (Phil. 2:5–8, 3:10).

Divine agitation for righteousness, in Paul's perspective, includes God's handing responsive people over to death for the sake of their manifesting life, in self-sacrifice, to God in Christ. God is set on manifesting such righteous life and power, for human benefit and for divine honor (Rom. 1:17, 3:21–6; cf. 1 Cor. 2:4–5). Paul's model, as suggested, is God's sacrificially handing over Jesus to death in his self-sacrifice, in turn, to God: "[God] did not withhold his own Son, but gave him up [παρέδωκεν αὐτόν] for all of us" (Rom. 8:32; cf. Rom. 3:25–6). The case of Jesus, Paul taught, is unique in divine redemption, given the unique filial and representative status of Jesus in relation to God (Rom. 5:15–20).

Jesus is to serve as a practical model for his disciples, according to the synoptic gospels (Mark 8:34–35; Matt. 10:38–39; Luke 9:23–24, 14:27). His disciples, too, are given up by God for death, courtesy of divine agitation for the redemption of God's people in righteousness. Paul affirms this sacrificial model, without regard for its popularity. Indeed, as suggested, he takes his ministry to include, in a "priestly service of the gospel," a sacrificial "offering" of its Gentile recipients to God (Rom. 15:16). This offering, as Chapter 1 noted, includes what Paul calls "the sacrifice and the offering of your faith [τῇ θυσίᾳ καὶ λειτουργίᾳ τῆς πίστεως ὑμῶν]" (Phil. 2:17). Paul thus suggests that a response to God in faith includes human sacrifice to God. We thus have an expectation of reciprocity with the divine self-sacrifice in Christ, including dying with Christ and carrying out the same kind of sacrificial love as Christ did in serving God (Rom. 12:9–11).

Paul finds a basis for divine agitation toward death in Psalm 44: "For your sake we are being killed all day long; we are accounted as sheep to be slaughtered" (Rom. 8:36; cf. Psalm 44:22). Even so, the intended outcome, from God's perspective, is life-giving through dying with Christ: "We are more than conquerors through him who loved us. For I am convinced that neither death, nor life, nor angels, nor rulers, nor things present, nor things to come, nor powers, nor height, nor depth, nor anything else in all creation, will be able to separate us from the love of God in Christ Jesus our Lord" (Rom. 8:37–39). The divine aim, then, is not death in itself. Instead, it is righteous life with God through the divine agitation toward human dying with Christ. The latter dying is for the sake of receiving "the life" of Jesus among humans (2 Cor 4:11; Phil. 3:10–11).

The cross of Christ, in Paul's perspective (following Jesus himself), is not a mere substitution for his disciples, if it is a "substitution" in any strict sense at all. It is, instead, a representational model from God for their reparative participation, for their sharing in the same divine power that guided and sustained Jesus through death to lasting life with God.[32] Robert C. Tannehill comments on Romans 8 in this connection:

> The Spirit has an active killing function. Through the Spirit what took place decisively in the death of Christ continually takes place: the believer dies to the old life "according to the flesh".... The believer is still a part of an untransformed world and through the body is subject to the attacks of the old powers. In the face of such attacks, the believer's past death with Christ must be maintained and affirmed in the present. Thus, the believer's existence continues to be characterized by dying with Christ.[33]

Paul regards the "sufferings of Christ," including the sufferings in his death, to be shared not just by apostles but by all disciples (2 Cor. 1:4–7). So, God agitates toward suffering and death in a human life in order to agitate toward new righteous life with God, after the model set by Jesus. The agitating seeks to be redemptive as reparative in setting people free to live with God in righteousness, with human trust and obedience toward God.

God might have removed or ended the worldly powers of death and disobedience (or "sin"). Instead, God agitates for obedient human dying to them through faith in God in order to bring people to cooperative life with God. In that dying of humans, God's life-giving power over death and disobedience emerges and shines forth, as in the case of Jesus crucified and risen. In Paul's perspective, the disciples of Jesus are thus implicated in a power struggle with death and disobedience, under agitation by contrary divine power for the sake of

---

[32] For an attempt to capture this theme, with special attention to the Lord's Supper, see C. F. D. Moule, "The Sacrifice of Christ," in Moule, *Forgiveness and Reconciliation*, pp. 163–73.

[33] Robert C. Tannehill, *Dying and Rising with Christ*, BZNW (Berlin: Töpelmann, 1966), p. 80; cf. Tannehill, "Participation in Christ," in Tannehill, *The Shape of the Gospel* (Eugene, OR: Cascade Books, 2007), pp. 223–37.

righteous life with God. Divine righteousness, then, does not come easy for wayward humans, even though it comes as an unearned gift of grace through faith based on divine self-sacrificial *agape* (Rom. 3:24). According to Paul, divine grace "reigns through righteousness" as found in Jesus Christ (Rom. 5:21). He thus exhorts disciples to "put on the Lord Jesus Christ," in obedient imitation of him, to avoid the corrosive effects of disobedience and death (Rom. 13:14; cf. Gal. 5:24–25).[34]

According to Paul, the redemptive core of Jesus's sacrificial death from the latter's perspective is not physical suffering. It is, instead, his humbly obeying God in a cooperative relationship, come what may: "He humbled himself and became obedient to the point of death – even death on a cross" (Phil. 2:8; cf. Rom. 5:18–19). Following suit, Paul reports his desire that "I may know him [Christ] and the power of his resurrection, and may share his sufferings, becoming like him in his death" (Phil. 3:10; cf. 2 Cor. 12:9-10; Rom. 8:17).

Jesus's self-sacrificial path of humble obedience to his death, in Paul's perspective, is the human path to righteous life with God. It is to be shared by all disciples as the way to receive divine redemptive power over disobedience and death. In this regard, Paul agrees with the psalmists and prophets who put obedience to God, in a cooperative relationship, ahead of merely ritual sacrifice and central to approved sacrifice to God (Psalms 40:6–8, 50:8–15, 51:16–19, 69:30–31; Micah 6:6–8; Amos 5:22–24; Hosea 6:6; Isa. 1:10–17; Jer. 7:21–23).

The redemptive key from the human side, as Paul suggests, is in Gethsemane, the place where Jesus humbly resolved to obey God in the divine call to his death, thereby putting God's will first: "Abba, Father, all things are possible to thee; remove this cup from me; yet not what I will, but what thou wilt" (Mark 14:36, RSV; cf. Rom.

---

[34] On being clothed with Christ, see Michael B. Thompson, *Clothed with Christ*, JSNTSS (London: Sheffield Academic Press, 1991).

8:13–16, 29).³⁵ Paul thus speaks of the righteousness of God as something to which people must "submit [ὑπετάγησαν]" (Rom. 10:3)

The filial responsiveness to God modeled in Gethsemane is at the heart of faith that includes trust in God. As the means to receiving divine redemptive power, it yields freedom from the corrosive effects of death and disobedience. God vindicates such responsiveness, according to Paul, by overpowering those corrosive effects to make room for voluntarily empowered obedience and divine resurrection through death. This is God's ratified way to empower righteous life with God, as shown by the obedience of Jesus and its vindication by God in resurrection. So, Jesus is God's approved model for a self-sacrificial human response to divine agitation for righteousness.³⁶

In Paul's portrayal of Jesus as God's model for humans, dying-and-rising with Christ has objective and subjective sides. On the objective side, Paul can say of Christ's death: "One has died for all; therefore, all have died" (2 Cor. 5:13). In addition: "We know that our old self was crucified with him [Christ] so that the body of sin might be destroyed, and we might no longer be enslaved to sin" (Rom. 6:6). Such remarks include a representational role for the crucified Christ, regardless of the response of humans.

The subjective side, being irreducible to the objective side, entails a voluntary human resolve to obey God humbly and thus a resolve to prioritize God's will over one's inferior human will. It

---

³⁵ For relevant discussion, see David Wenham, *Paul* (Grand Rapids, MI: Eerdmans, 1995), pp. 275–80.

³⁶ On the filial responsiveness of Jesus as the motivating center of his mission, see Moser, *The Divine Goodness of Jesus*, ch. 3. Frances Young misses the key role of Gethsemane in self-sacrifice by suggesting that "the central act of sacrifice performed by Christians is a fellowship-meal, through which believers share in the redemptive sacrifice of Christ by commemoration." Young, *Sacrifice and the Death of Christ*, p. 137. Similarly, see Vincent Taylor, *The Cross of Christ*, pp. 21–22, 45, 103–4. Paul, in contrast, considers filial obedience to God, rather than commemoration, as the "central act of sacrifice." The author of the Epistle to the Hebrews likewise gives a central role to obedience to God but appears, in contrast with Paul, to think of it as replacing sacrifice to God; see Hebrews 10:5–9. We need not think of it as a replacement, however, given the proper role of sincere obedience in sacrifice to God.

requires dying to ultimate self-trust, for the sake of trusting in God (2 Cor. 1:9), and to ultimate self-boasting, for the sake of boasting in God (cf. 1 Cor. 1:28–29; Gal. 6:14; Rom. 3:27). It puts God's will first in order to honor God as God and thereby to avoid the corrosive effects of idolatry toward false gods (Rom. 1:21–23), including the false gods humans sometimes make of themselves. Such dying-and-rising with Christ gives distinctive meaning to Paul's talk of human access to God. This meaning stems from the character of God as a righteous agitator for human good in redemption.

We can understand our access to God in terms of God's volitional agitation of Jesus in Gethsemane. The challenge is to abide "inside" – that is, in cooperation with – God's superior will. An analogy with the stained-glass windows of a church may help. Choosing to look at the windows only from their backside, without entering the church, is analogous either to ignoring or to dismissing the challenge of God's will in a Gethsemane episode. It includes a decision to remain "outside" the redemptive will of God, blocking its intended fruition in human cooperation after a brush with it. Such a decision is, in effect, for lasting death, apart from God. It puts a human will in the place of priority reserved, at least by Paul's message, for God alone.

Choosing to look at the stained-glass windows from their frontside, by entering the church, is akin to responding cooperatively to God's will agitating in human experience. From a perspective "inside" God's redemptive will, people can apprehend firsthand the life-giving power of divine righteousness as they enable it to come to fruition through their volitional cooperation. God intends it to come to such fruition, according to Paul, in order to change people by conforming them to Christ as God's righteousness and redemption for humans (Rom. 8:29; 1 Cor. 1:30). A positive response, including trust and obedience toward God, contributes to that desired goal, and it manifests responsible human agency before God.

Gethsemane access to God comes through divine volitional agitation combined with a cooperative human response, after the seminal example of Jesus in Gethsemane. Such access through Christ, in Paul's thought, is a trustworthy window to God, conveying divine power through human obedience and divine resurrection in the face of suffering and death. It thus relays the unique redemptive power, including the sacrificial love, motivating God's righteous kingdom.

We now see how Paul puts together some pieces of the puzzle involving divine *agapē*, human faith, and the law of God. In doing so, he acknowledges divine righteous *agapē* as the ground of human faith in God and as the center of fulfilling the law of God, in terms of its ultimate motivation and shared result. This widely neglected perspective enables us to understand Paul on the importance of faith as cooperatively receiving and expressing divine righteous *agapē* and on the conflict posed by "works of the law." It represents Paul on human relating to God in a way fitting toward, and receptive of, God's righteous character of *agapē*.

The grounding of faith and of the pursuit of the law in God's character is central to Paul's "putting all things in subjection" to God, so that "God will be all in all" (1 Cor. 15:27–28). This chapter's proposed understanding of Galatians 5:6, in terms of its semantic duality of passive and active factors, contributes to that end. It enables us to see the central role of self-sacrificial *agapē* in Paul's complex thinking about faith in a self-sacrificial God. We turn now to a distinctive incarnational element in Paul's understanding of ethics under a God devoted to self-sacrifice for the sake of righteousness.

3 Incarnational Ethics of Self-Sacrifice

> The law of the Spirit of life in Christ Jesus has set you free from the law of sin and of death.
>
> Romans 8:2

> I am again in the pain of childbirth until Christ is formed in you.
>
> Galatians 4:19

Paul gives a central theological role to divine incarnation, lawgiver, Spirit, and reconciliation, but New Testament scholars have given inadequate attention to how these theological realities enable us to make good sense of Paul on ethics and the law. Paul's idea of "the law of the Spirit of life in Christ Jesus" has long puzzled readers, perhaps since its first presentation among the early Roman Christians. This chapter contends, contrary to many interpreters, that Paul has a coherent approach to ethics and the law of God if understood with an incarnational and a reconciliatory component for Christ and his disciples.

The chapter relates Paul's approach to ethics and the law of God to reparative self-sacrifice. In doing so, it gives a primary role to a divine lawgiver in Paul's understanding, above the law itself, thus enabling the kinds of changes in the law and in the divine covenants acknowledged by him. In this connection, the chapter attributes a key role in Paul's perspective on ethics and the law to the promise of the new covenant in Jeremiah and Ezekiel. A theme of inwardness in self-sacrifice and even of incarnation emerges for the law, beyond any general covenantal nomism entailing that a covenant from God and its laws are the center of relating to

God.¹ The chapter also identifies five key desiderata for an account of Paul on theological ethics and the law.

UPHOLDING THE LAW

We cannot capture the subtlety of Paul's theology, as Chapter 2 suggested, if we portray him as antinomian or as advocating a "law-free" gospel. A difficult remark of Paul's for any such portrayal is: "Circumcision is nothing, and uncircumcision is nothing; but obeying the commandments of God [τήρησις ἐντολῶν θεοῦ] is everything" (1 Cor. 7:19). Paul made this statement to a Christian church, of course, and he could have said something just about faith instead, with no mention of God's commandments (cf. Gal. 5:6, 6:15).

Paul's praise of the law of God, as Chapter 2 noted, emerges more than once in his undisputed letters. For instance, he affirms: "The law is holy, and the commandment is holy and just and good .... We know that the law is spiritual .... I delight in the law of God in my inmost self ... With my mind I am a slave to the law of God" (Rom. 7:12, 14, 22, 25). Paul's endorsement of the law's holiness and goodness is not minimized at all by his acknowledgment of an anti-God power that accompanies the law among humans and influences them.

Paul remarks: "Sin, seizing an opportunity in the commandment, deceived me and through it killed me .... Did what is good, then, bring death to me? By no means! It was sin, working death in me through what is good, in order that sin might be shown to be sin, and through the commandment might become sinful beyond measure" (Rom. 7:11, 13). The law, then, is not sin or sinful, in Paul's perspective, and it does not deceive or kill. The power of sin, in contrast, brings death through the law. It is misleading, then, for E. P. Sanders to claim that "Paul virtually equates the law with Sin and the Flesh

---

¹ On covenantal nomism, see E. P. Sanders, *Paul and Palestinian Judaism* (Philadelphia, PA: Fortress Press, 1977), pp. 75, 236.

(Rom. 6:14; 7:5f.)."[2] In fact, Paul explicitly distinguishes the law from sin and sin-prone flesh.

The power of sin sets the context for Paul's following remark: "When the commandment came, sin revived and I died, and the very commandment that promised life proved to be death to me" (Rom. 7:9–10). The law, in Paul's thought, identifies sin, and it figures in the revival of sin by making it explicit. The law "proved to be death" only in the sense that the power of sin, when joined with the law, brings death. The law apart from the power of sin does not "prove to be death" or bring death. The law of God by itself, however, cannot give humans what they need in relation to God, as we shall see.

Even if Paul's view of the law developed between Galatians and Romans, to become more positive and less polemical, his following position was constant: "Is the law then opposed to the promises of God? Certainly not! For if a law had been given that could make alive [ζωοποιῆσαι], then righteousness [δικαιοσύνη] would indeed come through the law" (Gal. 3:21).[3] His notion of being made "alive" is clarified a bit in his following remark: "For through the law I died to the law, so that I might live to God" (Gal. 2:19; cf. Rom. 7:4). He has in mind something that could make a person alive to God, in a manner where a person has divine approval, or justification, in righteousness, including in a right, reconciled relationship with God. This involves, we shall see, dying to works of the law but not to the law of God as what Paul calls "the law of faith" or "the law of Christ."

Paul remarks: "Now it is evident that no one is justified [δικαιοῦται] before God by the law; for 'the one who is righteous

---

[2] E. P. Sanders, *Paul* (Oxford: Oxford University Press, 1991), p. 85; cf. Sanders, *Paul, the Law, and the Jewish People* (Minneapolis, MN: Fortress Press, 1983), p. 73.

[3] Here we have an indication that Paul can move from human plight to solution and not just from solution to human plight. It is a serious problem for him, even apart from his Christological solution, that the law cannot deliver reconciled life with God against the power of sin and death. E. P. Sanders thus oversimplifies the relevant story, in *Paul and Palestinian Judaism*, pp. 474–75, 497, 500–501, 506. My account, as suggested, allows for development in Paul's view on the law between Galatians and Romans, but development, of course, does not entail inconsistency.

[δίκαιος] will live by faith'" (Gal. 3:11, citing Hab. 2:4; cf. Rom. 1:17). Living with justification before God, then, comes by faith in God and not "by the law." In addition, "the law does not rest on faith [ἐκ πίστεως]; on the contrary, 'whoever does the works of the law will live by them'" (Gal. 3:12). The "works" of the law in Paul's special sense of the term identified in Romans 4 are not just acts of obedience.

Paul clarifies in Romans 4, as suggested, that the "working" in question is not reckoned according to divine grace but "according to debt" (κατὰ ὀφείλημα) or as "something due": "Now to one who works, wages are not reckoned as a gift but as something due" (Rom. 4:4). Paul then contrasts one who "works" with one who "without works trusts in" God (Rom. 4:5). It does not follow, however, that Paul took all of his fellow-Jews to advocate righteousness by works of the law; he had in mind a partly shared tendency within a highly diverse Judaism.[4] (Paul does use "works" to signify "deeds" on occasion, but this is not his special sense in Romans 4 that invites his criticism of "works" of the law.)

"Works" (of the law) in Paul's special sense of Romans 4 stem from neglecting a human need of divine grace as an unearned gift through faith. They thus are treated, by divine lights, as aiming to make God indebted to give divine approval as something owed or due, rather than having God give such approval as an undeserved gift of grace. Obeying God, however, need not seek to make God indebted to give approval as something owed from earning, despite the many

---

[4] For evidence of the diversity of Judaism in Paul's day, with a caution about normalizing talk of "common Judaism," see Martin Hengel and Roland Deines, "E. P. Sanders' 'Common Judaism', Jesus, and the Pharisees," *Journal of Theological Studies* 46 (1995), 1–70. I concur with C. E. B. Cranfield's defense of a general sense of "works of the law" in Romans; see Cranfield, "'The Works of the Law' in the Epistle to the Romans," *Journal for the Study of the New Testament* 43 (1991), 89–101. Cranfield takes exception to what he takes to be James D. G. Dunn's narrower sense restricted to Jewish identity-markers in the law, in Dunn, *Romans*, WBC (Dallas, TX: Word Books, 1988). In later work, Dunn favors a general sense allowing for varying emphases, in "Yet Once More – 'The Works of the Law,'" in Dunn, *The New Perspective on Paul*, rev. ed. (Grand Rapids, MI: Eerdmans, 2008), pp. 213–26. Further support for Cranfield's general sense can be found in Thomas R. Schreiner, "'Works of Law' in Paul," *Novum Testamentum* 33 (1991), 217–44.

commentators who miss this point. "Works" in Paul's sense of Romans 4 neglect a crucial role for divine grace through faith, but acts of obedience need not have that deficiency.[5] Paul regards the seeking of justification from God by (works of) the law to be incompatible with divine grace and righteousness: "I do not nullify the grace of God; for if justification comes through the law, then Christ died for nothing" (Gal. 5:4).

Paul corrects some members of Israel, as Chapter 2 noted: "Gentiles, who did not pursue righteousness, attained righteousness, even the righteousness which is by faith; but Israel, pursuing a law of righteousness, did not arrive at *that* law. Why? Because *they did not pursue it* by faith, but as though *it were* by works" (Rom. 9:30–32, NASB; the RSV and NRSV mistranslate here). So, how one pursues the law and righteousness matters: It should be by faith in God and Christ, according to Paul, and not by "works" as self-righteousness (Phil. 3:9) or as deeds of the law apart from grace through faith in God (as Chapter 2 explained). The law itself, then, is not the problem. It is "holy and just and good," by Paul's lights.

If the law is not a source of justification or righteousness from God for humans, what is its purpose, according to Paul? In his Epistle to the Romans, Paul takes the law to reveal sin for what it is and to draw out its sinfulness: "It was sin, working death in me through what is good [that is, "the commandment"], in order that sin might be shown to be sin, and through the commandment might become sinful beyond measure" (Rom. 7:13). A broader divine purpose lies in the background, according to Paul's perspective: "God has imprisoned all

---

[5] Rudolf Bultmann was a rare commentator who saw that deeds of obedience in Paul's thought should not be confused with "works" as earning approval from God. See Bultmann, *Theology of the New Testament*, trans. Kendrick Grobel (New York: Charles Scribner's Sons, 1955), vol. 1, pp. 283–84, 316. This distinction is neglected by, among others, Victor Paul Furnish, *Theology and Ethics in Paul* (Nashville, TN: Abingdon Press, 1968), p. 196; C.E.B. Cranfield, *A Critical and Exegetical Commentary on the Epistle to the Romans*, ICC (Edinburgh: T&T Clark, 1975), vol. 1, p. 90; and C. K. Barrett, *Paul* (London: Continuum, 1994), p. 82.

in disobedience so that [ἵνα] he may be merciful to all" (Rom. 11:32; cf. Gal. 3:22–23).

The law, in Paul's thinking, draws out a human tendency to disobedience for a divine redemptive purpose beyond condemnation. It is misleading, then, for Sanders to say: "Paul's major explanation – which he retracted ... in Romans 7 – was that the law was given to condemn."[6] At no point in his undisputed letters does Paul suggest or offer as his "major explanation" that the law's ultimate aim was to "condemn." Its aim to highlight disobedience was a means to a higher, redemptive end.[7]

Paul offers the following explanation in Galatians:

> Why then the law? It was added because of transgressions, until the offspring would come to whom the promise had been made ... Therefore, the law was our disciplinarian [παιδαγωγὸς] until Christ came, so that [ἵνα] we might be justified by faith. But now that faith has come, we are no longer subject to [ὑπὸ] a disciplinarian.
> (Gal. 3:19, 24–25)

In a similar vein, on not being under the law, Paul remarks: "If you are led by the Spirit, you are not subject to [ὑπὸ] the law" (Gal. 5:18; cf. Rom. 6:14).

God, according to Paul, intended the law to lead, eventually, to something more significant in redemption: to faith in God and in Christ and to divine approval on that basis. Its role as a "disciplinarian" against "transgression" set constraints aimed at guiding people toward faith in God. That guiding, however, depends on human cooperation and thus it can be corrupted and even resisted by humans. In any case, the fact that some people are no longer subject to law as a disciplinarian toward faith does not entail that the law has no other

---

[6] Sanders, *Paul*, p. 94; cf. Sanders, *Paul, the Law, and the Jewish People*, pp. 73–74.
[7] C. E. B. Cranfield is correct here; see his "St. Paul and the Law," *Scottish Journal of Theology* 17 (1964), 48–49.

relevance in relation to faith or what Paul calls "the obedience of faith" (Rom. 1:5, 16:26).[8]

Paul offers a case in Romans for upholding the law:

> What becomes of boasting? It is excluded. By what law? By that of works? No, but by the law of faith [νόμου πίστεως]. For we hold that a person is justified by faith apart from works prescribed by the law. Or is God the God of Jews only? Is he not the God of Gentiles also? Yes, of Gentiles also, since God is one; and he will justify the circumcised on the ground of faith and the uncircumcised through that same faith. Do we then overthrow the law by this faith? By no means! On the contrary, we uphold the law [νόμον ἱστάνομεν].
>
> (Rom. 3:27–31)

James D. G. Dunn captures one lesson here: "Paul's concern was precisely to reaffirm that faith and law were not at odds: the law is not to be understood in terms of works; but it can and should be understood in terms of faith."[9] We uphold, according to Paul, the "law of faith" not the "law of works." What, however, is the law of faith and how does it relate to the law of Moses? That twofold question will take us to the heart of Paul's incarnational view of the law of God and its sacrificial component.

LAW INCARNATE

Paul takes faith in God to include a human response to God and therefore to be interpersonal in focus. His talk of "the law of faith" should be understood accordingly, as inherently interpersonal between God and humans. The manner in which it is interpersonal, rather than just a matter of humans relating to inscribed commands, depends on Paul's contrast between "the old written code" and "the

---

[8] On Paul on "the obedience of faith," see Don Garlington, *Faith, Obedience, and Perseverance*, WUNT (Tübingen: Mohr Siebeck, 1994), pp. 10–31, 144–63; and Dunn, *The Theology of Paul the Apostle*, pp. 634–35.

[9] Dunn, *The Theology of Paul the Apostle*, p. 639. See also C. F. D. Moule, "Obligation in the Ethic of Paul," in Moule, *Essays in New Testament Interpretation*, pp. 263–75.

new life of the Spirit [of God]." He claims: "Now we are discharged from the law, dead to that which held us captive, so that we are slaves not under the old written code but in the new life of the Spirit" (Rom. 7:6). The old written code is the Mosaic law as written (cf. 2 Cor. 3:3, 6–7), whereas the new life of the Spirit is "the law of the Spirit of life in Christ Jesus [ὁ νόμος τοῦ πνεύματος τῆς ζωῆς ἐν Χριστῷ Ἰησοῦ]" (Rom. 8:2). We need to explain how the latter reality is a law if we are to understand how the law is "upheld," in Paul's thought.

I shall contend that Paul's talk of "the law ... in Christ Jesus" is incarnational, relying on a broadly person-locational sense of "in" (ἐν). This sense implies that the law "in Christ" exists and operates within the moral character, agency, and authority of the risen Jesus, in continuity with the earthly Jesus. I thus hold that the phrase "in Christ Jesus" modifies the locution "the law" in Romans 8:2, given that this makes the best available sense of our relevant evidence.[10] Commentators have neglected this perspective on Paul, but we shall see that it illuminates Paul's thinking about the law.

A key theme for Paul with regard to the law's fulfillment rests on a distinction between the law as "the old written code" and the law as "fulfilled" (in its purpose) by God. Both qualify as a "law," given their providing commands to be obeyed, but Paul contrasts the two in an important way. "God has done what the law, weakened by the flesh, could not do: by sending his own Son in the likeness of sinful flesh, and to deal with sin, he condemned sin in the flesh, so that the just requirement of the law might be fulfilled [πληρωθῇ] in us, who walk not according to the flesh but according to the Spirit" (Rom. 8:3–4). (Condemning sin here does not entail condemning Jesus.)

Leander Keck observes that "what the Spirit accomplishes is the *dikaiōma tou nomou*, the rightness, the right intent, of the

---

[10] Cranfield suggests that taking "the law" with "in Christ Jesus" is "unnatural." See his *A Critical and Exegetical Commentary on the Epistle to the Romans*, vol. 1, p. 374. We shall see, however, that it fits quite naturally with Paul's perspective on the law in his undisputed letters.

law – life."[11] The Spirit provides such intended life with God by overcoming the power of sin and death with God's life-giving power, as people walk "according to the Spirit." Even if the law's just requirement is fulfilled in certain humans, however, its fulfillment is courtesy of God's sacrificially sending his own Son as a powerful means of redemption. We need to clarify how God's sending his own Son fulfills the law in its divinely intended purpose.

God's sending his own Son is related significantly to Paul's following understanding of the fulfillment of the law:

> Owe no one anything, except to love one another; for the one who loves another has fulfilled the law. The commandments, "You shall not commit adultery; You shall not murder; You shall not steal; You shall not covet"; and any other commandment, are summed up in this word, "Love your neighbor as yourself." Love does no wrong to a neighbor; therefore, love is the fulfilling of the law.
> (Rom. 13:8–10; cf. Gal. 5:14, 6:2)

Since love is "the fulfilling of the law," God's redemptive work of righteous sacrificial love in Christ is, in Paul's thought, the climactic fulfilling of the law in its divine purpose. The latter view underlies Paul's previous remark that links God's sending his own Son in sacrificial love with the law's being fulfilled in certain humans.

The key link comes from the following assumption by Paul: "God proves his love for us in that while we still were sinners Christ died for us" (Rom 5:8; cf. Rom. 8:32, 39). God's sacrificial love in Christ toward humans, in "sending his own Son" for them, fulfills the law in its purpose by prompting cooperative people to reciprocate by responding in kind, with sacrificial love toward God and others. Christ, in Paul's thought, is the divinely appointed intentional agent who embodies the divine sacrificial love that fulfills God's redemptive

---

[11] Leander Keck, "The Law and 'the Law of Sin and Death,'" in *The Divine Helmsman*, eds. J. L. Crenshaw and Samuel Sandmel (New York: KTAV, 1980), p. 53.

purpose and thus the redemptive purpose of the law: to reconcile people to God and others in divine sacrificial love (2 Cor. 5:18–19).[12]

Christ as an intentional agent who is God's own Son can fulfill the divine redemptive purpose by enacting and showing God's sacrificial love and inviting love from others in response. An inscribed law, in contrast, cannot show love and thereby motivate or attract people to love others as God loves. Paula Fredriksen comments: "Paul's negative remarks about the Law are meant to discourage Gentiles from attempting to live according to its precepts in any way other than how *Paul* defines as 'in Christ.'"[13] Even so, Paul would have invoked Christ himself as the defining standard on God's behalf (1 Cor. 1:24, 30), given that he wants people to live "in (the power of) Christ," rather than "in Paul." He does not set himself up as the ultimate standard or authority for what it is to be "in Christ" (1 Cor. 1:13).[14]

The Mosaic law cannot give a life of reconciliation in divine love to people because it lacks the power from love to overcome the power of human sin and death. In contrast, Jesus, according to Paul, became a "life-giving Spirit" (1 Cor. 15:45) who can guide people with love and corresponding commands, and he thereby can empower them to "live to God" in the "obedience of faith." Regarding Paul's

---

[12] On the central role of divine-human reconciliation in Paul's theology, see Ralph P. Martin, *Reconciliation: A Study of Paul's Theology* (Atlanta, GA: John Knox Press, 1981); and Margaret Thrall, "Salvation Proclaimed: 2 Corinthians 5:18–21: Reconciliation with God," *Expository Times* 93 (1982), 227–32. P. T. Forsyth acknowledges the importance of this theme in Paul, and more generally, in his *The Work of Christ* (London: Hodder and Stoughton, 1910); likewise for James Denney, *The Christian Doctrine of Reconciliation* (London: Hodder and Stoughton, 1917).

[13] Paula Fredriksen, *Paul: The Pagans' Apostle* (New Haven, CT: Yale University Press, 2017), p. 126. An adequate account of Paul on the law must relate the topic to dying and rising with Christ as the way to overcome the corrosive effects of the powers of sin and death. On that important topic, see Robert C. Tannehill, *Dying and Rising with Christ*, BZNW (Berlin: Töpelmann, 1966); and Chapter 2 in this volume.

[14] For an illuminating treatment of Paul on being "in Christ," see Morna D. Hooker, "Raised for our Acquittal," in *Resurrection in the New Testament*, eds. R. Bierener, et al. (Leuven: Peeters, 2002), pp. 334–41. See also Dunn, *The Theology of Paul the Apostle*, pp. 396–404.

contrast between the law of Moses and the law of the Spirit in Christ, Joseph A. Fitzmyer remarks: "It is the risen person of Christ Jesus that makes the difference. Having become a 'life-giving Spirit' through his passion, death, and resurrection, he it is who brings about this freedom for humanity [from 'the law of sin and death']."[15] The contrast, then, is between the "law" of the Spirit in Christ that can bring reconciled life with God and the Mosaic law that lacks the power to overcome the power of sin and death for humans.

Fitzmyer, following Ernst Käsemann, overlooks an important feature of Paul's talk of the "law" of the Spirit in Christ. He comments:

> Paul indulges in oxymoron as he now applies *nomos* to the Spirit, which in his understanding is anything but "law." Rather, the law of the Spirit is nothing other than the "Spirit of God" (Rom. 8:9a, 14) or the "Spirit of Christ" (8:9b) in its ruling function in the sphere of Christ (Käsemann). It is the dynamic principle of the new life, creating vitality and separating humans from sin and death, indeed, supplying the very vitality that the Mosaic law could not give.[16]

Fitzmyer and Käsemann overlook how a distinctive functional feature of an intentional lawgiver underlies a distinctive kind of "law" in Paul's understanding. Their denial that the "law of the Spirit" is a law, strictly speaking (on the ground that it is "nothing other than the Spirit" of God ... in its "ruling function"), fails to convince."[17]

---

[15] Fitzmyer, *Romans*, p. 482.

[16] Fitzmyer, *Romans*, pp. 482–83. Käsemann states: "The law of the Spirit is nothing other than the Spirit himself in his ruling function in the sphere of Christ. He creates life and separates not only from sin and death, but also from their instrument, the irreparably perverted law of Moses." Käsemann, *Commentary on Romans*, pp. 215–16.

[17] Similarly, given my approach, it is misleading for BAGD, sub νόμος, to include Romans 8:2 and Galatians 6:2 as exemplifying a use of "law" as "figurative of Christianity as a 'new law.'" See Walter Bauer, W. F. Arndt, F. W. Gingrich, and F. W. Danker, *A Greek-English Lexicon of the New Testament and Other Early Christian Literature*, 2nd ed. (Chicago: University of Chicago Press, 1979), p. 543. The use of "figurative" regarding "law" begs a key question now. A related misgiving applies to Heikki Räisänen, *Paul and the Law*, WUNT (Tübingen: Mohr

Käsemann proposes that Paul is not speaking of the law of faith or the law of the Spirit as "a demand but [as] the rule, order, or norm of faith."[18] He claims that Paul here "plays on the word 'law,'" and uses it "in a transferred sense" that does not connote a law, strictly speaking. Fitzmyer similarly speaks of law "in its ruling function in the sphere of Christ," and he suggests, in keeping with Käsemann, that this is not a matter of law in any typical sense.

A problem for the view of Fitzmyer and Käsemann is that a person who is a lawgiver can give commands integral to, or at least causally emerging from, that person's moral character and authority, and those commands can constitute the law of that person. The commands call for obedience, and they signify the moral character and authority of the lawgiver. As a result, they may properly be called "the law of the person" in question, just as many historians of ancient Rome fittingly talk of "the law of (Julius) Caesar" (for instance, on municipalities, 44 BCE). So, there is no need to talk of an "oxymoron" or a "transferred sense" to something other than a law. We can make good sense of Paul's talk of the law of the Spirit "in Christ" and the law "of Christ" (1 Cor. 9:21; Gal. 6:2).[19] Our talk of a "lawgiver" concerns the giver of the content of a law, and it thus allows for

---

Siebeck, 1983), pp. 52, 80–81; and Richard Hays, "Christology and Ethics in Galatians: The Law of Christ," *Catholic Biblical Quarterly* 49 (1987), 268–90. For a similar questionable view on "the law of the Spirit" in Romans 8:2, see C. E. B. Cranfield, "The Freedom of the Christian according to Romans 8.2," in *New Testament Christianity for Africa and the World*, ed. Mark Glasswell (London: SPCK, 1974), p. 93.

[18] Käsemann, *Commentary on Romans*, p. 103. Douglas Moo agrees with Käsemann in "'Law,' 'Works of the Law,' and Legalism in Paul," *Westminster Theological Journal* 45 (1983), 78.

[19] For discussion of Paul's use of the genitive in "law of Christ," see J. Louis Martyn, "*Nomos* plus Genitive Noun in Paul," in *Early Christianity and Classical Culture: Comparative Studies in Honor of Abraham J. Malherbe*, ed. John T. Fitzgerald (Leiden: Brill, 2003), pp. 575–87. He remarks: "Paul coins that expression in order to speak of the Law as it has been taken in hand by Christ, thus being delivered from its lethal alliance with Sin and made pertinent to the church's daily life" (p. 583). See also Martyn, *Galatians*, AB (New York: Doubleday, 1997), pp. 556–57. I think of the relevant genitive as broadly a genitive of character-source implying formative authority over the law, owing to a causal source in Christ's authoritative moral character.

Paul's view of a role for intermediaries in the original delivery of the divine law to humans (Gal. 3:19).

Käsemann's background worry is that if the law of the Spirit (as in the case of a typical law) makes a demand, such as a demand of faith in God, it risks becoming a "religious work."[20] We already have noted, however, the importance of not confusing obedience to a command with a "work" in Paul's special sense in Romans 4. Obeying a command need not include an intended earning at all. For instance, the "obedience of faith," in Paul's thought is not a "religious work" as an intended earning from God. It demands intentional action from the person of faith, given that one's faith is to include trust that cooperates with God's will, but such action can be altogether free of intended earning of divine approval.

END OF LAW

The role of Christ in the fulfilled law of God prompts Paul to comment: "Christ is the end of the Law for righteousness [τέλος γὰρ νόμου Χριστὸς εἰς δικαιοσύνην] to everyone who believes" (Rom. 10:4, NASB). Paul does not mean that Christ terminates the law of God, especially given Romans 3:31. Instead, he has in mind the fulfilling of the law of God through Christ, including through his love commands.[21] Prior to Romans, Paul announced: "I am not free from God's law but am under Christ's law [ἔννομος Χριστοῦ]" (1 Cor. 9:21). So, the law of Christ exemplifies or instantiates the law of God. With similar language, Paul reported, again prior to Romans: "Bear one another's burdens,

---

[20] Käsemann, *Commentary on Romans*, p. 103.
[21] See Paul W. Meyer, "Romans 10:4 and the 'End' of the Law," in *The Divine Helmsman*, eds. J. L. Crenshaw and Samuel Sandmel (New York: KTAV, 1980), pp. 59–78; John M. G. Barclay, *Obeying the Truth: Paul's Ethics in Galatians* (Edinburgh: T&T Clark, 1988), pp. 127–34;, Graham Stanton, "The Law of Moses and the Law of Christ," in *Paul and the Mosaic Law*, ed. James D. G. Dunn, WUNT (Tübingen: Mohr Siebeck, 1996), pp. 99–116; and Martyn, *Galatians*, pp. 554–58. We thus need to correct Käsemann's striking claim that Paul "sees law and gospel nondialectically as mutually exclusive." *Commentary on Romans*, p. 282.

and in this way you will fulfill the law of Christ [ἀναπληρώσετε τὸν νόμον τοῦ Χριστοῦ]" (Gal. 6:2).

Christ is not the termination of the law of God, according to Paul, but instead is its goal or purpose. Christ serves that role as God's authoritative filial agent who guides and empowers the fulfillment of the law in the righteousness of divine–human reconciliation. This consideration underlies Paul's linking of "making alive" and "righteousness" in Galatians 3:21. The latter righteousness includes a life of reconciliation to God in Christ. So, Christ is the "end" as the redemptive "goal for righteousness" in reconciled relation to God. Paul thus comments: "In Christ God was reconciling the world to himself, not counting their trespasses against them, and entrusting the message of reconciliation to us" (2 Cor. 5:19).

Paul puts the intended relation with God in terms of adoption: "When the fullness of time had come, God sent his Son, born of a woman, born under the law, in order to redeem those who were under the law, so that we might receive adoption as children" (Gal. 4:4–5; cf. Rom. 8:15). This is adoption as children of God into God's "family of faith" (Gal. 6:10; cf. Gal. 3:26), of which Paul considered himself a capable builder (1 Cor. 3:9–11). A static written law cannot engage in forgiveness, reconciliation, or adoption in the way a personal lawgiver can. Hence, Paul gives primacy to the personal divine lawgiver, whether God or Christ, and this primacy is analogous to the priority he gives to God as gracious call-giver in election "not by works" (Rom. 9:11–12; cf. Rom. 11:6). (Chapter 5 returns to the topic of Paul on election.)

Paul's second letter to the Corinthians provides some confirmation of our proposed role for Christ in relation to the law of God. Paul comments on two kinds of "ministry" that correspond to two kinds of law, one temporary and the other permanent:

> If the ministry of death, chiseled in letters on stone tablets, came in glory so that the people of Israel could not gaze at Moses' face because of the glory of his face, a glory now set aside, how much

more will the ministry of the Spirit come in glory? For if there was glory in the ministry of condemnation, much more does the ministry of justification abound in glory! Indeed, what once had glory has lost its glory because of the greater glory; for if what was set aside came through glory, much more has the permanent come in glory!

(2 Cor. 3:7–11)

The ministry of "letters on stone tablets" includes the Mosaic law, and, in contrast, the ministry of "the Spirit" includes the law of Christ, guided and empowered by God's Spirit. The former is temporary, whereas the latter is permanent, being integral to the moral character of the divine lawgiver.

Paul comments on the role of Christ as the Spirit in relation to the two ministries (and, by implication, to the two kinds of law):

To this very day, when they [the people of Israel] hear the reading of the old covenant, that same veil is still there, since only in Christ is it set aside. Indeed, to this very day whenever Moses is read, a veil lies over their minds; but when one turns to the Lord, the veil is removed. Now the Lord is the Spirit, and where the Spirit of the Lord is, there is freedom. And all of us, with unveiled faces, seeing the glory of the Lord as though reflected in a mirror, are being transformed into the same image from one degree of glory to another; for this comes from the Lord, the Spirit.

(2 Cor. 3:14–18)

The law "in letters," according to Paul, resulted in spiritual blindness and death as a result of the power of human sin. The law of the Spirit in Christ, in contrast, results in spiritual sight and life in "the glory of the Lord." This is courtesy of Christ as Lord and life-giving Spirit, who exercises his lordship in leadership through the law of Christ. We thus may think of the law of the Spirit "in" Christ as Spirited, Christological law, able and intended to work inwardly on a person toward righteous reconciliation, through faith, with God and others.

Responding to the Corinthians, Paul pointed to the work of God's Spirit of Christ in fulfilling Jeremiah's promise of the new covenant: "You yourselves are our letter, written on our hearts, to be known and read by all; and you show that you are a letter of Christ, prepared by us, written not with ink but with the Spirit of the living God, not on tablets of stone but on tablets of human hearts" (2 Cor. 3:2–3). Paul echoes Ezekiel 11 and Jeremiah 31, the latter stating: "The days are surely coming, says the Lord, when I will make a new covenant with the house of Israel and the house of Judah .... This is the covenant that I will make with the house of Israel after those days, says the Lord: I will put my law within them, and I will write it on their hearts; and I will be their God, and they shall be my people" (Jer. 31:31, 33; cf. Ezek. 11:19–20, promising a "new spirit" within people to enable their obeying God's law).[22] Paul's incarnational nomism thus extends beyond the law incarnate "in Christ" to the law of God incarnate in the "hearts," or volitional centers, of the people of God. This theme is at the center of Paul's understanding of God's new covenant in Christ, including its extension beyond historical Israel, and it guided his new, post-Pharisee understanding of the law of God.

The incarnation of the law of God in willing humans comes courtesy of Christ as the "the Lord, the Spirit," who himself first incarnates God's law. These humans, however, must "walk according to the Spirit" (Gal. 5:16; Rom. 8:4), in reconciled interpersonal relation to God, with the cooperative trust of faith in God. Abraham is Paul's model example of faith, and his faith, unlike the Jewish provenance for the Mosaic law, can be universally shared, beyond Jewish believers: "For this reason it depends on faith, in order that the promise may rest on grace and be guaranteed to all his descendants, not only to the adherents of the law but also to those who share the

---

[22] On the Old Testament background here, see Victor Paul Furnish, *II Corinthians*, pp. 194–96; and Ralph P. Martin, *2 Corinthians*, WBC (Waco, TX: Word Books, 1986), pp. 52–55. See also Scott J. Hafemann, *Paul, Moses, and the History of Israel*, WUNT (Tübingen: Mohr Siebeck, 2005), ch. 2.

faith of Abraham (for he is the father of all of us)" (Rom. 4:16). The divine lawgiver, according to Paul, is the God of Gentiles as well as Jews, and therefore is not limited as lawgiver by the Jewish provenance of the Mosaic law (Rom. 3:29–30). As a result, Paul's understanding of God and redemption was transformed in relation to Christ.

In linking God's redemptive promise to divine grace, Paul also can link it to divine love as its motivation and ground and thus as the motivation and ground for faith in God. Hence, as Chapter 2 explained: "In Christ Jesus neither circumcision nor uncircumcision counts for anything; the only thing that counts is faith made effective [ἐνεργουμένη] by love" (Gal. 5:6, using the NRSV margin; see Chapter 2 for details). This love, according to Paul, is the love ultimately from Christ and God and thus it is irreducible to human love (2 Cor. 5:14; Rom. 5:5). This consideration fits with the NRSV margin's translation of Paul's participle with the passive voice, "made effective." Paul's comment thus echoes his remark that Christ "loved" him in Galatians 2:20. This translation, as Chapter 2 noted, also can capture what is frequently intended with the middle voice, because faith energized by divine love will "work through love," in its expression.[23] The energizing love is ultimately from God, but it can be embraced and extended through human cooperation.

The divine love in question becomes motivational for a receptive person as it becomes incarnate in the motivational center, "the heart," of that person (cf. Rom. 6:17). Paul holds that the source of that love, namely Christ, becomes incarnate, in at least one sense, in people of faith. He remarks: "It is no longer I who live, but it is Christ who lives in me [ζῇ ἐν ἐμοί]. And the life I now live in the flesh I live by faith in the Son of God, who loved me and gave himself for

---

[23] Support for the passive voice is found in George Duncan, *The Epistle of Paul to the Galatians*, MNTC (New York: Harper, 1934), p. 157. He translates: "faith that is quickened into life by a sense of God's love." Similarly in favor of the passive, see Kenneth W. Clark, "The Meaning of ἘΝΕΡΓΕΩ and ΚΑΤΑΡΓΕΩ in the New Testament," *Journal of Biblical Literature* 54 (1935), 99.

me" (Gal. 2:20; cf. Gal. 4:19). This love from the Son of God does not remove or eclipse Paul's distinctive personal identity (Paul has faith in Christ), but its direct causal influence (not causal coercion) became so central to Paul's moral-personal status that it prompted his striking talk of "Christ who lives in me." It also prompted his talk to the Galatian Christians of "Christ being formed in you [μορφωθῇ Χριστὸς ἐν ὑμῖν]" (Gal. 4:19).

Paul's mention of the Son of God who "loved me and gave himself for me" indicates self-sacrificial love from God and Christ. Such love is the divine righteous love Chapter 1 identified in the "sacrifice of atonement" of Romans 3:25. Paul's incarnational theme for Christ and his law entails an incarnational role for sacrificial love (as the law's fulfillment) among humans in reciprocal response to divine love. That sacrificial response is to come from within, from a human volitional center, and not just from visible behavior. The "formation of Christ" and his law "within" provides for reciprocal sacrifice of "the heart," thereby enabling the fulfillment of the grand promises of Jeremiah and Ezekiel for God's people. Paul's incarnational theme, then, is central to his call to reciprocal self-sacrifice to God.

The sacrificial love from Christ led Paul to embrace and promote divine–human reconciliation for his own life and for the lives of others (2 Cor. 5:14–19), and this included an incarnational theme. He sums up this theme for Christ and the Spirit in Romans: "If Christ is in you [ἐν ὑμῖν], though the body is dead because of sin, the Spirit is life because of righteousness" (Rom. 8:10). This, according to Paul, is the kind of unearned life and righteousness from God that sets one free from the corrosive power of sin and death that is impervious to the Mosaic law (Rom. 8:3). The freedom comes courtesy, as a powerful undeserved gift of grace, from the divine lawgiver who is not to be reduced to the law but who can promote not only Christ but also the law of Christ incarnate, inwardly. We turn next to a key, widely neglected motive behind Paul's incarnational nomism and its bearing on reciprocal self-sacrifice.

LAWGIVER FIRST

Paul's incarnational nomism stems from his concern not to separate the divine lawgiver from the divine law. If the law is incarnate in the divine lawgiver, the focus will tend to be at least as much on the lawgiver as on the law. This is important in Paul's perspective, because God can update divine commands as needed by the divine redemptive effort toward the reconciliation of wayward humans to God.

In Paul's apostolic mission to the Gentiles, circumcision and the food laws dropped out of the divine law, as least as it bears on Gentiles. Paul reports that the Jerusalem apostles (James, Cephas, and John) had no objection here (Gal. 2:1–14; cf. Rom. 14:13–15, 20–21). Similarly, the Sabbath laws dropped out for Gentiles, in Paul's judgment, on the ground that we (may) "live to the Lord" in different ways of regarding days (Rom. 14:5–7). Dunn observes that "where requirements of the law were being interpreted in a way which ran counter to the basic principle of the love command, Paul thought that the requirements could and should be dispensed with."[24] Paul reaffirmed various laws from the Torah, but as noted, he regarded them as "fulfilled" in loving one's neighbor (Rom. 13:8–10; cf. Gal. 5:14).

The central role of sacrificial love in Paul's approach to the law as rightly understood (and as fulfilled) stems from his view of the central role of love motivating the self-sacrificing lawgiver who loves all people. He holds that God teaches people to love one another (1 Thess. 4:9), and he uses the self-sacrificing actions as well as the teachings of Jesus as a main standard.[25] For instance: "Each of us must please our neighbor for the good purpose of building up the neighbor. For Christ did not please himself; but, as it is written, 'The insults of

---

[24] Dunn, *The Theology of Paul the Apostle*, p. 656.
[25] On Paul's allusions to the teachings of Jesus, see Furnish, *Theology and Ethics in Paul*, pp. 52–54; Wenham, *Paul*, pp. 380–408; and Dunn, *The Theology of Paul the Apostle*, pp. 650–53.

those who insult you have fallen on me'" (Rom. 15:2–3). Similarly, writing to the Corinthians, Paul says: "I am testing the genuineness of your love against the earnestness of others. For you know the generous act of our Lord Jesus Christ, that though he was rich, yet for your sakes he became poor, so that by his poverty you might become rich" (2 Cor. 8:8–9; cf. 1 Thess. 5:21–22). These are actions of self-sacrificial love by Christ the lawgiver, the one to whom Paul is "en-lawed [ἔννομος]" and ascribes "the law of Christ" (1 Cor. 9:21; Gal. 6:2).

Unlike Christ as intentional lawgiver, an inscribed law ("in letters") is a static artifact of history and not an intentional agent with variable redemptive purposes for its readers or hearers. A written law can have value, of course, but Paul insists that such a divine law be understood and pursued in terms of the redemptive purposes of its lawgiver. Otherwise, we would have law without the "law of the Spirit" of God in Christ. That would leave us, Paul suggests, with a law ineffective against the powers of sin and death. He thus gives priority to an intentional lawgiver, who fulfills the law with self-sacrificial righteous love.

Pursuing the law through faith in God and Christ contributes to honoring and loving the divine lawgiver above the law. The same holds for Paul's view of the law incarnate in Christ. His distinctive view goes against separating the law of God from God in Christ, and it honors God's prerogative to update the law with a new covenant introduced by Christ, the lawgiver under his divine father, the ultimate lawgiver. Paul's aforementioned echo of Jeremiah's promised new covenant shows his acknowledgment of this divine prerogative and its bearing on the law incarnate. The law, in Paul's perspective, is not an end in itself; it is a means to relate to God (and others) as God desires and commands. Honor and love of God are thus to come first (Rom. 1:21), prior to certain secondary features of the law.

Our talk of the law "incarnate" to capture Paul's talk of "the law (of the Spirit of life) in Christ" does not invite speculative metaphysics. It does include the idea of the law being "encompassed" or "embodied" in Christ and thereby in his disciples, but this notion of incarnation does not depend on abstract philosophical theory. Instead, it rests on an understanding of the directness and proximity of God's (and Christ's) causal influence on one's will, an influence that includes psychological inwardness for the recipient, even when physical inwardness does not apply. This is causal influence and not coercion, because it must be received inwardly by cooperative trust in its source, God or Christ. This consideration fits with Paul's position that the inward reception of God's Spirit comes through faith and not through works of the law (Gal. 3:2–4; cf. Gal. 3:14). It enables Paul to speak of "setting the mind on the Spirit" (Rom. 8:6) and "having the mind of Christ" (1 Cor. 2:16). His emphasis on inwardness emerges clearly in his view that "a person is a Jew who is one inwardly, and real circumcision is a matter of the heart – it is spiritual and not literal" (Rom. 2:29; cf. Phil. 3:3; Rom. 7:6).

The proposed understanding of law incarnate can make sense of talk of the law embodied "in Christ" and thereby in his disciples. It also can illuminate Paul's aforementioned talk of "Christ who lives in me" and "Christ is in you." The same holds for his interchangeable talk of the indwelling "Spirit of God" and "Spirit of Christ":

> You are not in the flesh; you are in the Spirit, since the Spirit of God dwells in [ἐν] you. Anyone who does not have the Spirit of Christ does not belong to him. But if Christ is in [ἐν] you, though the body is dead because of sin, the Spirit is life because of righteousness. If the Spirit of him who raised Jesus from the dead dwells in [ἐν] you, he who raised Christ from the dead will give life to your mortal bodies also through his Spirit that dwells in [ἐν] you.
> (Rom. 8:9–11; cf. 1 Cor. 6:19–20; Col. 1:27)

If the inwardness in question is a matter of direct causal proximity in influence, we can avoid any misleading physical portrait of the law incarnate in its lawgiver or in a recipient.

The language of inwardness has a metaphorical feature, but it still can illuminate the relevant kind of causal influence. It also can bear on the kind of "leading" by God's Spirit that Paul deemed central to being a child of God (Rom. 8:14), particularly in the Spirit's guiding influence through conscience (Rom. 9:1; cf. 2 Cor. 4:2). It thus can figure in Paul's understanding of redemption as including human adoption by God (Rom. 8:15–16).

Paul's Christological approach to the law is eschatological in its fulfillment theme that Jesus has launched the new and final Earthly age as a new domain of divine power. We have noted Paul's mention of God's sending his Son in the fullness of time to redeem those under the law (Gal. 4:4–5; cf. Rom. 8:3). This time or age of fullness, according to Paul, has begun with Christ, while its culmination in final judgment and restoration awaits a future time. As a result, people of faith live with hope in God for promised final redemption, including bodily redemption (Rom. 8:23; cf. Gal. 5:5). Paul calls the new covenant ministry of the Spirit "a hope," in its enduring beyond "the letter" of the law to future redemption and full reconciliation (2 Cor. 3:12).

Hope in God, according to Paul, is not wishful thinking, because, as Chapter 2 indicated (and Chapter 4 will develop), it is grounded in what ultimately motivates and grounds faith in God: divine righteous love courtesy of the Spirit of God. Thus: "Hope [in God] does not disappoint us, because God's love has been poured into our hearts through the Holy Spirit that has been given to us" (Rom. 5:5). This remark is central to Paul's epistemology of knowing God because it identifies what saves hope (and faith) in God from being arbitrary and thus cognitively "disappointing": namely, experiential evidence from divine love presented to "us" by God's Spirit.[26] This kind of experiential evidence enabled Paul to say of Christ, as indicated, that "he loved me" in giving his life through self-sacrifice for divine redemption (Gal. 2:20). (Chapter 4 returns to the topic of grounded hope, in Paul's thought.)

---

[26] I have explained this approach to evidence of divine reality in Moser, *Understanding Religious Experience*, chs 7–8. Chapter 6 returns to the topic of Paul's epistemology of knowing God.

Paul's epistemology rests on a distinction between knowing Christ from two different perspectives: from a fleshly, human point of view and from God's point of view. Paul remarks: "From now on, therefore, we regard no one from a human point of view [κατὰ σάρκα]; even though we once knew Christ from a human point of view, we know him no longer in that way. So, if anyone is in Christ, there is a new creation: everything old has passed away; see, everything has become new!" (2 Cor. 5:16–17). Knowing "according to flesh" is knowing antithetical to God's redemptive self-sacrificial love in Christ. It typically includes a kind of self-seeking knowledge at odds with the self-sacrificial character of God and Christ. In some way, it disregards in knowing Christ his special status arising from the distinctive divine love characteristic of him.[27]

The correction to knowing "according to flesh" comes from receiving and reciprocating, cooperatively, the kind of divine sacrificial redemptive love on offer in Christ. Paul takes such receiving to be integral to receiving cooperatively "the law of faith" or "the law of Christ" and thus to "new creation" by God. He also takes such receiving to proceed with human reciprocating toward the self-sacrifice of Christ in obedience to God (Phil. 2:5, 8), even given human imperfections. In such human receiving and reciprocating, divine love among humans can become inward and motivational in a way that enables their fulfilling the law of God and of Christ, even aside from parts of the Mosaic Law as written. Paul thus holds that human reciprocating toward divine self-sacrifice figures in knowing God and Christ aright, from God's point of view rather than "according

---

[27] For support for such a proposal to understand Paul on knowing from a human point of view, see Margaret E. Thrall, "Christ Crucified or Second Adam? A Christological Debate between Paul and the Corinthians," in *Christ and Spirit in the New Testament*, eds. Barnabas Lindars and Stephen S. Smalley (Cambridge: Cambridge University Press, 1973), pp. 152–56. See also Thrall, *A Critical and Exegetical Commentary on the Second Epistle to the Corinthians*, ICC (London: T&T Clark, 1994), vol. 1, pp. 413–20.

to flesh." (Chapter 6 returns to the latter topic, in assessing Paul's gospel of divine self-sacrifice.)

DESIDERATA

In sum, my case for Paul's commitment to incarnational nomism depends on five desiderata for capturing Paul's position:

(1) Paul aimed to uphold the law of God, not to nullify it, through faith in God (Rom. 3:27–31).
(2) Paul acknowledged "the law of Christ" as exemplifying the law of God (Gal. 6:2; cf. 1 Cor. 9:21).
(3) Paul recognized the law of God in terms of "the law of the Spirit of life" in Christ Jesus (Rom. 8:2).
(4) Paul understood the law of God in terms of Jeremiah's promised new covenant that would bring inwardness to the law of God for God's people, thus assuming that God would improve on the Mosaic law and hence exercise authority over it (2 Cor. 3:2–3).
(5) Paul acknowledged his dying to (the works of) the law in order to "live to God" and to Christ, in a way that reciprocates divine self-sacrificial love (Gal. 2:19; cf. Rom. 7:4).

The best available explanation of the desiderata is that Paul embraced incarnational nomism of the kind outlined in this chapter. The key role for incarnational inwardness, explained in terms of the direct causal proximity of God and Christ through their commands, sets this position apart from any version of covenantal nomism that neglects an incarnational component. It also brings out the superiority of God and Christ over the Mosaic law, in Paul's thought, thus leading to Paul's recognition of "the law of Christ," focused on Christ's love commands and human reciprocating of divine self-sacrificial love in Christ.

Paul's incarnational nomism serves a divine goal: building God's universal kingdom as anticipated to Abraham, including Gentiles as well as Jews (Rom. 3:29–30; 4:16–18). God is thereby set on "the reconciliation of the world" (Rom. 11:15), and Paul follows suit. Paul's nomism thus has a social direction for universal divine redemption in righteousness, beyond merely individual redemption. His gospel may go to "the Jew first," but it also goes to the Gentile world (Rom. 1:16) and hence to the whole world.[28]

The law incarnate is not forced on people by God but can be rejected or ignored by them. It calls, in Paul's perspective, for their "turning to the Lord" in cooperative trust (2 Cor. 3:16).[29] In this regard, at least, it is "the law of faith" and "the law of Christ." It is interpersonal and reconciliatory toward humans and the divine lawgiver, who may relinquish parts of the written law at odds with divine–human reconciliation in divine love. Paul understood the divine law accordingly, although the occasional nature of his letters can make it difficult to put the pieces of the interpretive puzzle together.

We now have an account showing that the pieces fit well in a distinctive portrait of the enduring redemptive value of the divine law in Paul's thought. In this portrait, the divine lawgiver has first place for honor and love and calls for one's understanding and pursuing the law of God accordingly, in reciprocity of divine sacrificial love. We turn now to how grounded hope in God informs Paul's self-sacrificial approach to redemption and counters an obstacle from human fear toward divine self-sacrifice.

---

[28] For a case for Paul as an apostle to Jews and Gentiles, see Michael F. Bird, *An Anomalous Jew: Paul among Jews, Greeks, and Romans* (Grand Rapids, MI: Eerdmans, 2016).

[29] On the role for a voluntary human decision in response to God's love in Christ, see Thrall, *A Critical and Exegetical Commentary on the Second Epistle to the Corinthians*, vol. 1, p. 409. Chapter 5 returns to the topic of Paul on a voluntary human response to his gospel.

4 Hope and Fear toward Divine Self-Sacrifice

In hope we were saved.

Romans 8:24

Various New Testament writings assume an important role for hope in God. The role of eschatology in those writings includes a role for hope regarding what God will accomplish by way of redemption. The apostle Paul goes further to identify a widely neglected evidential ground for hope in God. This ground is in divine righteous *agapē* toward humans in their experience, and it anchors, as supporting evidence, not only human hope in God but also divine promises for humans.

In Paul's view, divine epiphany and divine promise belong together as constituents of grounded human hope in God. His view provides a needed corrective to Jürgen Moltmann's influential but unduly sharp contrast, in *Theology of Hope* and elsewhere, between a God of epiphany and a God of promise. This chapter clarifies Paul's position on an important kind of experience-grounded hope in God neglected by Moltmann and many other commentators. In doing so, it identifies a key role for divine self-sacrifice in grounding human hope in God.

The chapter explains how a kind of fear toward divine self-sacrifice yields an obstacle to hope in God. It distinguishes two kinds of fear of God in order to clarify a command from Paul (and Jesus before him) to fear God. In doing so, it makes sense of a suggestion of 1 John that human love in relation to God "casts out fear." The chapter illuminates why one kind of fear, even when combined with felt abandonment by God, need not yield despair about God's reality or goodness. The chapter finds that Paul avoids two influential extremes: treating fear of God as experiencing an "ineffable" object that is "wholly other" (Rudolf Otto and others) and treating it as mere obedience to God (Gerhard von Rad and others). It identifies a central but widely neglected role in Paul's thought for affective distress experiences in fear of God that can be motivational for obeying God and for reconciliation with God. Divine self-sacrifice in righteous love anchors Paul's perspective on hope and fear toward God.

TOWARD GROUNDED HOPE

Hope includes a desire regarding the future. *The Oxford English Dictionary*, 3rd ed., offers this lead definition: "Expectation of something desired; desire combined with expectation." Perhaps expectation distinguishes hope from a mere desire. It seems that I can desire to become a billionaire but not have any expectation, and thus any hope, of becoming one. The OED allows for thinking of hope in this way, as requiring desire even though desire is insufficient for hope. We shall follow suit, while allowing the required expectation in hope to be minimal rather than strong or high. Ordinary English is somewhat loose in its use of "hope," but we can proceed with the lead definition of the OED.

Hope need not have a ground indicating the eventual realization of its object, and thus it can be akin to wishful thinking. Grounded hope, in contrast, is reasonable, or reason-based, to some extent, and thus it has some support from a ground. The support can be either for the hoping (as a psychological event or state) or for what is hoped for (as an object of hoping). When it is for the hoping, it can be a matter of mere psychological benefit, with no indicator of its being realized or satisfied with regard to its object or what is hoped for.

I might hope to become a billionaire, and I might even have some indication that this hoping will be psychologically beneficial for me (say, in terms of its giving me a positive psychological outlook for my financial prospects). Even so, nothing in my evidence indicates that I actually will become a billionaire; in fact, all of my evidence indicates that I will not. If we want to be constrained by likely reality, we will do well to give a priority to reasons supporting the eventual actualization of an object of hope and not merely an event or state of hoping. We shall be concerned mainly about the kind of ground in Paul's thought that supports the eventual actualization of an object of hope: an "object-ground," for short, in contrast with a "state-ground."

Object-grounds for hope can come with variable degrees of support for an object of hope. Some are strong (such as my ground for the object of my hoping to have milk to drink tomorrow), and others are relatively weak (such as my ground for the object of my hoping to live to be 100). We can think of very weak grounds as bad grounds overall from the standpoint of the likely realization of an object of hope. They fail to indicate adequately that the object of hope will be realized (such as my living to be 100). As for how "eventual" the actualization must be indicated, in terms of delayed time, that will be a function of the content of a particular case of hope. We need not assume a single standard of "eventual" here.

Discussions of hope in God typically fail to distinguish between object-grounds and state-grounds. Inquirers about God, however, ordinarily care about the object-grounds, because those grounds bear on the question of the reality of God's present and future intervention in human affairs. A mere belief, even if called "faith," will not serve as a good object-ground, because questions about the ground of the relevant belief or faith itself need good answers.

A source of hoping is a causal basis of hoping, but it need not be an object-ground that indicates (with evidence) the eventual realization of the object of hoping. A source of hoping could be a report from a person who lacks needed supporting evidence and is unreliable on the realization of the relevant object of hoping. So, a source of hoping can yield an object-ground, but it need not do so. Some sources of hoping are good, but others are not, from the standpoint of supplying an object-ground for the realization of what is hoped for.

Jürgen Moltmann has referred to "the hope that is continually led on further by the promise of God." He adds that "the hope which arises from faith in God's promise will become the ferment in our thinking, its mainspring." At the same time, he suggests that "it is hope that maintains and upholds faith," and that "hope ... is the mobilizing and driving force of faith's thinking."[1] We need not digress to the issue of whether faith has causal priority over hope or vice versa. Our concern now lies with the matter of an object-ground for hoping. We need to ask whether either a promise or faith in a promise can provide such an object-ground.

The terms "led on," "arises from," "mainspring," "upholds," and "mobilizing and driving force" suggest causal influence on hoping and believing, but they do not suggest evidence as an object-ground for hoping. Similarly, talk of "the hope which arises from faith in God's promise" does not suggest an object-ground. Even so, that kind of hope needs such a ground if it is to stand in contrast with a kind of wishful thinking. We need to identify what can underwrite such a contrast.

A promise by itself does not supply an adequate object-ground for hope. A promise can be altogether ungrounded regarding an indicator of its object being eventually realized. Ungrounded promises are familiar among humans, and thus we often learn in pain that promises need to earn their keep from an evidential object-ground. The same holds for faith in a promise. Faith can be ungrounded regarding an indicator of its object being real or true. In that respect, it can be akin to wishful thinking. Faith thus needs an object-ground and, in that respect, it is similar to hope. The requirement of an object-ground for hope in God, we shall see, need not threaten the freedom or the authority of God. Instead, it can contribute to the confirmation of that freedom and authority.

---

[1] Jürgen Moltmann, *Theology of Hope*, trans. James Leitch (London: SCM Press, 1967), p. 33. Hereafter: TH.

Moltmann speaks of "the ground of the promise" of God and of "the ground of the hope which carries faith through the trials of the godforsaken world and of death" (TH, 85). He finds this ground in "the fact that in all the qualitative difference of cross and resurrection Jesus is the same," adding that "this identity in infinite contradiction is theologically understood as an event of identification, an act of the faithfulness of God" (TH, 85). The talk of "infinite contradiction" seems hyperbolic from a logical point of view, given that Moltmann affirms the actuality, rather than the logical impossibility, of the crucifixion and the resurrection of Jesus.[2] He evidently has in mind not a literal contradiction but God's enigmatic intervention in human affairs via the crucifixion and the resurrection of Jesus. The divine "faithfulness" of that distinctive intervention is his proposed "ground" for God's redemptive promise and human hope in God.

Moltmann rejects any position implying that an appearance or an epiphany of God is at the center of the object-ground for hope in God's promise. He finds such a position to be inspired typically by Parmenides who identified ultimate reality with a changeless presence devoid of movement toward a promised future. Moltmann adds:

> The real language of Christian eschatology is not the Greek *logos*, but the *promise* which has stamped the language, the hope, and the experience of Israel. It was not in the *logos* of the epiphany of the eternal present, but in the hope-giving word of promise that Israel found God's truth. That is why history was here experienced in an entirely different and entirely open form. Eschatology as a science is therefore not possible in the Greek sense, nor yet in the sense of

---

[2] Moltmann's talk of "infinite contradiction" is inspired by Kierkegaard writing as Climacus in his *Concluding Unscientific Postscript*, trans. H. V. Hong and E. H. Hong (Princeton: Princeton University Press, 1992). For reasons not to take such talk literally, see Paul K. Moser, "God *De Re et De Dicto*: Kierkegaard, Faith, and Religious Diversity," *Scottish Journal of Theology* 74 (2021), 135–46; and Paul K. Moser and Mark McCreary, "Kierkegaard's Conception of God," *Philosophy Compass* 5 (2010), 127–35.

modern experimental science, but only as a knowledge in terms of hope, and to that extent as a knowledge of history and of the historic character of truth.

(TH, 40–41)

Moltmann's signature contrast is: "It was not in the *logos* of the epiphany of the eternal present, but in the hope-giving word of promise that Israel found God's truth."

Moltmann adds: "The point of the appearance [of God to people] lies not in itself, but in the promise which becomes audible in it, and in the future to which it points …. The sense and purpose of his 'appearances' lies not in themselves, but in the promise and its future" (TH, 100; cf. TH, 143). He faults Kierkegaard and Bultmann, among others, for neglecting his sharp contrast (TH, 29–31, 58–69). We shall see, however, that a false disjunction is at work in his contrast, particularly from the standpoint of the apostle Paul on grounded hope in God's redemptive promise.

Moltmann cites Luther on Romans 8:19, with regard to "the earnest expectation of the creature" (TH, 35), to support his exclusive contrast between divine epiphany and divine promise. He portrays God's redemptive intervention as aimed at prompting that kind of "earnest expectation" as a hope. He also applies his sharp contrast to the presence of Christ and the coming of Christ: "The parousia of Christ is conceived in the New Testament only in categories of expectation, so that it means not *praesentia Christi* but *adventus Christi*, and is not his eternal presence bringing time to a standstill, but his 'coming'" (TH, 31). Moltmann's exclusive contrast fails, however, because it neglects that the divine promise has its object-ground in divine intervention, including divine presence, in human experience and thus not "only in categories of expectation." The problem comes from the use of the word "only." Paul acknowledges an object-ground in divine presence, as we shall document, and thus Moltmann captures only one side of Paul on grounded hope in God's redemptive promise.

Paul straightforwardly endorses an object-ground for hope in God: "Hope does not disappoint us, because God's love has been poured into our hearts through the Holy Spirit that has been given to us" (Rom. 5:5). This is an acknowledgment of divine presence with self-manifested divine *agapē* in human experience; it is not about human love of God. The love acknowledged by Paul here is a divine self-manifestation, an epiphany, of God's moral character of righteous love toward humans. Paul thought of it as not only experienced but also motivating, or leading, toward a goal for a person and thus a basis for hope in God. He remarks: "The love of Christ urges us on," on the assumption that this is God's love from Christ (2 Cor. 5:14). This kind of divine motivating guidance for willing people figures in Paul's understanding of being a child of God: "All who are led by the Spirit of God are children of God" (Rom. 8:14; cf. Gal. 5:18).

The divine righteous love "poured into our hearts" shows, in Paul's perspective, God's perfectly good and trustworthy character as a ground for hope in God, that is, hope in God's good character and its future ends. Paul has in mind experience-based hope in God, including God's redemptive promise, and he identifies an object-ground in the self-manifestation of God's perfect character in divine love poured into human hearts. This object-ground serves to ground not only God's redemptive promise but also human hope in God.

C. E. B. Cranfield comments: "The hope which is thus strengthened and confirmed does not put those who cherish it to shame by proving illusory."[3] This talk of a counter to "proving illusory" captures Paul's thinking of an object-ground for hope in God. God's own perfect character of righteous love, suitably manifested to humans in their experience, serves as the needed object-ground among humans for their hope in God and God's redemptive promise. This character shows God's goodness, including righteous love, in

---

[3] C. E. B. Cranfield, *A Critical and Exegetical Commentary on the Epistle to the Romans*, ICC (Edinburgh: T&T Clark, 1975), vol. 1, pp. 261–62.

human experience, and it thereby shows God's trustworthiness for human hope in God and God's redemptive promise.

Moltmann neglects the importance of God's self-manifested character of righteous love as an object-ground for God's promise and human hope in God. Instead, he puts the focus on God's "faithfulness" to the divine promise (TH, 116). As a result, he misses the importance of self-manifested divine *agapē* of the kind embraced by Paul as an object-ground for hope in God. Falling short of Paul's point, Moltmann says: "'God himself' cannot be understood as reflection on his transcendent 'I-ness,' but must be understood as his selfsame-ness in historic faithfulness to his promises" (TH, 116). He adds: "Our hope in the promises of God is not hope in God himself or in God as such, but it hopes that his future faithfulness will bring it also the fullness of what has been promised" (TH, 119).

Paul's lesson missed by Moltmann is that God's perfect character of righteous love is more basic to God than divine promises. God's perfect character does not depend on those promises, because it could exist without them (as it would prior to the making of promises). Those promises, however, depend on God's perfect character of righteous love for not only their reality but also their object-ground. We misrepresent Paul if we give promises a priority over the divine perfect character behind them.

Moltmann gets the direction of grounding dependence exactly backwards from Paul's perspective when he says: "The *pro-missio* of the kingdom is the ground of the *mission* of love to the world" (TH, 224). According to Paul, as indicated in Romans 5:5, God's mission of righteous love self-manifested to the world supplies the object-ground for the promise of the kingdom announced by Jesus. The promise itself, contrary to Moltmann, does not ground the divine mission of self-manifested love.

Moltmann's mistaken reversal of Paul accounts for his neglect of the fundamental role of presented divine righteous *agapē* in Paul's message, including: "God proves his love for us in that while we still were sinners Christ died for us" (Rom. 5:8). Moltmann's interpretation does not go deep enough in stressing God's "faithfulness" to a divine promise (TH, 116), because it does not identify the divine moral character of sacrificial *agapē* that grounds the faithfulness and the promise. According to Paul, the relevant divine faithfulness is, ultimately, faithfulness to God's perfect moral character of righteous love (cf. Rom. 3:4), and we have seen that this divine character is self-sacrificial for righteousness.

DOWN PAYMENT FOR HOPE

Paul offers an alternative both to a claim of hope's "fulfillment already" and to a claim of no present realization of a hope to be fulfilled. The familiar talk of "now, but not fully yet" captures Paul's approach to hope in God and God's promise. Moltmann wrongly suggests that a proponent of divine epiphany must think of that epiphany as "already fulfillment" (TH, 155). This goes against Paul's understanding of currently experienced divine *agapē* as an object-ground of hope in God that awaits fulfillment. He thinks of it not as "already fulfillment" but as an actual down payment on a promise that God will fulfill, or bring to "already fulfillment," only in the fullness of time (Rom. 8:18–25).

Regarding the Spirit of God who has poured divine love into human hearts, Paul speaks of God's "putting his seal on us and giving us his Spirit in our hearts as a guarantee [ἀρραβῶνα]" (2 Cor. 1:22, RSV; cf. 2 Cor. 5:5). The experience of divine *agapē*, courtesy of God's Spirit, is thus a down payment on a promise to be fulfilled. So, it would be mistaken to characterize it as "already fulfillment." Paul thus endorses "abounding in hope by the power of the Holy Spirit" (Rom. 15:13), and he has in mind currently experienced power. Moltmann acknowledges an important role for the Spirit of God in Christian life, in various ways. Even so, he fails to appreciate Paul's perspective that an experience of God's Spirit is crucial for grounding hope in God (as Romans 5:5 confirms).

We have no evidence of "already fulfillment" in Paul's understanding of a person's being led by God as a child of God toward the ultimate redemptive goal. Such a person is attracted through experience of God's righteous love to cooperate with God's will self-manifested in human experience. According to Paul, this kind of "being led" guides a person, without coercion, toward the goal of conformity to God's (and Christ's) moral character in reconciliation with God (see Gal. 5:16–18, 25; Rom. 8:3–5).[4] In being thus led, a human moral character is integrated with God's righteous love, thereby bringing unity to a person's moral experience and conscience. A person then also receives experiential evidence of God's presence in a human life via experienced divine goodness and love, while undergoing moral renewal through human cooperation with God. The evidential and the moral realities work together in a transformative manner as humans cooperate with an intervening God toward a prized redemptive goal. A significant transformation thus occurs in human moral character, and this bears on human evidence of God's reality and presence, in Paul's account.[5]

Paul comments on hope in relation to creation as follows: "The creation waits with eager longing for the revealing of the children of God; for the creation was subjected to futility, not of its own will but by the will of the one who subjected it, in hope that the creation itself will be set free from its bondage to decay and will obtain the freedom of the glory of the children of God" (Rom. 8:19–21). In this perspective, God subjects creation to futility, but the subjection is accompanied by hope for a kind of freedom to be fulfilled in the fullness of time. Leander Keck notes Paul's suggestion that God did so "in hope," that is, "with an eye to its eventual liberation and participation in the same future that God's children will enjoy."[6]

---

[4] I thus take exception to the reading "driven by the Spirit" proposed by Ernst Käsemann, *Commentary on Romans*, p. 226. I share Käsemann's view that divine righteousness in Paul's perspective is a power, and not a mere idea, but I deny that this power coerces human wills to obey.

[5] On Paul's understanding of "being led" by the Spirit in comparison with obeying a law, see Dunn, *The Theology of Paul the Apostle*, pp. 668–69.

[6] Keck, *Romans*, p. 211.

The future time of fulfillment will include the volitional freedom of the glory of God's children, but their volitional freedom does not apply directly to inanimate "creation." Volitional freedom (to be discussed in Chapter 5) is not a feature of things that do not have a will or make decisions, such as trees, rocks, and clouds. Even so, the volitional freedom in question can be part of a larger context for creation in general, and inanimate creation can be freed of its "bondage to decay." In addition, one may, with good ground, hope for the latter freedoms, in Paul's perspective.

The promise of eschatological freedom does not float free of an object-ground in Paul's thinking. He remarks:

> We know that the whole creation has been groaning in labor pains until now; and not only the creation, but we ourselves, who have the first fruits [ἀπαρχὴν] of the Spirit, groan inwardly while we wait for adoption, the redemption of our bodies. For in hope we were saved. Now hope that is seen is not hope. For who hopes for what is seen? But if we hope for what we do not see, we wait for it with patience.
>
> *(Rom. 8:22–25)*

Joseph A. Fitzmyer puts Paul's lesson as follows: "The Spirit, which has been received, is the guarantee or pledge of the glory assured for Christians. Though thus assured, they still have to wait, as long as they are alive 'in the flesh,' for the full payment" (cf. Gal. 5:5).[7] This observation captures the "now, but not fully yet" feature of Paul's perspective on redemption. The "redemption of our bodies" in resurrection awaits a future time; so, it does not allow for thinking of the experienced "first fruits" of God's Spirit as "already fulfilment" for God's redemptive promise.

Paul's position on hoping for what we do not see finds its basis in his following perspective: "We look not to the things that are seen but to the things that are unseen; for the things that are seen are

---

[7] Fitzmyer, *Romans*, p. 510.

transient, but the things that are unseen are eternal" (2 Cor. 4:18). The latter perspective also underlies his remark that "we walk by faith, not by sight" (2 Cor. 5:7). Being led by God toward conformity with God's moral character entails, in Paul's thinking, being led by and toward something unseen.

Paul's God is not an object of typical human vision. So, hope in this God is hope in someone unseen: in an unseen God, as well as in an unfulfilled, and thus unseen, scenario promised by this God. Hope, faith, and being led regarding God, then, do not reduce to visual or other sensory processes. They depend, instead, on human discernment of things unseen, although they can find a needed ground in divine love experienced by humans, courtesy of God's Spirit (as Romans 5:5 indicates). So, Paul is discouraging an expectation for visual evidence, but not evidence altogether, in the ground of hope in God.

God's Spirit can serve as the needed down payment because this Spirit, according to Paul, is the source of the divine leading of the children of God to God's main redemptive goal for them. The goal is to be glorified with Christ as God's children and heirs. Paul remarks:

> For all who are led by the Spirit of God are children of God. For you did not receive a spirit of slavery to fall back into fear, but you have received a spirit of adoption. When we cry, "Abba! Father!," it is that very Spirit bearing witness with our spirit that we are children of God, and if children, then heirs, heirs of God and joint heirs with Christ – if, in fact, we suffer with him so that we may also be glorified with him.
>
> (Rom. 8:14–17)

Paul makes a similar point in an earlier letter: "Because you are children, God has sent the Spirit of his Son into our hearts, crying, 'Abba! Father!' So, you are no longer a slave but a child, and if a child then also an heir, through God" (Gal 4:6–7).

As in Romans 5:5, Paul looks to a distinctive experience of God's Spirit as confirming or guaranteeing God's promise of redemption: "When we cry, 'Abba! Father!,' it is that very Spirit bearing witness with our spirit that we are children of God." God's love "poured into our hearts," in Paul's perspective, prompts our calling God "Abba! Father!," and God's Spirit empowers that interactive and inter-relational filial encounter.

The Spirit of God serves the purpose of the down payment because that Spirit provides the means of fellowship (κοινωνία, 2 Cor. 13:13) with God now, in advance of the later full glory promised to God's people. Paul remarks: "The Spirit helps us in our weakness; for we do not know how [better: *what*] to pray as we ought, but that very Spirit intercedes with sighs too deep for words. And God, who searches the heart, knows what is the mind of the Spirit, because the Spirit intercedes for the saints according to the will of God" (Rom. 8:26–27). The Spirit of God thus represents the will of God to humans in seeking to have them commune with God, if at times with "sighs too deep for words" (cf. Rom. 8:23). Paul considers this work of God's Spirit to be part of his experience of God and not just a feature of a theory.

Experienced divine love from God's Spirit can serve as a down payment or a guarantee for the future glory for God's children, according to Paul, because it gives a partial, if imperfect, foretaste now of that future glory. It does so by giving an experienced sample of the divine righteous love to be realized in fullness later. Paul identifies that Spirit with the Spirit of Christ, thus suggesting that its power is Christ-like.[8] The power in question includes the effort of God's Spirit now to have people willingly cooperate with and thereby share in God's character of righteous love.

VARIABLE HOPE

Hope in God varies among people, according to Paul, to the extent that some people "have no hope" (1 Thess. 4:13). We now can explain

---

[8] This identification figures in the later talk of "Christ in you, the hope of glory" (Col. 1:27), while Paul elsewhere assigns the same role in human hope in God to the Spirit of God. Part of the background here is Paul's view that Jesus Christ "became a life-giving Spirit" (1 Cor. 15:45).

some of the variation. People can resist the divine redemptive effort, and they often do (Rom. 1:18, 25, 29), thereby excluding or obscuring the object-ground for hope in God. Paul thus commands the Thessalonian Christians: "Do not quench [σβέννυτε] the Spirit" (1 Thess. 5:19; cf. Eph. 4:30). He also commanded the Galatian Christians: "Walk by the Spirit, and do not gratify the desires of the flesh" (Gal. 5:15, RSV). If the Spirit worked coercively, apart from human cooperation, there would be no point to Paul's commands.

Paul's commands assume that humans can choose voluntarily not to cooperate by ignoring or rejecting the effort of God's Spirit to attract them with divine goodness and love. They can decide either to cooperate or to disobey. They are therefore responsible, or accountable, to God for their settled response, in Paul's perspective. The previous command applies to Galatian Christians, but Paul assumes a voluntary response to God available to people in general, as suggested by Romans 1:18–23, 28. (Chapter 5 returns to this topic.)

Paul thinks of divine goodness as aimed at challenging people to exercise their will, by way of response, to turn to God in repentant cooperation. He asks regarding God: "Do you despise the riches of his kindness and forbearance and patience? Do you not realize that God's kindness is meant to lead you to repentance [εἰς μετάνοιάν σε ἄγει]?" (Rom. 2:4–5). Paul's question assumes that God has a purpose or goal in showing divine goodness to people: to lead them, by way of their response, to repentant cooperation with God, in what he calls the "obedience of faith" (Rom. 1:5, 16:26; cf. Rom. 10:16).

We have noted that the obedience of faith is neither a "work" that earns divine approval (Rom. 4:3–4) nor mere intellectual assent but trust and volitional cooperation toward God's redemptive will.[9] Paul thus can talk of "obedience which leads to righteousness" (ὑπακοῆς εἰς δικαιοσύνην) (Rom. 6:16) and of believing in God with one's volitional center, one's "heart" (Rom. 10:10; cf. 2 Thess. 1:8). Paul

---

[9] For discussion of Paul's view of faith in God, see Chapter 2. Cf. John M. G. Barclay, *Paul and the Gift* (Grand Rapids, MI: Eerdmans, 2015), pp. 378–83.

denies that "works of the law" lead to righteousness before God (Rom. 3:20); so, we should deny, as Chapter 2 suggested, that such works are to be identified with what Paul takes to be actions obedient to God.

The importance of human volitional cooperation in Paul's perspective is often neglected by commentators. It emerges, however, in his following illuminating remark about receiving God's Spirit: "Indeed, to this very day whenever Moses is read, a veil lies over their minds; but when one turns to the Lord, the veil is removed. Now the Lord is the Spirit, and where the Spirit of the Lord is, there is freedom" (2 Cor. 3:15–17). The key phrase is: "when one turns to the Lord." Paul has in mind a voluntary human action, in response to divine intervention, and it involves the volitional center, the will, of a person for a life-direction, beyond reflection or contemplation.

Paul (as Chapter 5 will explain) has no place for God's causing human disobedience, unbelief, or ultimate exclusion in relation to redemption. Instead, he assigns the problem to "the god of this world" (2 Cor. 4:4) and to human "unbelief," and he acknowledges that humans can change their unbelief in relation to God (Rom. 11:20, 23). Drawing from the book of Isaiah (65:2), he states regarding God: "Of Israel he says, 'All day long I have held out my hands to a disobedient and contrary people'" (Rom. 10:21). This is not the conduct of a God who causes the disobedience, unbelief, or exclusion of people. We should interpret Paul's understanding of God's redemptive will accordingly.

The divine redemptive effort, we have noted, includes the Spirit's power to kill evil deeds incompatible with divine goodness and love. Paul thus says: "If by the Spirit you put to death the deeds of the body, you will live" (Rom. 8:13). People can choose, however, not to extinguish such deeds, thereby opting to live at odds with God's Spirit. In that case, they will lack firsthand experience of the power of God in its fruition intended by God that includes their cooperating with it.

The power of self-presented divine goodness and love is intended by God to be joined with human cooperation for its humanly experienced fruition. Such cooperation is a vital part of the divine–human reconciliation portrayed by Paul. In blocking the intended fruition of divine power, people obstruct their experienced reception of the divine goodness and love that ground hope in God by removing disappointment in such hope (Rom. 5:5). They thus block the unique evidence available to them of God's reality and goodness presented in human experience. The proper reception of that evidence, we have suggested, is sensitive to human cooperation with it, given the divine aim for human cooperation with it for the sake of fruition in reconciliation.

We now can see why grounded hope in God varies among humans and does not arise just from human reflection or contemplation. Its object-ground varies as a result of different human volitional responses to presented divine goodness and love. Some of those responses are uncooperative and thus at odds with divine goodness or love that comes to fruition in human cooperation with it. Jesus told the parables of the sower and the great banquet to illustrate this concern (see Mark 4:3–20; Luke 14:15–24).[10] Paul, as noted, acknowledges a similar role for an accountable human response to the intervention of God's Spirit in experience.

The perspective being developed is not Pelagian, because it attributes no role to the earning or meriting of human approval before God. Cooperating with God does not entail earning, or intending to earn, something from God. Instead, this perspective acknowledges a key role in Paul's thought for human responsiveness and responsibility toward the gracious evidence of divine self-manifestation that is the object-ground for hope in God.

What we value figures in whether we will cooperatively receive a grounded hope with regard to God. This fits with God's redemptive aim for willing and cooperative divine–human reconciliation that

---

[10] For relevant discussion, see Moser, *The Divine Goodness of Jesus*, ch. 5.

preserves human responsibility. If we do not value God's kind of goodness, including divine love, we will not receive this goodness cooperatively as our object-ground for hope in God. In that case, we will not receive it for what it is intended by God to be: a power that comes to fruition in human cooperation with it. In failing to value that power, we will lose enduring access to the needed object-ground for hope in God. We then will fail to value, and to participate in suitably, the cooperation intended by God to bring presented divine power to fruition for human redemption.

We now can see how we ourselves can contribute to our lacking grounded hope for lasting goodness for our lives and how this can lead to variation among humans in grounded hope in God. If we recognize the needed ground to include divine epiphany as well as divine promise, with respect for human cooperation, we can make good sense of the human redemptive predicament and its hopeful solution acknowledged by Paul. We turn to an influential obstacle to hope in God: self-protective fear.

HOPE AND FEAR

Paul writes to the Roman Christians: "You did not receive a spirit of slavery to fall back into fear [φόβον], but you have received a spirit of adoption" (Rom. 8:15; cf. 2 Tim. 1:7). In this context, Paul comments on hope in relation to the kind of adoption (including the redemption of our bodies) he contrasts with fear: "In hope we were saved. Now hope that is seen is not hope. For who hopes for what is seen? But if we hope for what we do not see, we wait for it with patience" (Rom 8:24–25). Paul suggests that the debilitating fear he has in mind is at odds with waiting for God's full redemption "with patience," and thus that it is inimical to suitable hope for that redemption. The relevant fear, in short, is an obstacle to human hope in God and the divine redemption of humans.

We need to clarify Paul's suggestion about fear as an obstacle to hope in God, because he shares in his letter to the Romans a criticism of humans from Psalm 36:1: "There is no fear of God before their eyes" (Rom. 3:18). He also remarks: "Knowing the fear of the Lord [τὸν φόβον τοῦ κυρίου], we try to persuade others" (2 Cor. 5:11). He repeats his positive attitude toward fear of God as follows: "Since we have these promises, beloved, let us cleanse ourselves from every defilement of body and of spirit, making holiness perfect in the fear of God [ἐν φόβῳ θεοῦ]" (2 Cor. 7:1). Similarly, he commands the Christians at Philippi: "Work out your own salvation with fear [φόβου] and trembling" (Phil. 2:12). So, Paul has positive as well as negative views about fear in relation to God. We need to ask whether they are coherent and how they bear on hope in God.

Paul's position on fear of God raises an important motivational problem: What will motivate, or empower, a person to obey God, especially when obeying is difficult and stressful? Self-motivation often falls short, particularly when people prefer not to obey. Fear of God can play a key role here, figuring in human motivation to obey God or at least to respond to God in some way. We will consider the importance of such motivational fear of God and its value in challenging human moral and cognitive inadequacy, such as complacency or arrogance, before God. This will enable us to clarify Paul's position on hope and fear toward God, in relation to his gospel of divine self-sacrifice.

Two influential approaches to human fear of God stand in sharp contrast, but both miss the mark on the motivational problem for obeying God. In characterizing "the fear of God," Rudolf Otto cites the book of Job: "If [God] would take his rod away from me, and not let dread of him terrify me" (Job 9:34). In addition: "Withdraw your hand far from me, and do not let dread of you terrify me" (Job 13:21). Otto remarks: "Here we have a terror fraught with an inward shuddering such as not even the most menacing and overpowering created thing can instill."[11] He adds that "shuddering is something more than natural, ordinary fear. It implies that the mysterious is already

---

[11] Rudolf Otto, *The Idea of the Holy*, trans. John W. Harvey (London: Oxford University Press, 1923), p. 14.

beginning to loom before the mind, to touch the feelings."[12] The mysterious object in fear of God, according to Otto, is "beyond our apprehension and comprehension"; it is "the ineffable something that holds the mind," and it is "inherently wholly other."[13] It thus escapes any of our thoughts or other conceptualizations.

Otto deserves credit for identifying fear of God as an affective response that can motivate a person, but he goes astray on two matters. First, the fear of God in the biblical narratives, including in Paul's letters, is not always portrayed as "terror fraught with an inward shuddering" toward "an ineffable something" that is "inherently wholly other." That may be a feature of some mystical religious experiences, but the biblical narratives are more diverse in their portrayals of human fear of God. For instance, they include this instruction to Abraham: "He said, 'Do not lay your hand on the boy or do anything to him; for now I know that you fear God, since you have not withheld your son, your only son, from me'" (Gen. 22:12). In addition: "Moses said to the people, 'Do not be afraid; for God has come only to test you and to put the fear of him upon you so that you do not sin'" (Exodus 20:20). The contexts of such passages do not include "terror fraught with an inward shuddering" toward "an ineffable something" that is "inherently wholly other."

The second problem for Otto's account is that it does not adequately connect fear of God with a motivational response to the righteous God of the Jewish and Christian scriptures. For the sake of righteousness, that God is morally demanding and even testing toward humans in a way that includes definite moral content, even if God is not completely comprehensible by them. Moral demands from God reveal God's righteous moral character; they thus remove God from the domain of the (completely) "ineffable," strictly speaking. Shuddering in fear of God, then, must be shuddering toward, and prompted by, a being with a certain kind of righteous moral character who is morally demanding. Otto's account is too morally

---

[12] Otto, *The Idea of the Holy*, p. 15. [13] Otto, *The Idea of the Holy*, pp. 18, 28.

indeterminate regarding the object of human fear of God to capture the motivational significance of God's presented moral character. It thus falls short in accounting for the motivational significance of fear of God for obeying God.

A second influential approach to human fear of God identifies such fear with obedience to God. Gerhard von Rad has explained fear of God simply in terms of obeying God, suggesting that talk of such fear is replaceable, without loss, with talk of obeying God.[14] Following von Rad, and dissenting from Otto, Jason A. Fout has proposed: "The fear of God is specifically connected with … commandments [e.g., from Leviticus] in a way that strongly suggests it ought to be understood as obedience (and therefore involving human agency to a high degree), as not involving a visceral response to a numinous experience, and as correlated to justice and goodness."[15]

Fout correctly suggests a relation of fear of God to divine justice and goodness, given God's righteous moral character. This improves on Otto's approach. We should add that a God of self-sacrificial righteousness will prompt fear from many people, owing to a common human fear of self-sacrifice, including self-sacrificial love. Such fear will leave many people with a tendency to avoid God, as a result of fearing a loss of something good, perhaps even one's life, from righteous self-sacrifice. We thus may think of it as avoidance-fear. The feared loss seems to need an antidote, however, such as divine vindication of righteous self-sacrifice (cf. Rom. 3:24–26). In the absence of God's vindication, avoidance-fear can increase and prevail. Human trust or faith in God can figure in the antidote, in its countering avoidance-fear. So, a divine call for faith in God finds a practical rationale in relation to avoidance-fear of God.

Humans need something to motivate, or empower, their obedience to God, but fear of God will not serve that purpose if it is

---

[14] Gerhard von Rad, *Old Testament Theology*, trans. D. M. G. Stalker (New York: Harper and Row, 1962), vol. 1, pp. 433, 438.

[15] Jason A. Fout, "What Do I Fear When I Fear My God?," *Journal of Theological Interpretation* 9 (2015), 32.

"understood as obedience." The needed motivation for obedience cannot come from the obedience itself needing motivation. Fout holds that "the fear of God as found in Scripture is not best understood by analogy with the typical human emotion of fear."[16] That may be true, but we still should consider how fear of God can serve as a needed motivation for obedience to God.

Otto's approach falls short on needed motivation to obey God (that is, the morally demanding God of the Jewish and Christian scriptures), whereas the approach of von Rad and Fout falls short on the needed motivation to obey God. R. W. L. Moberly takes exception to Otto and von Rad, proposing that we understand fear of God as "integrity and faithfulness of relationship" with God.[17] That may be a feature of a kind of fear of God, but we are looking for the role of such fear as a motivation for obedience and faithfulness to God.

C. Stephen Evans rightly has linked fear of God to accountability for obedience, citing Deuteronomy 6:13, Joshua 24:14, and 1 Samuel 12:14. He remarks: "We are to fear the Lord because God has authority over us, the right to command and to expect us to be obedient. Perhaps we should say that to fear God is to recognize and respect his authority, to understand that we are *accountable* to him."[18] This is correct as far as it goes, but we need to acknowledge an experiential affective component of fear. The same lesson applies to the suggestion of Job Y. Jindo: "The fear of God is a reflective response attained through an internalization of [a] certain kind of knowledge ... a recognition of one's status within the universe, of which YHWH is the absolute authority."[19] Even so, an experiential component of fear, going beyond anything merely intellectual, should be introduced here as crucial to its motivational value.

---

[16] Fout, "What Do I Fear When I Fear My God?," 35.

[17] R. W. L. Moberly, *The Bible, Theology, and Faith: A Study of Abraham and Jesus* (Cambridge: Cambridge University Press, 2000), pp. 88, 96.

[18] C. Stephen Evans, "Accountability and the Fear of the Lord," *Studies in Christian Ethics* 34 (2021), 316–23.

[19] Job Y. Jindo, "On the Biblical Notion of Human Dignity: Fear of God as a Condition for Authentic Existence," *Biblical Interpretation* 19 (2011), 449.

Walther Eichrodt has offered a helpful suggestion, citing Deuteronomy 20:20: "The religious feeling of terror does not have the character of panic, nor even that of servile anxiety, but contains a mysterious power of attraction which is converted into wonder, obedience, self-surrender, and enthusiasm."[20] We need to clarify this "power of attraction" in motivational fear of God, in order to understand Paul on fear and hope toward God.

MOTIVATIONAL FEAR

Some biblical writers suggest that the fear of God is good as "the beginning of wisdom" (Proverbs 9:10), whereas other biblical writers appear to dissent in holding that, in relation to God, "there is no fear in love" and "perfect love casts out fear" (1 John 4:8). We have seen that Paul shares such apparent ambivalence, discouraging one kind of fear of God and encouraging another kind (Rom. 3:18, 8:15). We can resolve the apparent conflict with a distinction between two kinds of motivational fear and of human response to such fear: conforming motivational fear and response and nonconforming motivational fear and response.

The relevant conforming or nonconforming is to the object of the fear. Fear accompanied by a response that conforms to God's good moral character and will, we shall see, is morally good fear. In contrast, fear accompanied by a nonconforming response, such as an avoiding response, to God is morally bad. This position fits with the nature of fear in general relative to the goodness or the badness of an object of fear. It also allows, we shall see, for the goodness of a kind of redemptive fear motivated by God, and it accommodates a distinction between voluntary, controllable fear and involuntary, uncontrollable fear. We shall support a distinction between fear of God and despair toward God, and we shall identify a neglected role for affective distress experiences in motivational fear of God.

---

[20] Walther Eichrodt, *Theology of the Old Testament*, trans. J. A. Baker (Philadelphia, PA: Westminster Press, 1967), vol. 2, p. 270.

Some fear is morally good, such as some fear of evil, including the evil of murderous terrorists of the kind represented by ISIS. Fear of the evil of murderous terrorists can be morally good in motivating people away from undergoing morally bad destruction and toward receiving something morally good for all concerned. We need to clarify how morally good fear and morally bad fear relate to motivational human fear of God. In doing so, we will make sense of what seem to be Paul's contrasting attitudes toward fear.

Motivational fear of God includes a state of felt, or experienced, distress toward a perceived danger regarding God, accompanied by an inclination either to avoid or to oppose ("flee or fight") that danger. The felt distress makes for an experiential affective response that includes a person's being moved, beyond anything merely intellectual, by something perceived as dangerous regarding God. We should distinguish, however, between fear with an inclination either to avoid or to oppose its object and fear with actually avoiding or opposing its object. The former can be morally good even if the latter is not.

Motivational fear of God typically includes a felt distress arising from a perceived danger in God's good moral character as it bears on one's attitudes and actions. The felt distress concerns the apprehended prospect of falling short of God's moral approval and perhaps even the felt actuality of eliciting divine judgment. Such distress does not require actually disobeying God, but it does counter undue confidence toward earning divine moral approval. It also challenges presumed moral authority or equality in relation to God and thus moral complacency or arrogance toward God. Such felt distress can repel and attract in relation to God. It can create felt distance from God when one insists on earning divine moral approval by one's own moral merit. It also can yield felt attraction to God when a person values obedience as a response to God's unearned merciful goodness.

By analogy, consider a teenage boy who is seeking his own moral identity and thus feels uneasy toward a perceived danger from his morally good father. As a result, the boy is inclined either to ignore or to oppose his father. It is morally good, however, that he is uneasy and thus carefully attentive toward his father, because he is morally accountable to his father and will be held morally accountable by him for wayward decisions. This is true even though his distress includes an inclination either to ignore or to oppose his good father for the sake of forging his own moral identity. The boy can control that inclination, however, and thus it need not block his ultimately conforming to his father's better moral judgment. Even so, the boy can undermine the moral goodness of his distress in a particular case by using it to prompt his actually ignoring or opposing his father's better moral judgment. Motivational fear of God can be analogous to that kind of distress of perceived danger.

Some psychologists link fear to a "freeze or fawn" tendency in a person toward a feared object. This tendency, however, evidently accompanies traumatic fear of a severe sort but not either fear in general or motivational fear of God. We should not confuse either fear in general or motivational fear of God with severe trauma or terror, even though trauma and terror include fear. In any case, the tendency to "freeze or fawn" is not central to the kind of motivational fear of God we are exploring in connection with Paul's thought. The same is true of fear that includes despair as hopelessness toward its object.

We should distinguish motivational fear as a state of distress toward a perceived danger from a human response to such a state of fear. The latter response, given its object, differs from that state and its variable inclinations. A state of distress and its inclinations are not always under voluntary control, as in the case of a fear state underlying fearful recoiling from large deadly spiders near one's face. A response to such a fear state is a response typically to an inclination either to avoid or to oppose a perceived danger. The fear state and its inclinations can be involuntary in a way akin to a habit to behave in a certain way. They thus need not be under a person's direct control, even if some fear states are under human control.

A human response to a fear state of distress can be voluntary, even if the fear state and its inclinations are not voluntary. In general, we can have a voluntary response to our habits or other dispositions even though they themselves are not voluntary. For instance, with due time and effort, I can train myself not to flee, or even to be inclined to flee, from large deadly spiders near my face, particularly when my research project is to study them up close. Similarly, with adequate preparation, I can habituate myself not to avoid, or even to be inclined to avoid, the murderous ISIS terrorists whom I need to interview for my research on religious terrorism. In the same vein, we shall see, I can bring myself not to flee from or even to avoid divine interventions in my life. My voluntary response to fear may involve indirect rather than direct control, but it can involve control nonetheless over my response to my fear states, even when they are involuntary.

When a motivational fear state is not under a person's control, directly or indirectly, that person will not be morally responsible or irresponsible for it. Even so, an involuntary fear state or its inclination can be morally good or bad, apart from the issue of moral responsibility. The moral goodness or badness of a person's psychological state does not depend on a person's being morally responsible regarding that state. Instead, it depends on the worthiness of a state for being morally valued, regardless of whether a person can control the state. Even if I cannot control a particular state of fear, such as my fear of death, that state still could be morally good or bad, given its worthiness of being valued or disvalued from a moral point of view. In addition, I still could seek to formulate a morally good response to it, despite my inability to change it.

Motivational fear admits of two noteworthy kinds of response: conforming and nonconforming responses to an object of fear. A nonconforming response to a state of fear responds with an effort either to avoid or to oppose the object of fear. This is an effort not to conform to it, by not going along with the presence, character, or will of its object. A conforming response, in contrast, responds to a state of fear with an effort to side with the object of fear, that is, to conform to its presence, character, or will. Such efforts are irreducible to a mere inclination; they include intentional actions, given the relevant effort toward a goal in response to fear.

Fear states themselves can be conforming or nonconforming, owing to whether they conform or fail to conform their subject or bearer (a personal agent) to their object of fear. In some cases, a human will can contribute to the conforming or the nonconforming of a fear state to its object, whether it be a murderous ISIS terrorist or God. Conforming and nonconforming need not be perfect, of course, but they can come in degrees. We can proceed now with a rough but workable standard of on-balance or overall conforming or nonconforming to an object of fear.

Neither a nonconforming nor a conforming response to an object of fear or to a state of fear is automatically good or bad. By way of a response, we can be conforming in our character and will to an object of fear that is bad, such as to a murderous terrorist and his evil will. We also can be nonconforming in our character and will toward an object of fear that is good, for instance to God and God's perfect will. The goodness of a fear-state and of a response to a fear-state depends on the goodness of their object and on their conforming their subject or bearer (a personal agent) to their good object. The goodness of a fear-state, as suggested in the previous case of the teenage boy, is also overridable by an agent's actually avoiding or opposing something good. These considerations, we shall see, figure in the goodness of human motivational fear of God and of a human response to such fear. They will contribute to clarifying Paul's position on fear and God.

The Oxford English Dictionary, 3rd ed., offers some definitions of "fear" that fit with the approach under development: "the emotion of pain or uneasiness caused by the sense of impending danger, or by the prospect of some possible evil" and "apprehensive feeling towards anything regarded as a source of danger, or towards a person regarded as able to inflict injury or punishment." These definitions are helpful as far as they go, but they omit the key role of an inclination either to avoid or to oppose an object of fear perceived to be harmful. Our suggested approach to motivational fear, in contrast, maintains that key role, thereby capturing the way that fear typically has a tendency to avoid or oppose its object. Our approach thus fits well with typical behavioral responses to fear with an inclination either to avoid or to oppose. It serves better, as a result, in explaining ordinary fearful behavior. We turn to how the idea of motivational fear can illuminate fearing God.

FEARING GOD

The OED offers the following on fearing God: "A mingled feeling of dread and reverence towards God (formerly also, towards any rightful authority)." It adds: "Wyclif has always *drede* in this sense. The distinction between *servile* and *filial fear*, in Latin *timor servilis, filialis*, is stated (as already generally current) by Thomas Aquinas, *Summa* ii. ii. xix." This general approach to fearing God has led to a distinction between two kinds of fear of God: fear as awe or reverence and fear as felt distress toward perceived danger. Some theologians hold that both kinds of fear properly apply to human fear of God, whereas other theologians hold that the proper fear of God is just awe or reverence toward God. The latter theologians are often guided by the claim of 1 John that, in relating to God, "perfect love casts out fear."

Aquinas allows for the relevant distinction between two kinds of fear in relation to Christ's fear of God as reverence: "In this way it is said that in Christ there was the fear of God, not indeed as it regards the evil of separation from God by fault, nor as it regards the evil of punishment for fault; but inasmuch as it regards the Divine pre-eminence, on account of which the soul of Christ, led by the Holy Spirit, was borne towards God in an act of reverence."[21] He adds: "Filial fear which shows reverence to God, is a sort of genus in respect of the love of God, and a kind of principle of all observances connected with reverence for God."[22] We need to draw out, however, an

---

[21] Thomas Aquinas, *Summa Theologica* (New York: Benziger Brothers, 1947), IIIa, q. 7, a. 6.
[22] Thomas Aquinas, *Summa Theologica*, IIa–IIae, q. 22, a. 2. For discussion of Aquinas's position on Christ and the fear of God, see Dylan Schrader, "Christ's Fear

experiential feature that prompts and guides conforming fear of God, if we are to capture Paul's position.

Some theologians propose that we understand fear of God as awe or reverence of God in terms of God's being mysterious in a certain way. Pieter de Villiers claims that "numinous awe" before God "provides the reason why awe is linked with fear. It is because it has to do with an encounter with God as the *mysterium* . . . . The fear points towards the *mysterium* that evokes the *fascinans*."[23] In various encounters with God, according to de Villiers, "the divine is experienced as the totally Other so that the fear is a *tremendum* as a reaction to the unique, numinous and awesome presence of God that created 'great' fear."[24] This position is influenced by Rudolf Otto, and behind him, Kierkegaard's pseudonymous author, Johannes Climacus.[25]

The position of de Villiers (and Otto) prompts two misgivings. First, the proposal to think of God as "the totally Other" is a recipe for trouble. It divorces divine moral goodness from human moral goodness in a way that neglects the interrelation between the two. The dominant Jewish and Christian views of God portray humans as made in the moral image of God with due moral responsibility and similarity in relation to God, even given serious human moral imperfection. If God is "the totally Other," strictly speaking, this key moral relation is severed, and the category of divine moral goodness becomes "totally" foreign to general human understanding of moral goodness.

Humans, of course, do not have moral authority over God, but the dominant biblical narratives assume a moral similarity between

---

of the Lord according to Thomas Aquinas," *Heythrop Journal* (2017), doi.org/10.1111/heyj.12487.

[23] Pieter G. R. de Villiers, "In Awe of the Mighty Deeds of God," in *Saving Fear in Christian Spirituality*, ed. Ann W. Astell (Notre Dame, IN: University of Notre Dame Press, 2020), p. 34.

[24] De Villiers, "In Awe of the Mighty Deeds of God," p. 28.

[25] See Rudolf Otto, *The Idea of the Holy*, pp. 12–41; and Søren Kierkegaard (as Johannes Climacus), *Philosophical Fragments*, trans. H. V and E. H. Hong (Princeton: Princeton University Press, 1985 [1844]), pp. 37–48, using "absolutely different" instead of "totally Other."

God and humans and thereby hold humans morally accountable before God. The language of "the totally Other" is thus misleading relative to that context of interpersonal moral interaction. Even so, we should acknowledge, as does Paul, the mystery of God's ways and human lack of full comprehension of God.

Second, an encounter with God as "the *mysterium*" invoking "the *fascinans*" is inadequate to yield fear of God, even if it yields fascination, amazement, or puzzlement. We risk confusing matters if we identify fear with fascination, amazement, or puzzlement. Mathematical and scientific inquiries, for instance, can be motivated by fascination, amazement, or puzzlement, but it does not follow that they are motivated by fear or lead to fear. An awe-inspiring mystery of the sort suggested by Otto and de Villiers, even if from an encounter with God, need not either presuppose or provoke fear, or a felt danger at all. Fear in an encounter with God differs from any accompanying fascination, amazement, or puzzlement. So, an awe-inspiring human encounter with God need not be an encounter including a human state of fear. Whatever fear of God is, then, it is not just an awe-inspiring encounter.

In the Gospels of Luke and Matthew, Jesus commands human fear of God: "I will warn you whom to fear: fear him who, after he has killed, has authority to cast into hell. Yes, I tell you, fear him!" (Luke 12:5; cf. Matt. 10:28). This is a command by Jesus to fear God, and not, as some commentators have mistakenly suggested, a command to fear an evil power.[26] Jesus assigned the ultimate power and authority in question to God, not to an evil power. The human fear of God commanded by Jesus is no mere state of being fascinated, amazed, or puzzled. The same is true of Paul's command to "make holiness perfect in the fear of God" (2 Cor. 7:1). Paul, as suggested, considers this to be good, commendable fear of God.

---

[26] For support for interpreting Jesus to give a command to fear God, see Joseph A. Fitzmyer, *The Gospel according to Luke*, AB (New York: Doubleday, 1985), vol. 2, p. 959; and W. D. Davies and Dale C. Allison Jr., *The Gospel according to Saint Matthew*, ICC (Edinburgh: T&T Clark, 1991), vol. 2, pp. 206–7.

The relevant fear is not just awe or reverence before God. Instead, it includes human distress with being held morally accountable by God. This distress typically arises from human moral inadequacy and weakness before God, in addition to God's utter seriousness about the moral direction of a human life, either conforming or not conforming to God's character and will. Luke's Gospel puts the lesson in terms of God's "authority" (ἐξουσίαν), and this is the authority of holding people morally accountable by divine standards. Paul agrees with this theme of divine authority entailing moral accountability for humans, including Jews: "Now we know that whatever the law says, it speaks to those who are under the law, so that every mouth may be silenced, and the whole world may be held accountable to God" (Rom. 3:19).

Jesus and Paul command something morally good, rather than something bad, regarding human fear of God. In commanding fear of God, they were considering a kind of fear that is under human control, at least indirectly. Otherwise, their command would be pointless, having no prospect of a responsible human reply. We may think of the relevant kind of fear as redemptive fear. Its accompanying distress toward God brings attention, in a good way, to human moral or cognitive inadequacy before God. On the cognitive side, the distress indicates serious human shortcomings in knowledge of God's profound redemptive will. On the moral side, it indicates the moral gravity of neglecting or disobeying a life-sustaining God who holds humans morally accountable for their own benefit.

God can intend redemptive fear to challenge a person for moral inadequacy as either complacency or arrogance toward God. The moral goodness of such fear stems from its involving people firsthand with divine goodness and moral accountability for them. So, the command from Jesus and Paul seeks, in effect, to allow God's profound goodness to instill enough distress to reorient you, volitionally and affectively, to make God's will your priority.

Redemptive fear is morally good for humans in relation to the felt opportunity of (what Paul considers) their being reconciled to God in the presence of their moral accountability from God (2 Cor. 5:18–20). Such reconciliation, however, is not automatic. Humans can undermine the goodness of fear of God, just as they can corrupt free will, by using it (in going beyond its inclination) actually to avoid or to oppose God. Its defeasible moral goodness, then, depends on its motivational value for the human condition of moral inadequacy and weakness before God and divine accountability. Just as it can lead, by way of human resolution, to avoiding or opposing God, it can lead to yielding to God in obedience. Its motivational value allows for bad effects from its motivational inclination, such as when humans decide to avoid or to oppose God out of fear, thereby undermining the goodness of fear of God. They thereby avoid good fear of God, as Paul acknowledges, by implication, with his worry about "a spirit of slavery to fall back into fear" (Rom. 8:15).

The distress in human fear of God fits the human moral condition of tending either to avoid or to oppose God's moral character or will under certain conditions. For instance, since God's moral will, as morally perfect, is for humans to love (including to will what is good for) their enemies as well as other people, that can be perceived as dangerous by humans not inclined to love their enemies. This conflict of wills, divine and human, can yield fear of God for humans aware of their falling short of God's will while being accountable to God for this moral failure. Even so, humans need not avoid or oppose God as a result of their fear of God. They typically can opt for conforming fear of God.

God is not just a perceived danger by typical humans. Instead, as suggested in Chapter 1, God as righteous is an actual source of moral challenge to them, including a danger to the satisfaction of their intentions contrary to God's will. God's perfectly righteous will conflicts with any morally inferior human will, and it thus poses a danger to satisfying such an inferior will. So, humans should fear God in this regard, so long as their moral inadequacy, such as complacency or arrogance, yields a conflict, or even a likely conflict, with God's superior will. God's righteous will emerges, then, as dangerous for their morally inferior will.

The fear-making danger from God does not come from God as the "*mysterium.*" God's being mysterious, awesome, fascinating, or puzzling is not the source of the relevant fear of God. Instead, the fear comes in response to God's perfect righteousness, or moral goodness, and its serious accountability for humans in relation to their moral inadequacy before God. This fear stems from reacting to divine moral accountability, including potential redemptive judgment, for humans, and it typically inclines a morally wayward human either to avoid or to oppose God in some way.

Divine redemptive judgment, in Paul's perspective, typically aims for divine–human reconciliation, and not mere retribution or merited punishment. This is shown by Paul's mention of divine patience in judgment and wrath; such patience indicates divine seeking of the repentance of humans (Rom. 2:2–4, 9:22–23).[27] A key feature of redemptive judgment arises from the mercy and forgiveness patiently offered for the sake of interpersonal reconciliation. This offer stems from the background of divine redemptive judgment in the New Testament love commands, which extend even to loving one's enemies (Mark 12:29–31; Matt. 5:43–8).[28]

God, according to Jesus and Paul, is dangerous in a good, redemptive way relative to human moral shortcomings. So, human fear is typically fitting in relation to God. Jesus therefore commanded people to fear God for their own benefit relative to God, and Paul followed suit. Lacking the relevant fear of God is not morally good for humans, given its omitting an avenue of a morally and redemptively

---

[27] For discussion of how a retributive approach to judgment fails to capture much of divine judgment in the biblical writings, see Stephen H. Travis, *Christ and the Judgment of God* (Peabody, MA: Hendrickson, 2008); and Christopher Marshall, *Beyond Retribution* (Grand Rapids, MI: Eerdmans, 2001). It is undeniable, however, that some of the biblical remarks on judgment are retributive; see Travis, pp. 13–24.

[28] On the historical background of the synoptic love commands, see John Meier, *A Marginal Jew, vol. 4: Law and Love*, AYBRL (New Haven, CT: Yale University Press, 2009), pp. 499–527. See also Victor Paul Furnish, *The Love Command in the New Testament* (Nashville, TN: Abingdon Press, 1972), pp. 62–69.

good motivational challenge from God for them. It omits a source for challenging human moral inadequacy before God.

Jesus told a parable of the laborers in the vineyard to illustrate a typical oppositional human attitude toward God's perfect moral goodness.

> Now when the first [of the laborers in the vineyard] came [to be paid], they thought they would receive more [payment than the late-comers]; but each of them also received a denarius. And on receiving it they grumbled at the householder, saying, "These last worked only one hour, and you have made them equal to us who have borne the burden of the day and the scorching heat." But he replied to one of them, "Friend, I am doing you no wrong; did you not agree with me for a denarius? Take what belongs to you, and go; I choose to give to this last as I give to you. Am I not allowed to do what I choose with what belongs to me? Or do you begrudge my generosity?"
>
> (Matt. 20:10–15, RSV)

The parable illustrates a typical human attitude of "begrudging" God's goodness, if by setting the moral bar too low for God's perfect goodness.

The extravagance of God's generosity, or grace, does not fit well with typical human attitudes regarding moral goodness in relationships. This lesson is confirmed in grudging human attitudes toward enemies and people needing forgiveness. Jesus highlighted this lesson about God's challenging moral character in his teachings and actions, and Paul took a similar approach to love of enemies and people needing forgiveness (Rom. 12:14–20; cf. 1 Cor. 4:12–13).

Suitable fear of God allows for divine redemptive judgment on wayward humans for their benefit toward reconciliation with God. Paul acknowledges the role of judgment in fear of God: "All of us must appear before the judgment seat of Christ, so that each may receive recompense for what has been done in the body, whether good or evil. Therefore, knowing the fear of the Lord, we try to persuade others"

(2 Cor. 5:10–11). This fits with Paul's commendation of "making holiness perfect in the fear of God" (2 Cor. 7:1). His central view of redemption as reconciliation with God (2 Cor. 5:17–20) sets the context for his comments on divine judgment and the fear of God.[29] When judgment is morally good and motivates fear of God toward redemption as reconciliation, such "fear of the Lord" likewise can be morally good.

God's redemptive judgment of a person does not entail the "condemnation" of that person, according to Paul, if condemnation aims for the harm or destruction of the person (Rom. 8:1). Redemptive judgment typically identifies wrongdoing or something bad in order to prompt moral correction of a person toward reconciliation with God, for that person's moral good. Some interpreters confuse judgment and condemnation, to the detriment of perceiving the moral value of divine redemptive judgment.

Even if the condemnation of persons is suspect from a moral point of view, the same does not follow for redemptive judgment. In many cases, our failure to offer redemptive judgment of harmful persons calls in to question our morally good caring or courage toward them. In particular, a God with no redemptive judgment toward wayward humans would be a candidate for moral indifference and failure and thus for unworthiness of worship. That would be a false god, by Paul's lights.

Redemptive judgment from God need not await a final judgment in the fullness of time. It can come now in the moral experience of a wayward person, via a redemptive challenge in conscience. A person can try to avoid a moral challenge from God, through diversion or dismissal, but God also can frustrate a person's contrary will. Paul thought of this as God's subjecting parts of the created world to "futility" in the hope of people recognizing and cooperating with

---

[29] On Paul's view of divine–human reconciliation in relation to the position of Jesus, see Ralph P. Martin, *Reconciliation*, pp. 201–33.

needed reconciliation to God (Rom. 8:20–21).[30] In this regard, God is dangerous, and thus worthy of fear, in relation to anti-God human ways, including complacency toward God. Divine perfect goodness would be questionable if God did not care enough for humans to undertake redemptive judgment of them for their benefit.

FEAR, JUDGMENT, AND LOVE

According to the writer of 1 John: "God is love, and those who abide in love abide in God, and God abides in them. Love has been perfected among us in this: that we may have boldness on the day of judgment, because as he is, so are we in this world. There is no fear in love, but perfect love casts out fear; for fear has to do with punishment, and whoever fears has not reached perfection in love" (1 John 4:16–18). The writer of 1 John thus relates perfect love, judgment, fear, and punishment, arguing that "perfect love casts out fear; for fear has to do with punishment," involving "the day of judgment." He is arguably correct in the following claim: "Whoever fears has not reached perfection in love." We can grant that claim for now, if only for the sake of argument, but we should ask whether some humans actually have "reached perfection in love."

Jesus's teachings assumed that his disciples need moral improvement and thus have not reached moral perfection. He said to his disciples: "If you then, who are evil, know how to give good gifts to your children, how much more will your Father in heaven give good things to those who ask him!" (Matt. 7:11; cf. Luke 11:13). Jesus thus did not assume that his disciples have "reached perfection in love." Even so, he did command perfection for his disciples: "Be perfect as your heavenly Father is perfect" (Matt. 5:48; cf. Luke 6:36). This command, however, assumes that they have not reached moral perfection, including perfection in love. The commanded

---

[30] See C. E. B. Cranfield, *A Critical and Exegetical Commentary on the Epistle to the Romans*, vol. 1, pp. 413–16.

perfection is an ideal but (to state the obvious) not an ideal fully realized now.

Paul agreed with Jesus about humans not having reached moral perfection, including perfection in love. He remarked: "Not that I have already obtained this [the resurrection from death] or am already perfect; but I press on to make it my own, because Christ Jesus has made me his own. Brethren, I do not consider that I have made it my own; but one thing I do, forgetting what lies behind and straining forward to what lies ahead" (Phil. 3:12–13, RSV). In Paul's perspective, humans are, at best, works in progress, courtesy of divine leading (Rom. 8:14), and thus, at best, human moral perfection awaits the fullness of time. Paul and Jesus concurred on this important matter, avoiding any suggestion of human moral perfection now.

Both Jesus and Paul acknowledge a place for divine redemptive judgment in human lives, including those of the people of God. It is thus a mistake to put the role of divine judgment in conflict with the good news of divine redemption preached by Jesus and Paul. Marius Reiser, for instance, comments: "The central focus of [Jesus's] speech and action is not judgment and the way to avoid it, but the reign of God and how to gain it; it is not fear of judgment that should move Israel to repentance, but the fascination of the reign of God."[31]

We should acknowledge that Jesus differed from John the Baptist in having a "central focus" on the kingdom of God and its appropriation by humans.[32] It is a false contrast, however, to say: "It is not fear of judgment that should move Israel to repentance, but the fascination of the reign of God." Both should be motivating in repentance before God, according to the teaching of Jesus and Paul. Given this "both-and" approach to repentance, we can accommodate not only Jesus's command to fear God but also his parables of judgment,

---

[31] Marius Reiser, *Jesus and Judgment*, trans. L. M. Maloney (Minneapolis, MN: Fortress Press, 1997), p. 255.

[32] For the role of a two-phased kingdom of God in the teaching of Jesus, with an initial redemptive stage and a final stage of completion, see Paul Moser, *The Divine Goodness of Jesus*, ch. 7.

such as the parable of the unjust manager (Luke 16:1–8). That parable calls for a shrewd commitment of repentance before God in an emergency situation of impending judgment, illustrated by putting wealth in its subsidiary place relative to the kingdom of God.[33]

Reiser plausibly explains the main point of the parable but in a way that challenges his previous claim contrary to my proposed "both-and" approach to repentance.

> It is difficult to assert that this parable speaks of the reign of God as something that brings salvation, but not judgment.... The threatening character that the future brings for the manager must correspond to the threatening character of the impending event. Jesus is saying that just as the threat of ruin forces the manager to immediate and resolute action, so the impending judgment... must compel everyone to act immediately and decisively. But by that action Jesus can mean nothing other than repentance in a concrete sense.... This is the precondition for escaping judgment and achieving the salvation of the reign of God.[34]

This parable thus goes against Reiser's previous claim that "it is not fear of judgment that should move Israel to repentance." It is precisely fear of "impending judgment," as Reiser notes, that moves the manager to repent and "to act immediately and decisively." Likewise, fear of divine judgment should figure in an immediate cooperative response to the kingdom of God announced by Jesus. This is a key lesson of the parable, which should not be read as mainly financial advice for managing money.

Jesus did not regard fear of divine judgment as the only factor motivating repentance before God. He characterized God's role in offering the divine kingdom to humans as follows: "Do not be afraid, little flock, for it is your Father's good pleasure to give you the

---

[33] For details, see Arland J. Hultgren, *The Parables of Jesus* (Grand Rapids, MI: Eerdmans, 2000), pp. 146–57.
[34] Reiser, *Jesus and Judgment*, pp. 300–301.

kingdom" (Luke 12:32). This command may appear at first glance to contradict Jesus's aforementioned command to fear God, but it does not. His command, "Do not be afraid," was not an unqualified command not to fear God. Instead, it was a command not to be afraid regarding God's gladly offering humans the divine kingdom. This command allows for fearing God in relation to the moral accountability of wayward, morally inadequate humans before God. Indeed, God's offering the kingdom could include the divine aim to challenge people toward moral improvement before God and to use proper fear of God as a motivation. We should understand Jesus and Paul as having assumed that view.

Fearing God is helpfully understood as fearing God with regard to something perceived to be at risk from God. If, as suggested, my will is in conflict with God's morally superior will, then God should be perceived as a risk, a danger, to my satisfying my will. For a good, redemptive purpose, God actually would be such a danger for my will in that case. Even so, with regard to another matter, such as God's graciously offering the divine kingdom to humans, I would not need to fear God. God's generosity in that regard is not a danger for me, even if God's moral goodness is dangerous for me in other areas, such as areas where my will conflicts with God's will. Fear of God, accordingly, should correspond to areas where God is dangerous for my intentions contrary to God's. As long as we are morally imperfect before the God of perfect righteousness, fear of God is fitting in relation to various moral matters.

We should understand the kind of divine judgment announced by Jesus and Paul to seek, out of divine love, the redemption of humans as reconciliation to God. It is a serious mistake to portray such judgment as stemming from divine hate or condemnation toward humans. Jesus's parable of the great banquet (Luke 14:16–24; cf. Matt. 22:1–14) sets the background for divine redemptive judgment, and that background includes the divine invitation of humans to enter God's kingdom in divine–human reconciliation. Humans have a role to play, a decision to make, in this process, according to

Jesus and Paul, and they can ignore or reject the invitation to their own detriment. When they ignore or reject the invitation, they invite divine redemptive judgment on themselves, owing to their doing self-harm and thus needing a divine challenge toward reconciliation with God. Jesus's consistency and intensity in presenting that challenge figured, ultimately, in his being condemned to death.

Divine redemptive judgment prompted by human conflict with God's will applies to current human life and not just to the eschatological fullness of time. It can include God's "giving up" humans to their anti-God ways for a time, as Jesus illustrated in the parable of the prodigal son (Luke 15:11–32) and as Paul emphasized to the Roman Christians (Rom. 1: 24, 26, 28).[35] It also can include more active challenges from God, such as felt volitional frustrations prompted by God in human moral experience, including conscience (Rom. 2:15; 2 Cor. 1:12). In any case, such judgment calls for a human response, and human fear of God should figure in that response, owing to human moral inadequacy before God.

Fear of God does not exhaust the needed response, because God seeks divine–human reconciliation that includes human cooperation with God's superior will. Such cooperation will take a person beyond mere reflection on God to willing participation in God's perfect moral life and will. This kind of volitional cooperation, free of human earning or merit, is central to what Jesus and Paul considered to be faith in God. Paul called it "the obedience of faith" (Rom. 1:5, 16:26; cf. Matt. 7:21).

The model for responding obediently to God's intervening redemptive will was set by Jesus in Gethsemane. Luke's Gospel portrays Jesus as being in a state of intense distress, including fear: "In his anguish [ἀγωνίᾳ] he prayed more earnestly, and his sweat became like great drops of blood falling down on the ground" (Luke 22:44). Joseph

---

[35] On Paul's understanding of God's "giving up" humans in judgment, see Travis, *Christ and the Judgment of God*, pp. 60–62; and Cranfield, *A Critical and Exegetical Commentary on the Epistle to the Romans*, vol. 1, pp. 120–21. See Psalm 106:41 for an analogue from the Hebrew Bible.

A. Fitzmyer notes in this connection that "ἀγωνία" is "well attested for a state of mind associated with fear or anguish because of some impending, uncertain experience or phenomenon."[36] This fits with the portrait of Jesus in Gethsemane by Mark's Gospel: "[He] began to be distressed [ἐκθαμβεῖσθαι] and agitated" (Mark 14:33). The distress of fear would be natural for Jesus, given a cognitive shortcoming from his lack of full knowledge of the troubling effects of God's redemptive will for him in Jerusalem.[37] Such fear is not a moral defect before God, but it does allow for Jesus's having been tempted and having learned from what he suffered (Heb. 4:15, 5:8).

Jesus's settled response to his distressed fear, which did not remove the fear, was his resolve to put God's will first, above his own initial request to avoid his impending death: "Father, if you are willing, remove this cup from me; yet, not my will but yours be done" (Luke 22:42; cf. Mark 14:36; Matt. 26:39). His obedient response to fear is compatible with human fear of God, including conforming fear of God's perfect will. Luke's Gospel suggests that Jesus showed distressed fear in relation to God's redemptive will for his own future, particularly the terrifying death God called him to undergo in Jerusalem. Jesus had shown awareness of his impending death at the Last Supper (Luke 22:19–22; cf. Mark 14:24–7; Matt. 26:28–31), but this awareness did not prevent his fear expressed in Gethsemane.

Jesus's Gethsemane response to fear led to God's vindicating him for his faithful obedience to God's will for him. Paul expresses God's vindication of the obedient Jesus as follows: "[Jesus] humbled himself and became obedient to the point of death – even death on a cross. Therefore, God also highly exalted him and gave him the name that is above every name" (Phil. 2:8–9). God, according to Paul, did not

---

[36] Joseph A. Fitzmyer, *The Gospel according to Luke*, AB (New York: Doubleday, 1985), vol. 2, p. 1444. See also Raymond E. Brown, *The Death of the Messiah*, ABRL (New York: Doubleday, 1994), vol. 1, pp. 189–90.

[37] This lack of full knowledge of God's redemptive plan coheres with Jesus's own acknowledgment of such a lack in Mark's and Matthew's Gospels (Mark 13:32; Matt. 24:36).

fault Jesus for his fear in Gethsemane but instead looked for and approved his faithful obedience in response to his fear.

In Gethsemane, Jesus showed his response to his fear toward God's redemptive will, and he intended his response to be a model for his disciples. He urged his disciples to respond with his kind of Gethsemane prayer for obedience, but, notoriously, they fell short, and fell asleep, in Gethsemane (Luke 22:40–42, 45–46). We find a similar instruction from Jesus in Matthew's version of the Lord's prayer: "Thy will be done" (Matt. 6:10).[38] This instruction fits with his comment on worry, which often accompanies fear: "Strive first for the kingdom of God and his righteousness, and all these things will be given to you as well. So, do not worry about tomorrow, for tomorrow will bring worries of its own" (Matt. 6:33–34).

Jesus commanded his disciples not to fear or worry about their future, but he did not extend this to a command not to fear God. Indeed, his command to fear God was joined with his Gethsemane response to his fear that put other fears in subsidiary perspective. He expected his disciples to follow suit, as the way to cooperate with God's will in their lives. He did not offer to do this by proxy for them; instead, he provided a model and means for them to follow, in his Gethsemane prayer and obedience. He aimed for his disciples to have a relationship, if imperfectly, of filial reconciliation with God, and no one else could have this relationship for them. If atonement with God includes divine–human reconciliation, we should expect such atonement to be not completely by proxy but directly interpersonal between God and individual humans. Paul agrees with Jesus on this matter.

We now can identify what it is about God that can prompt human fear, including the kind of fear Jesus showed in Gethsemane. If we acknowledge God's redemptive will to show self-sacrificial love,

---

[38] For some historical background to the Lord's Prayer, and how the Gethsemane prayer of Jesus "harmonises easily" with the Lord's prayer, see David Catchpole, *Jesus People: The Historical Jesus and the Beginnings of Community* (London: Darton, Longman, and Todd, 2006), pp. 121–68.

as Jesus and Paul assumed, we can identify a role for human fear of God and divine self-sacrificial love. We get a hint from Matthew's and Luke's versions of the parable of the talents: "Master, I knew that you were a harsh man, reaping where you did not sow, and gathering where you did not scatter seed; so, I was afraid" (Matt. 25:24–5; cf. Luke 19:20–1). There is often a severity about divine self-sacrificial love that prompts human fear.

Understandably, humans sometimes fear what divine love, in sacrificially willing what is good for people, will demand they give up or undergo for that good. For instance, will it demand that we either face our moral failure by God's standard or experience felt abandonment by God (as Jesus did), if not some other kind of suffering? God's self-sacrificial love is notorious for going deeper than what is comfortable for us, thus prompting our fear of God and divine love. It is no accident, then, that the injunction "Fear not" recurs throughout the biblical writings. We need to ask if hope can endure in combination with human fear of divine self-sacrificial love.

In the aftermath of Gethsemane, Jesus showed a feeling of abandonment by God, and fearful distress would have been a natural component. Regarding his cry of abandonment in Mark's and Matthew's Gospels: "At three o'clock Jesus cried out with a loud voice, 'Eloi, Eloi, lema sabachthani?' which means, 'My God, my God, why have you forsaken me?'" (Mark 15:34; cf. Matt. 27:46–47). Jesus felt forsaken by God, and that was a kind of frightening disappointment with God, regardless of Jesus's expectations for God's future intervention for him. He predicted three times in Mark's Gospel that God would raise him from death (Mark 8:31, 9:31, 10:34), but that allowed for his felt abandonment by God on the cross.

Jesus did not express complete despair before God, and this is important for combining hope in God with fear of God. God was still, from Jesus's perspective, "My God, my God," despite his feeling that God had abandoned him at that time. Richard Bauckham comments: "In crying out to God from his abandonment, Jesus, desperately we must suppose but really, trusts God to be still his God, the 'My God, my God' of the cry."³⁹ We can speculate about Jesus's theology behind this distressed situation, but the reality is that Jesus felt abandoned by God. A plausible approach is that God was showing, at least, that a faithful relationship with God does not depend on a constant experience of God's presence.⁴⁰ If we trust the Gospels of Mark and Matthew here, the word "trauma" applies to the dying experience of Jesus, and this includes a kind of distressed fear.

According to the dominant New Testament message, God did not forsake Jesus ultimately. In addition, that message does not teach, contrary to Markus Barth, that "God has turned against his own Son" or that "God openly stands against God, the Father against the Son."⁴¹ Instead, the dominant message is that God vindicated Jesus with resurrection from death. Even so, Jesus felt abandoned by God, according to the Gospels of Mark and Matthew. The candor of the two Gospel writers is remarkable, because it bluntly expresses the weakness of Jesus before God.

Paul would suggest an important theological lesson: God allowed the felt abandonment of Jesus to show that the power, authority, and timing of divine rescue and vindication are solely from God and can come even in human powerlessness. Paul offers a similar lesson about divine redemptive power for God's people in general: "We have this treasure in clay jars, so that it may be made clear that this extraordinary power belongs to God and does not come from us. We are afflicted in every way, but not crushed; perplexed, but not driven to despair; persecuted, but not forsaken; struck down, but not destroyed; always carrying in the body the death of Jesus, so that the life of Jesus may also be made visible in our bodies" (2 Cor. 4:7–10).

---

[39] Richard Bauckham, "God's Self-Identification with the Godforsaken," in Bauckham, *Jesus and the God of Israel* (Grand Rapids, MI: Eerdmans, 2008), p. 268. See also Brown, *The Death of the Messiah*, vol. 2, pp. 1043–65.

[40] For relevant discussion, see Gérard Rossé, *The Cry of Jesus on the Cross*, trans. S. W. Arndt (New York: Paulist Press, 1987).

[41] Markus Barth, *Justification*, trans. A. M. Woodruff (Grand Rapids, MI: Eerdmans, 1971), p. 47. For a view similar to Barth's, see Jürgen Moltmann, *The Crucified God*, trans. R. A. Wilson and John Bowden (New York: Harper and Row, 1974).

This is an illuminating comment on Paul's own experience of how God works in human lives.

Paul reports being "perplexed but not driven to despair." He has in mind distressful puzzlement toward God that coexisted with grounded hope in God, a hope contrary to despair. The relevant hope, we have seen, is grounded in an experience of God's self-sacrificial love, according to Paul (Rom. 5:5), but the perplexity arises from the same love. Perhaps this consideration led the writer of Ephesians to speak of the love from Christ that "surpasses knowledge" (Eph. 3:10). It may have figured also in Paul's remark: "Now we see in a mirror, dimly, but then we will see face to face. Now I know only in part" (1 Cor. 13:12).

A full explanation of God's ways in relation to humans is beyond our capacity now (Rom. 11:33; cf. 1 Cor. 2:16). We still may suggest the following: God allows human felt abandonment to show that God is faithful to rescue God's people, with divine timing, even when they have nothing left to contribute. Helmut Thielicke has put the general Pauline idea succinctly: "The afflictions of your life and mine are the hollow ground under our feet which gives way because God wills to catch us."[42] Paul testified to such a lesson from his own experience, particularly in 2 Corinthians.

The rigorous obedience of Jesus to God is not fully shared by his followers, given their moral weakness. In addition, Jesus did not advise them to seek felt abandonment by God. Even so, Jesus can serve, according to Paul, as a model for typical humans to approximate in their relating to God (1 Cor. 1:11). Despite his felt abandonment by God, Jesus was rescued by God in resurrection, and not in the restoration of his earthly life, according to a central New Testament theme. The same kind of rescue, in Paul's message, can apply to various other humans faced with felt abandonment by God, even if they fail by the standard of Jesus's rigorous obedience. The special importance of divine resurrection of humans, in this perspective, is

---

[42] Thielicke, *Out of the Depths*, trans. G. W. Bromiley (Grand Rapids, MI: Eerdmans, 1962), p. 20.

that it can rescue them even in their perceived divine abandonment. Humans need not recognize God's resurrection of them for God to undertake it solely with divine life-giving power.

Jesus offered something that can stop felt abandonment from leading to human despair about God's reality and goodness. The key is: Jesus willingly experienced the perfect goodness of God as his caring Father, the one who seeks for and rescues the lost and downtrodden children of God. He immortalized this experience of his in his parable of the lost sheep, identifying divine seeking and "joy in heaven" for divine–human reconciliation: "Which one of you, having a hundred sheep and losing one of them, does not leave the ninety-nine in the wilderness and go after the one that is lost until he finds it? When he has found it, he lays it on his shoulders and rejoices. And when he comes home, he calls together his friends and neighbors, saying to them, 'Rejoice with me, for I have found my sheep that was lost'" (Luke 15:4–6; cf. Matt. 18:12–14). Given his grounding experience of God's goodness, and allowing for God's own good timing in rescue, Jesus did not yield to complete despair about God's reality or goodness. Paul identifies a similar experience of divine sustaining love when he gives a reason for not despairing about God (Rom. 5:5).[43]

Human fear of God for divine moral accountability of humans needs an antidote to human despair about God, lest it collapse into something harmful to humans. That antidote, according to Jesus, is in how a person relates to God's intervening with divine self-sacrificial goodness in human experience. One can relate to such intervening with indifference, opposition, or cooperation. Jesus's parable of the sower identifies the main options for human response. Those options will bear on whether a person has an anchor against despair. That anchor, according to the parable, will be in experiencing the fruition of divine redemptive goodness in a person's cooperatively receiving it.

---

[43] For Paul's approach to human experience of divine grace through faith, see Chapter 2. On the relevant experience had by Jesus, with regard to God as Abba, see Moser, *The Divine Goodness of Jesus*, ch. 3.

Such experiencing, Jesus taught, figures in the heart of redemption as divine–human reconciliation. Paul agrees with this perspective (Rom. 2:4; 2 Cor. 5:14–15).

Avoiding despair from felt abandonment by God is good, but it calls for humans becoming "good soil," that is, "the ones who, when they hear the word [from God], hold it fast in an honest and good heart, and bear fruit with patient endurance" (Luke 8:15). Such "hearing" is experiential regarding divine intervention with goodness, and such "holding fast" is volitionally cooperative toward God. Humans thus have a voluntary role to play in whether fear collapses into despair. They thus have a contribution in whether fear of God leads to bad trouble for them. (Chapter 5 takes up the topic of voluntary human agency in Paul's thought.) Despair is evidently the fate of humans without their cooperating with the divine goodness on offer, if only because such goodness alone will last beyond the world's troubles. Even so, the option of due cooperation as conforming to God's goodness entails that humans need not fear their fearing God.

Finally, we have seen that fear of God can have good motivational value toward reconciliation with God. This value can emerge from a distress experience of divine goodness, including self-sacrificial love, that challenges moral complacency and arrogance toward God. In that context, a moral agent can decide whether to conform or not to conform to God's presented moral character and will. In deciding to conform, a person will favor reconciliation with God, with aid from motivational fear of God. As a result, such fear of God was commanded by Jesus and, in his wake, commended by Paul. It can coexist, we have seen, with grounded hope in God, and both can benefit from a ground in divine goodness and its self-sacrificial love. Perhaps conforming fear of God can enhance hope in God, owing to a heightened expectation for divine rescue from distress. That will depend, however, on a person's actual expectations for such rescue. Even so, human hope in God, according to Paul, has nothing to fear from human fear of God. We turn to the role of human agency in his perspective on divine redemption in self-sacrificial love.

5 Responsible Agency toward Divine Self-Sacrifice

I do not frustrate [ἀθετῶ] the grace of God.

Galatians 2:21

Paul's gospel of divine self-sacrifice, however promising for human redemption, is rejectable by humans. In fact, many people do reject it, for various reasons, even after careful reflection. The lion's share of scholarly attention to Paul on God focuses on his position on divine grace and promised triumph, leaving neglect of his position on divine frustration and failure in redemptive purpose. This chapter counters that neglect with a presentation of Paul's case, in his undisputed letters, for human frustration of God and God's redemptive aim. It identifies how this case bears on Paul's understanding of the divine redemption of humans, and it observes how many commentators have missed the important role of human frustration of God in Paul's theology.

The chapter acknowledges a role for human power in redemption, according to Paul, as a response to the gospel of divine self-sacrifice. The result does not compromise, however, Paul's understanding of redemption by divine grace through faith in God. The human power in question enables God to be blameless, by Paul's lights, in the human frustration of the intended divine redemption for humans.

DIVINE PURPOSE

Paul presented himself to Christians at Rome as representing a divine purpose, including: "I tell you that Christ has become a servant of the circumcised on behalf of the truth of God in order that he might confirm the promises given to the patriarchs, and in order that the Gentiles might glorify God for his mercy" (Rom. 15:8–9). Paul's use of "in order that" (εἰς) is significant here. God, according to Paul, aimed to confirm the divine redemptive promises to Abraham and his immediate successors and to extend divine redemption to the Gentiles. This aim, in Paul's perspective, is a central part of the divine redemptive purpose for humans.[1]

As we have seen, Paul said of the redemptive promise to Abraham: "For this reason it depends on faith, in order that [ἵνα] the promise may rest on grace and be guaranteed to all his descendants, not only to the adherents of the law but also to those who share the faith of Abraham (for he is the father of all of us)" (Rom. 4:16). Paul expressed the same divine purpose, as noted previously, to the Galatian Christians: "The scripture, foreseeing that God would justify the Gentiles by faith, declared the gospel beforehand to Abraham, saying, 'All the Gentiles shall be blessed in you.' For this reason, those who believe are blessed with Abraham who believed" (Gal. 3:8–9). So, Paul portrays God as aiming to redeem the world by grace through faith, and this aim includes Gentiles as well as Jews. In addition, he regards human justification by law apart from faith in a God of grace as incompatible with divine grace in redemption (Gal. 5:4; Rom. 4:4–5; cf. Phil. 3:9).

We have seen that God's aim for human redemption, according to Paul, seeks divine–human reconciliation: "All this is from God, who reconciled us to himself through Christ, and has given us the ministry of reconciliation; that is, in Christ God was reconciling the world to himself, not counting their trespasses against them, and entrusting the message of reconciliation to us" (2 Cor. 5:18–19). The desired reconciliation is for humans to conform to God's good

---

[1] For some elaboration, see James D. G. Dunn, *Jesus, Paul, and the Gospels* (Grand Rapids, MI: Eerdmans, 2011), pp. 154–62.

character and purpose, and this reconciliation is to be "received" (ἐλάβομεν) by humans (Rom. 5:11).

The reconciliation in question does not require that humans rise to the level of God's character to be reconciled. On the contrary, as noted, God seeks to "justify the ungodly": "Now to one who works, wages are not reckoned as a gift but as something due. But to one who without works trusts him who justifies the ungodly, such faith is reckoned as righteousness" (Rom. 4:4–5). By a divine standard of perfect goodness, if humans are to be justified, God will need to justify "the ungodly," and "it is God who justifies" (Rom. 8:33). These considerations are central to God's redemptive plan and promise of grace through faith, according to Paul.

We have seen that a key standard for redemption, in Paul's perspective, is divine righteousness. This is not just a standard satisfied by God; it also is a standard, according to Paul, that God manifests or shows to humans with an aim to righten, or rectify, them in relationship. Divine righteousness seeks to righten in that way. Thus:

> All have sinned and fall short of the glory of God; they are now justified by his grace as a gift, through the redemption that is in Christ Jesus, whom God put forward as a sacrifice of atonement by his blood, effective through faith. He did this to show [ἔνδειξιν] his righteousness, because in his divine forbearance he had passed over the sins previously committed; it was to prove [ἔνδειξιν] at the present time that he himself is righteous and that he justifies the one who has faith in Jesus.
>
> (Rom. 3:23–26)

So, God does not keep divine righteousness to God as a secret but instead seeks to show it to people, according to Paul.

God shows righteousness to humans in different circumstances, but Paul offers God's putting forward the sacrificial offering of Jesus Christ for others as a decisive example of showing divine righteousness. This fits with Paul's previously noted remark that "in Christ God was reconciling the world to himself." God presents

Christ as a "sacrifice of atonement" for humans, in order to show the divine righteousness that motivates and characterizes divine–human reconciliation.

The self-manifestation of divine goodness, including righteousness and kindness in self-sacrifice, aims to attract people to reconciliation with God. We have noted two questions important to Paul: "Do you despise the riches of [God's] kindness and forbearance and patience? Do you not realize that God's kindness is meant to lead you to repentance [μετάνοιάν]?" (Rom. 2:4). The divine intention in self-manifestation is "to lead [people] to repentance," and such repentance, in Paul's understanding, includes voluntarily turning to God to receive reconciliation with God.

The reconciliation in question, we have seen, includes a human response of reciprocity toward divine self-sacrifice. Paul does not speak much of repentance explicitly in his letters, but the turning of repentance is included in his approach to reconciliation with God.[2] Paul assumes that voluntary turning by a responsible person includes that person's power to do otherwise, to refrain from such turning (cf. Rom. 10:21). The responsibility of persons in relation to responding to God has that feature and thus takes them beyond being mere effects of outside causes.

The intended leading of people to repentance by divine goodness stems from what Paul calls God's "grace as a gift [δωρεὰν]" (Rom. 3:24). He explains it as follows:

> The free gift is not like the trespass. For if the many died through the one man's trespass, much more surely have the grace of God

---

[2] For discussion of the relation between justification and reconciliation in Paul, see Victor Paul Furnish, *Theology and Ethics in Paul* (Nashville, TN: Abingdon Press, 1968), pp. 148–53, Ralph P. Martin, *Reconciliation: A Study of Paul's Theology* (Atlanta, GA: John Knox Press, 1981), pp. 32–37, 153–54; and Margaret Thrall, "Salvation Proclaimed: 2 Corinthians 5:18–21: Reconciliation with God," *Expository Times* 93 (1982), 227–32. For Paul on repentance, see C. F. D. Moule, "Obligation in the Ethic of Paul," in Moule, *Essays in New Testament Interpretation* (Cambridge: Cambridge University Press, 1982), pp. 263–75; and Eckhard J. Schnabel, "Repentance in Paul's Letters," *Novum Testamentum* 57 (2015), 159–86.

and the free gift in the grace of the one man, Jesus Christ, abounded for the many. And the free gift is not like the effect of the one man's sin. For the judgment following one trespass brought condemnation, but the free gift following many trespasses brings justification [δικαίωμα]. If, because of the one man's trespass, death exercised dominion through that one, much more surely will those who receive the abundance of grace and the free gift of righteousness [δικαιοσύνης] exercise dominion in life through the one man, Jesus Christ.

(Rom. 5:15–17)

So, Paul acknowledges "those who receive ... the free gift of righteousness" (τῆς δωρεᾶς τῆς δικαιοσύνης λαμβάνοντες) from God to humans. This raises an important question: Do some people, at least according to Paul, have the power not to receive this gift, either to ignore it or to reject it? In addition, does an affirmative answer, at least according to Paul, pose a threat to divine power or sovereignty or somehow undermine the reality of divine grace? We turn to these questions.

GRACE FOR VOLUNTARY FAITH

Paul considers God's grace to require that divine righteousness for humans come through their faith in God or Christ: "Now, apart from law, the righteousness of God has been disclosed, and is attested by the law and the prophets, the righteousness of God through faith in Jesus Christ for all who believe [πιστεύοντας]" (Rom. 3:21–32). How does such faith relate to the kind of "work" that Paul contrasts with grace and faith? Does it introduce a kind of human power that can curb or even block divine control over humans, including a divine redemptive purpose for them?

C. E. B. Cranfield has offered an interpretation of Paul that attributes full power to God in redemption as "altogether God's work":

> Faith ... is wrongly conceived if it is thought of as being, as a man's response to the gospel, a contribution from his side which, by

fulfilling a condition imposed by God, enables the gospel to be unto salvation for him. In that case, faith would itself be in the last resort a human meritorious work, a man's establishment of his own claim on God by virtue of something in himself.... For Paul, man's salvation is altogether – not almost altogether – God's work; and the faith spoken of here is the openness to the gospel which God himself creates, the human response of surrender to the judgment and unmerited mercy of God which God himself brings about – God who not only directs the message to the hearer but also Himself lays open the hearer's heart to the message. And yet this faith, as God's work in a man... is the expression of the freedom which God has restored to him – the freedom to obey God. So, the human freedom comes *as a result* of God's creating salvation for a human as "altogether God's work."[3]

Cranfield attributes all of the causal power in redemption to God: "For Paul, man's salvation is altogether – not almost altogether – God's work; and the faith spoken of here is the openness to the gospel which God himself creates." Even if some human freedom "comes as a result of God's creating salvation," the salvation, including the faith, is "altogether God's work." This position precludes voluntary frustration of God's redemptive aim by humans. It entails that God causes human salvation solely by God's own causal power.

Cranfield's reading of Paul arises from a concern about making faith a "human meritorious work" of the kind that Paul disowns in connection with Abraham's faith (Rom. 4:4–5). Even so, this reading goes to an extreme that misrepresents Paul, who acknowledges a role for human power that can frustrate divine grace and redemption.

---

[3] C. E. B. Cranfield, *A Critical and Exegetical Commentary on the Epistle to the Romans*, ICC (Edinburgh: T&T Clark, 1975), vol. 1, p. 90. A similar approach to Paul on divine power is found in Ernst Käsemann, *Commentary on Romans*, trans. G. W. Bromiley (Grand Rapids, MI: Eerdmans, 1980), p. 226. As indicated previously, I share Käsemann's view that divine righteousness in Paul's perspective is a power, and not a mere idea, but I shall present evidence against the interpretation of Paul that this power fully causes some human wills to obey God.

Cranfield mistakenly assumes that a voluntary human role in faith would make faith a meritorious work. This amounts to a confusion of the conditions for earning something and the conditions for (actively) receiving an unearned or undeserved gift. Paul, we shall see, does not make such a confusion.

Paul acknowledges a voluntary human role in receiving a divine gift of grace through faith, without any human earning or meriting of divine approval. This fits with his view of humans who have not "submitted" (ὑπετάγησαν) to the righteousness of God (Rom. 10:3), where submitting would be voluntary. The divine gift includes God's approval of a human in relation to God without human earning or meriting, but the gift is to be "received" by a human, and not left free of cooperative human responsiveness. Paul thus uses an active participle to signify those who are believing or trusting in God: πιστεύοντας (Rom. 3:22; cf. Rom. 1:16).

Faith in God, according to Paul, includes human doing, or genuinely acting, at least in actively trusting God (for Paul's use of the passive voice to indicate "being trusted with," see Rom. 3:2). Such doing is not earning or meriting divine approval or favor; instead, it includes actively receiving a gift. Paul does not hold that actively receiving a gift from God is earning or meriting that gift.

It is a harmful category mistake to subsume the notion of human acting under a concept of works as earning or meriting approval. Paul avoids that mistake, and his interpreters should too. A version of the mistake occurs in Victor Paul Furnish, who interprets Paul as follows on the qualities collectively called "the fruit of the Spirit": "They are not to be regarded as qualities which may be successively achieved by human effort ('works') but as manifestations of the gift of God."[4] With regard to faith, he adds: "For Paul, faith's obedience neither achieves nor attains righteousness, but receives it as a gift."[5] Such a contrast, however, will not convincingly

---

[4] Furnish, *Theology and Ethics in Paul*, p. 87.
[5] Furnish, *Theology and Ethics in Paul*, p. 196.

accommodate Paul's talk of "obedience which leads to righteousness [ὑπακοῆς εἰς δικαιοσύνην]" (Rom. 6:16). We shall see that nothing is lost in taking Paul's talk at face value here. In fact, we gain explanatory value by not identifying human actions or efforts with Paul's works of earning mentioned in Romans 4.

Furnish acknowledges that Paul's "exhortations seek to summon believers to that kind of *deliberate response* to God's claim without which faith forfeits its distinctive character as obedience."[6] He does not intend, however, to take this claim at face value in suggesting human power at work. He thus adds: "Paul understands man's response to be an expression of God's power to redeem and transform, not of man's power to comply and perform."[7] So, Furnish's position agrees with the previous remarks of Cranfield implying that only God's power, and not human power, brings about a human response to God in faith and obedience. This position may seem puzzling, given a familiar sense of "deliberative response," but it seems motivated by a clear intention not to allow human power to limit divine power in redemption.

In connection with Abraham's faith, we noted, Paul does not understand "works" simply in terms of a result of "human effort." Instead, he links "works" in Romans 4:4–5 to a disregard of the human need of divine grace as an undeserved gift through faith in God. He thus represents God to treat such works, apart from faith, as God's owing something to humans as a result of their earning or merit. By that presumptuous standard, humans do not fare well before God. People, however, can exercise "human effort" in actively receiving an undeserved divine gift, but that would not entail "works" (of the law) in Paul's special sense of disregarding needed grace through faith. Otherwise, the gift in question would be earned when received, and that is clearly an unacceptable result. This lesson falsifies the

---

[6] Furnish, *Theology and Ethics in Paul*, p. 227.
[7] Furnish, *Theology and Ethics in Paul*, p. 238; cf. p. 239.

position on "works" (of the law) assumed by Furnish, Cranfield, and various other commentators on Paul.

We find some evidence of Paul's voluntary understanding of a human response to God in this chapter's opening quotation: "I do not frustrate [ἀθετῶ] the grace of God" (Gal. 2:21, KJV). Paul would not affirm this view if voluntary rejection of divine grace were not a live option for humans. His affirmation would be trivial without that option. In addition, as noted, Paul acknowledges a voluntary human role in receiving illumination from God. Regarding the people of Israel, he remarks: "To this very day whenever Moses is read, a veil lies over their minds; but when one turns [ἐπιστρέψῃ] to the Lord, the veil is removed" (2 Cor. 3:15–16). Such "turning" is a voluntary action performed by a human, but it does not earn or merit God's removing the veil of misunderstanding. Paul holds that it is the way a human actively and voluntarily receives the gift of God's removing the veil of misunderstanding.

If the process of illumination were "altogether God's work," as implied by the perspective of Cranfield and Furnish, Paul would have no point in mentioning the condition of human "turning to the Lord." His mentioning it reveals that the voluntary responsiveness of humans is significant to his understanding of redemption by grace. It also reveals that he understands divine grace to leave room for voluntary human action in response, without human earning.

Offering a "motif of transformation through contemplation" to interpret Paul, Volker Rabens has proposed that "believers are transformed by means of deeper knowledge of an intimate encounter with the (glory of the) Lord."[8] He offers the following paraphrase of 2 Corinthians 3:18: "As a result of the work of the Spirit, we are all transformed into the same image, for one glory to another. The transformation takes place by means of an unveiled face and by beholding the glory of the Lord as in a mirror, just as this is accomplished from

---

[8] Volker Rabens, *The Holy Spirit and Ethics in Paul*, 2nd ed. (Minneapolis, MN: Fortress Press, 2014), p. 190.

the Lord, the Spirit." He adds that, in Paul's view, "the believer is brought into the presence of the Lord" (note the passive voice here, in contrast with Paul's use of the active voice in "turning to the Lord"), and that "the Spirit creates this intimate relationship."[9] The problem with such an interpretation of Paul on illumination is its neglect of the significant role for voluntary human "turning to the Lord" (2 Cor. 3:16). It gives no significant attention to that volitional role for humans, and it therefore misses an important component of Paul's understanding of divine self-revelation as actively received by humans.[10]

Paul gives a range of imperatives or injunctions that assume a voluntary and responsible human role in responding to God's intervention in human experience. They include: "Do not quench the Spirit" (1 Thess. 5:19) and "Walk by the Spirit, and do not gratify the desires of the flesh .... If we live by the Spirit, let us also walk by the Spirit" (Gal. 5:16, 25, RSV; cf. Rom. 8:4). Such injunctions assume a role for active human power in responding to God, without the earning of approval. That role, however, is incompatible with the commanded human response being, in Cranfield's language, "altogether God's work." The relevant injunctions would be beside the point if the matter were "altogether God's work." We should derive a similar lesson from Paul's talk of active human "sowing to the Spirit" (Gal. 6:7–8) and his injunction to "present yourselves to God" as being alive from the dead (Rom. 6:13; cf. Rom. 12:1-2). It makes no sense to say that Paul assumes such responsive matters to be "altogether God's work." He assumes a voluntary and responsible human role here.

An important question concerns what kind of action Paul assumes to be voluntary in relation to God. In particular, is it a purely

---

[9] Rabens, *The Holy Spirit and Ethics in Paul*, pp. 191, 192.

[10] The same shortcoming marks the relevant discussions in Grant Macaskill, *Union with Christ in the New Testament* (Oxford: Oxford University Press, 2013), pp. 219–50; and Craig S. Keener, *The Mind of the Spirit: Paul's Approach to Transformed Thinking* (Grand Rapids, MI: Baker Academic, 2016), pp. 210–16.

receptive action, an action of merely receiving, rather than something more? Herman Ridderbos has offered the following interpretation of Paul on faith: "Faith stands over against works as that which is absolutely receptive and dependent, over against that which is productive, which is able to assert itself.... The functional significance of faith as human act in justification is of course not thereby denied."[11] In this perspective, faith is an "absolutely receptive" human act. This act, according to Ridderbos, includes a decision merely to receive something offered as a gift of grace from God: God's gracious gift of righteousness as a (divinely imputed) right relationship with God.

Paul, as Chapter 2 noted, characterizes faith as follows in response to a misunderstanding of the Mosaic Law among the Galatian Christians: "In Christ Jesus neither circumcision nor uncircumcision counts for anything; the only thing that counts is faith working through love [πίστις δι' ἀγάπης ἐνεργουμένη]" (Gal. 5:6). Paul's talk of faith "working through love" (if taken as having at least a middle voice; on which see Chapter 2) does not suggest that faith is "absolutely receptive."[12] Instead, given at least a middle voice, it suggests that faith is active beyond mere reception, active as loving, owing to its "working through love." Such active loving combined with active faith is no mere reception, because it includes at least a kind of active trust that positively wills something good in relation to God. It thus wills in a way cooperative (at least to some extent) with God's self-sacrificial loving will that attracts such faith uncoercively. This kind of faith is positively active, beyond mere reception, but it is not a matter of earning or meriting divine approval.

---

[11] Herman Ridderbos, *Paul: An Outline of his Theology*, trans. J. R. De Witt (Grand Rapids, MI: Eerdmans, 1975), p. 172. Ridderbos cites G. C. Berkouwer to support his interpretation; see Berkouwer, *Faith and Justification*, trans. L. B. Smedes (Grand Rapids, MI: Eerdmans, 1954), pp. 178–79.

[12] Likewise, with endorsement of the middle voice for the participle, see J. Louis Martyn, *Galatians*, AB (New York: Doubleday, 1997), pp. 473–74.

Paul's understanding of the working of faith in response to God, according to Robert C. Tannehill, is active as follows: "The believer is not simply dragged along by the Spirit as if he had no choice. The believer is actively enlisted in the struggle [against the powers of the old dominion]."[13] Tannehill, however, seems to favor the following kind of approach offered by J. Louis Martyn, which he calls "Bultmannian":

> Were the Galatians to fail to continue the life they are being given in the Spirit (5:22–23), they would not be exercising freedom of will. On the contrary, they would find that they are again slaves of the Flesh, and thus in the state properly called bondage of the will. For there is only one form of free will, and that is obedience to the leading of the Spirit.[14]

Paul himself, however, does not limit the relevant voluntary response to God to the time after divine power has changed a life.

Paul regards some people as responsible for their voluntary opposition to God apart from their yielding to God (Rom. 1:21–25, 32). He does not assign the source of this opposition to the power of God rather than to the power of humans.[15] At the same time, he holds that these people cannot obey God adequately on their own, without receiving divine power (Rom. 8:7). It does not follow, however, that he attributes full causal power to God in bringing about human responses. Humans can lack the power to obey God adequately on their own, according to Paul, but they still have the power, courtesy of a divine prevenient gift, either to seek (or receive) or not to seek (or receive) divine power for adequate obedience to God.

---

[13] Robert C. Tannehill, *Dying and Rising with Christ*, BZNW (Berlin: Töpelmann, 1966), p. 81.

[14] Martyn, *Galatians*, p. 535, n. 184. See also Martyn, *Theological Issues in the Letters of Paul* (Edinburgh: T&T Clark, 1997), p. 264.

[15] For relevant discussion, see Leander Keck, "The Accountable Self," in Keck, *Christ's First Theologian* (Waco, TX: Baylor University Press, 2015), pp. 133–45.

Paul explains his understanding of active faith, beyond mere reception, in connection with the faith of Abraham.

> [Abraham] did not weaken in faith when he considered his own body, which was already as good as dead (for he was about a hundred years old), or when he considered the barrenness of Sarah's womb. No distrust made him waver concerning the promise of God, but he grew strong in his faith as he gave glory to God, being fully convinced that God was able to do what he had promised. Therefore, his faith "was reckoned to him as righteousness."
> (Rom. 4:19–22)

In Paul's understanding, Abraham's strengthening in faith included the fact that "he gave glory to God, being fully convinced that God was able to do what he had promised." This is more than mere reception of divine input of some kind, but it does not undermine grace. In fact, Paul holds that God's redemptive promise proceeds by such faith "in order that the promise may rest on grace and be guaranteed to all [Abraham's] descendants" (Rom. 4:16).

John M. G. Barclay has suggested that in Romans 4 Abraham's "faith amounts to the declaration of incompetence, or total dependence on the competence of God (4:20–22)."[16] This suggestion may seem to approach what Paul has in mind, but it falls short if it does not go beyond a "declaration." The kind of trust Paul has in mind goes beyond a "declaration" of dependence, because it is akin to counting on God (actively). Paul talks of Abraham's "believing in God" (ʼΕπίστευσεν δὲ ʼΑβραὰμ τῷ θεῷ), with the dative and no indicated declared content (Rom. 4:3; cf. Gal. 3:6). Such believing thus goes beyond believing or declaring about something. Declaring, then, does not go far enough, because it omits the active trust of Abraham's faith suggested by Paul.

A clear indication of Paul's understanding of a suitable human response to God as active rather than merely receptive arises from his

---

[16] John M. G. Barclay, *Paul and the Gift* (Grand Rapids, MI: Eerdmans, 2015), p. 489.

injunction to Christians at Philippi. He commands: "Therefore, my beloved, just as you have always obeyed me, not only in my presence, but much more now in my absence, work out [κατεργάζεσθε] your own salvation with fear and trembling; for it is God who is at work in you, enabling you both to will and to work for his good pleasure" (Phil. 2:12–13). Paul thus suggests that the relevant kind of faithful obedience to God includes "working out" of one's salvation from God.

Noting that Paul deems the salvation of the Christians at Philippi to be "from God" (Phil. 1:28), Gordon D. Fee observes that, according to Paul, "salvation is not only something they receive; it is something they *do*."[17] "Working out" of salvation, of course, is not to be confused with "working for" salvation as "earning" divine approval. Instead, it is the voluntary action of human obedience to God, if with "fear and trembling." It would be a confusing mistake to identify such obedience with earning approval from God. Instead, it is the kind of obedience that Paul deems, as noted, to "lead to righteousness" (Rom. 6:16), that is, righteousness "under grace" (Rom. 6:14).[18]

DIVINE REGRET

Paul emphasizes the voluntary and responsible human frustration of God in order to protect God's righteousness and to save God from blame for human opposition to God. The aforementioned interpretation offered by Cranfield and Furnish implicates God in the human frustration of God. It assigns only divine power to a human response

---

[17] Gordon D. Fee, *Paul's Letter to the Philippians*, NICNT (Grand Rapids, MI: Eerdmans, 1995), p. 234.

[18] Rudolf Bultmann, as Chapter 3 noted, saw that deeds of obedience in Paul's thought are not to be confused with "works" as earning approval from God. See Bultmann, *Theology of the New Testament*, trans. Kendrick Grobel (New York: Charles Scribner's Sons, 1955), vol. 1, pp. 284, 316. For elaboration on Bultmann's position on faith and obedience, see Barclay, *Paul and the Gift*, pp. 135–40, taking exception to the interpretation in E. P. Sanders, *Paul and Palestinian Judaism* (Philadelphia, PA: Fortress Press, 1977). For an illuminating assessment of Bultmann's broader approach to faith, see Leander Keck, *A Future for the Historical Jesus* (Philadelphia, PA: Fortress Press, 1981), pp. 50–58.

to God, including a response opposed to God. Paul offers a contrary approach, without misplaced fear of undermining divine grace or sovereignty.

With regard to opponents of God's redemptive purpose within Israel, Paul explains:

> They were broken off because of their unbelief, but you stand only through faith. So do not become proud, but stand in awe. For if God did not spare the natural branches, perhaps he will not spare you. Note then the kindness and the severity of God: severity toward those who have fallen, but God's kindness toward you, provided you continue in his kindness; otherwise you also will be cut off. And even those of Israel, if they do not persist in unbelief, will be grafted in, for God has the power to graft them in again.
> (Rom. 11:20–23)

Paul does not say or suggest that God's power caused the unbelief of the Israelites in question. He could have supported such a view, but he clearly avoids that approach. Instead, he refers to the human need to "continue in [God's] kindness" as the active alternative to being "cut off" as a result of "unbelief." Paul thus attributes the relevant causal power and corresponding responsibility to humans and not to God. So, he does not make this process a matter of only God's power.

Referring to Isaiah 65, Paul portrays God to take an opposing, and not a causally supporting, position toward voluntary human frustration of God: "Of Israel he says, 'All day long I have held out my hands to a disobedient and contrary people'" (Rom. 10:21). This, of course, is not the attitude of a God who exercises all of the power in a human response to God and thereby causes some people, in a negative response, to disobey God and not to trust God. In addition, if this God exercised all of the power in a positive response of faithful obedience, we have a serious problem from Paul's perspective, a problem of divine partiality toward the redemption of humans.

God, according to Paul, is the God of all people (Rom. 3:29–30) and "shows no partiality" in the desired redemption of humans:

"Glory and honor and peace for everyone who does good, the Jew first and also the Greek. For God shows no partiality" (Rom. 2:10–11).[19] So, if this God fully caused some people to respond positively and thereby receive redemption, then God out of impartiality would give this divinely caused gift to all people. Otherwise, God would not have the status of being the redemptive God of all people. In that case, God would be the inevitable destroyer, and not the desired redeemer, of some people. This is not the God portrayed by Paul. Paul's God "shows no partiality" in this matter of ultimate life and death. Paul thinks of this divine impartiality to include God's "holding out hands" of welcome to all people, leaving them with a responsible decision to make in response.

We have seen that Paul does not consider divine grace to be threatened by human freedom either to frustrate or to receive that grace. Voluntary reception of divine grace includes a voluntary human deed, but a deed, even when obedient, should not be confused with an effort to earn divine approval. Interpreters of Paul who miss this lesson distort, if by implication, the impartial redemptive love of Paul's God. They thereby sell short Paul's striking portrait of God, borrowed from Isaiah, as holding out divine hands to a disobedient and contrary people. Paul took this as sincere, and not play-acting, on God's part. Interpreters of Paul do well to follow suit. In doing so, they will come to appreciate the human challenge posed by the role of divine self-sacrifice in Paul's understanding of redemption. Reciprocal self-sacrifice for humans, we have noted, can prompt fear of loss in humans and therefore rejection of God's redemptive plan. We turn to divine reckoning of righteousness to humans as an alternative to human rejection of divine goodness, including redemptive self-sacrifice.

---

[19] For relevant discussion, see Dunn, *Jesus, Paul, and the Gospels*, ch. 8; Dunn, *The Theology of Paul the Apostle*, pp. 341–44; and Joseph A. Fitzmyer, *Romans*, pp. 302–3.

VOLUNTARY CREDIT IN ELECTION

If, as argued, human faith in God is voluntary and responsible in Paul's thought, then the divine reckoning of faith as righteousness assumes a voluntary and responsible human role, in his thought. We need to clarify how such reckoning figures in Paul's gospel of divine self-sacrifice.

Paul holds that righteousness from the Mosaic law is a package deal, requiring obedience to the whole law. He remarks to the Galatian Christians: "Once again I testify to every man who lets himself be circumcised that he is obliged to obey the entire law [ὅλον τὸν νόμον]" (Gal. 5:3). In the same vein: "Circumcision indeed is of value if you obey the law; but if you break the law, your circumcision has become uncircumcision" (Rom. 2:25). So, Paul thinks of righteousness from the Mosaic law to depend on keeping the law and not just a part of the law. This would be complete obedience from the standpoint of the Mosaic law and thus a tall order by any standard. Paul, of course, denies that humans succeed here. He states: "We know that whatever the law says, it speaks to those who are under the law, so that every mouth may be silenced, and the whole world may be held accountable to God. For 'no human being will be justified in his sight' by deeds prescribed by the law" (Rom. 3:19–20).

According to Paul, God needs an alternative to the Mosaic law for humans if they are to receive divine righteousness. The power of sin figures in human failure to obey the law as a whole, even if isolated acts of obedience occur (Rom. 3:23). So, God reckons, or credits, righteousness to humans on a basis other than obeying the Mosaic law. That basis is faith in God, as represented by Abraham, according to Paul's understanding of Genesis: 15:6: "What does the scripture say? 'Abraham believed God, and it was reckoned to him as righteousness.' Now to one who works, wages are not reckoned as a gift but as something due. But to one who without works trusts him who justifies the ungodly, such faith is reckoned as righteousness" (Rom. 4:3–5; cf. Gal. 3:6).

The NIV translates Romans 4:3 as: "Abraham believed God, and it was credited to him as righteousness." The 1995 NASB uses similar language of "credit," and such language is fitting. Paul has in mind God's giving credit for something (counted by God) as righteousness. Contrary to some commentators, Paul is not thinking of, and does not speak of, God's "imputing" the righteousness of Christ to humans with faith.[20] Instead, he is thinking of God's giving humans with the faith of Abraham credit for righteousness. Such faith "was credited to him as righteousness."

Neither Abraham nor other similar humans have or exhibit God's righteousness as perfect moral goodness. So, from the standpoint of their own moral characters, they are morally inadequate before God. They are thus at odds with a reconciled relationship with God. Paul makes this clear in Romans 3. God's redemptive solution, according to Paul, is to identify a means of a reconciled relationship in humans and to credit it as righteousness. Human faith in God and Christ, Paul holds, is that means. We shall see that this is not a matter of fictional crediting, because it is anchored in actual, if incomplete, righteousness.

We have noted that some commentators deny the active human role of faith in Paul's thought. A result has been misunderstanding of the role of human agency in the faith by which righteousness is reckoned according to Paul. We shall clarify this active role with a distinction between action that constitutes righteousness and action that receives already constituted righteousness. This distinction will illuminate credited divine righteousness in terms of faith that is voluntary and active in receiving such righteousness without constituting it.

Paul contends that in dealing with human disobedience, God is both righteous and the one who justifies people who have faith in

---

[20] For doubts about a thesis of imputation of Christ's righteousness in Paul, see Michael F. Bird, *The Saving Righteousness of God* (Milton Keynes: Paternoster, 2006), ch. 4.

God. He takes that justifying activity to include God's justifying ungodly people, that is, people who fall short of divine righteousness (Rom. 4:5; cf. Rom. 5:6). We might have assumed that God would justify only righteous people, but this is not Paul's view. God, according to Paul, extends redemption to humans by not crediting sin to them, while maintaining divine righteousness through the sacrifice of atonement in Jesus. Paul finds the idea of God's not crediting sin to sinful humans in the Psalms (32:1–2, LXX; cf. Rom. 4:8). He also finds God's crediting righteousness to the ungodly, apart from human works of earning, in the Genesis story of Abraham (Gen. 15:6, LXX; cf. Rom. 4:3). This crediting avoids a juridical fiction, because it includes a morally relevant change in a human recipient.

Paul focuses on a kind of divine righteousness that "leads to ... life for all" (Rom. 5:18; cf. 4:16, 5:21). He finds God's unique trademark in the fact that God "gives life to the dead and calls into existence the things that do not exist" (Rom. 4:17). He holds that, in contrast with God, a law cannot yield the relevant kind of righteousness, because a law itself cannot give life to people (Gal. 3:21). Paul holds that the righteousness needed by humans must be life-giving, given the opposing power of death, and that only God can fill this order.

Paul identifies a divine means of righteousness for humans that does not depend on the Mosaic law leading to human condemnation. Faith in God, in contrast with both "works" of earning and "works of the law" without faith (see Chapter 2), enables God's promise of life in Genesis 15 to rest on an unearned gift of grace and to be offered to all people, not just to the physical descendants of Abraham (Rom. 4:16). Paul opposes in Romans 4 a kind of working whereby a person (supposedly) obligates God to satisfy a debt of approval of that person. His conception of works in that context, we have seen, is not the same as the broader notion of human acts or deeds, such as acts of obedience.

Not all human acts, even acts of obedience, aim to obligate someone to give approval. In addition, works as intended earnings, according to Paul, have no role in a gift of divine grace or credited righteousness from God. It does not follow, however, that the same holds for human actions or deeds in the human reception of divine grace. Human faith in God, in Paul's thinking, includes human deeds in such reception of grace, without either constituting or meriting that grace.[21]

Some proponents of the "new perspective" on Paul recommend that we understand his talk of "works" of the law in terms of Jewish identity-markers. James Dunn, for instance, claims that "'works of the law are an outward mark indicative of ethnic solidarity.'"[22] This interpretation, as Chapter 2 noted, is too narrow. Paul's exclusion of human "works" of the law from divine grace is not limited to deeds required by the law as ethnic identity-markers. Paul excludes from grace human works of any sort that neglect a needed role for divine grace as an undeserved gift through human faith in God.[23] This is confirmed by Romans 9:31–32, which assumes that parts of Israel pursued righteousness via "works" based on the Mosaic law rather than via faith in God and its corresponding divine grace. Paul seeks a correction here to pursuing righteousness, to make room for righteousness by divine grace as an undeserved gift to humans.

Paul faults a tendency in Israel: "Being ignorant of the righteousness that comes from God, and seeking to establish their own, they have not submitted to God's righteousness" (Rom. 10:3). He thus assumes a distinction between two kinds of righteousness: the righteousness "from God," specifically from an undeserved divine gift of grace, and the righteousness humans "seek to establish" apart from grace through faith, such as with their own works to constitute or

---

[21] It is potentially misleading, then, to translate Romans 11:6 with "deeds done" (NEB) or "deeds" (REB and Fitzmyer, *Romans*).

[22] James D. G. Dunn, *Romans 1–8*, WBC (Dallas, TX: Word Books, 1988), p. 158.

[23] For further support, see C. E. B. Cranfield "'The Works of the Law' in the Epistle to the Romans," *Journal for the Study of the New Testament* 43 (1991), pp. 89–101; and Seyoon Kim, *Paul and the New Perspective* (Grand Rapids, MI: Eerdmans, 2002), pp. 57–66.

earn their righteous standing with God. Paul suggests that the latter righteousness via human works is a failure to "submit" to the righteousness from God by grace through faith.

Paul claims, as suggested, that "God credits righteousness apart from works," and that "to the one who does not work but trusts God who justifies the ungodly ... faith is credited as righteousness" (Rom. 4:5-6, NIV). Paul's talk of "faith" here relies on an active participle (πιστεύοντι) signifying an action contributed by a human to a situation where God reckons righteousness. This contribution is action-involving: It includes a human's doing something, that is, trusting in God. Faith in God is not just a human action and so is not merely an action of trust. It includes state-like dispositional features that can exist when a person is not acting at all, such as when sleeping. Even so, Paul's use of an active participle indicates that his understanding of faith cannot be characterized accurately apart from an active human response to God.

We would have a puzzling result if Paul identified "works" with human action. He then would leave us with the following claim in Romans 4:5: "To the person who without doing any action performs the action of trusting him who justifies the ungodly, that person's faith is credited as righteousness." This claim entails a contradiction, but we have no good reason to assign it to Paul. Romans 4:5 gives us good reason not to confuse Paul's idea of "works" with a notion of human actions in general.

Faith in God, according to Paul, is the divinely approved means for receiving God's crediting of righteousness to willing humans (Rom. 4:11, 16, 22-24). It includes humans being active in their redemption by God, as a result of their actively receiving the divine righteousness offered as a free gift. Paul says of Abraham, as noted: "No distrust made him waver concerning the promise of God, but he grew strong in his faith as he gave glory to God, being fully confident that God was able to do what he had promised. Therefore, his faith 'was reckoned to him as righteousness'" (Rom. 4:20-22). Paul stresses the active resolve of Abraham in his trusting response to God's promise. This active resolve, in Paul's understanding, is a central factor for the divine crediting of righteousness to Abraham.

Paul suggests that Abraham "was empowered [ἐνεδυναμώθη] in his faith" by God (Rom. 4:20).[24] This is part of his view of human faith in God as a person's actively receiving God's free gift of righteousness and being empowered by God on that basis. The available empowerment of a human by God through human faith saves Paul from promoting a legal fiction in the divine crediting of righteousness to humans. The divine power of righteousness received as a divine gift by faith starts and supports a real process in a person of being made righteous by God (Rom 5:19; 2 Cor. 5:21). So, in Paul's perspective, God's crediting of righteousness to humans is not a legal fiction. It includes an actual change in receptive humans, courtesy of God's redemptive power, even if maturation in righteousness is required.

Paul's gospel of divine grace precludes the constituting or earning of righteousness before God by human activity. We have noted, however, that it includes an active human role, via faith, in the human receiving of divine righteousness. Although humans are not active in constituting or earning the righteousness being offered to them by God, they still can be active in the reception of such righteousness. In other words, there can be receptive actions, such as trusting in God, that do not involve any intention to constitute or to earn a status before God. In addition, such actions need not be merely receptive. These distinctions are central to Paul's thinking on grace, faith, and works.

In his brief autobiography as "a member of the people of Israel" (Phil. 3:5), Paul acknowledges pursuit "not [of] a righteousness of my own that comes from the law, but ... [of] the righteousness from God based on faith" (Phil. 3:9). Paul is not accusing all of the Jews before him or contemporaneous with him as seeking to constitute or to earn

---

[24] In Philippians 4:13, Paul uses the corresponding active participle with reference to a divine source of the empowering of himself.

righteousness before God via the law. Instead, he is identifying this tendency in his own earlier life as a law-observant Jew who was "as to righteousness under the law, blameless" (Phil. 3:6). Paul assumes, quite plausibly, that he is not alone in this tendency, but this is no denunciation of Judaism properly understood or of all or even most other Jews as promoting righteousness via human earning. Under the lordship of Christ, Paul had come to count his aforementioned "gain" of blamelessness relative to the law as "loss," as irrelevant, for the sake of having the righteousness from divine grace through faith (Phil. 3:7-9). The righteousness from divine grace comes as an undeserved gift, and therefore leaves no room to be either constituted or earned via works of the law.

Paul's talk of "works" takes on different meanings in different contexts in his letters. So, he does not use "works" or "work" in all contexts to signify the paying of a debt that is due. For instance, he refers to the "work of faith" in 1 Thessalonians 1:3 and to the "work of God" in Romans 14:20. Neither of these contexts concerns the human constituting or earning of a status before God. Paul's language thus conflicts with sweeping generalizations; it calls for careful attention to the individual contexts of his use of terms.

We should avoid two extremes in the interpretation of Paul on righteousness by grace through faith. The first extreme dehumanizes faith, and the other reduces it to a mere action. The first extreme denies that faith includes human action, on the assumption that a role for human action would make righteousness depend on a work and thus undermine grace. This extreme is encouraged by the NEB and REB translations of Romans 11:6, and it emerges in various Reformed Protestant interpreters of Paul.

Ridderbos comments on Paul on faith: "There can be no doubt whatever that faith, however much it bears the character of obedience and submission to the divine redemptive will, nevertheless does not rest on the assent of man himself... but on the renewing and re-creating power of divine grace. Were it otherwise, then the gospel would be a new law, and the whole problem of the impotence of the law would recur."[25] Ridderbos claims that faith "does not rest on the assent" of humans, on the ground that otherwise the gospel preached by Paul would be "a new law" promoting works. Such reasoning confuses a law as a human means of constituting or earning righteousness before God and a law as a commandment to receive righteousness by grace through faith in God. Paul promotes the latter kind of commandment, apart from human earning of righteousness.

Paul speaks of "obeying the gospel," and he uses this talk interchangeably with talk of "believing" the gospel (Rom. 10:16-17; cf. 2 Thess. 1:8). He holds that the Roman Christians received their freedom from slavery to sin by becoming "obedient from the heart" to the good news preached to them (Rom. 6:17). We have noted, in addition, that Paul speaks of "obedience which leads to righteousness" (Rom. 6:16; cf. Rom. 10:10). These remarks count against any interpretation that divorces Paul's notion of faith from his notion of obedience. Of course, Paul would reject talk of "works which lead to righteousness." So, his talk of "obedience" in Romans 6:16 contrasts with his talk of works constituting or earning righteousness. Paul, then, can talk of "the obedience of faith" (Rom. 1:5, 16:26) while accommodating his key remarks about "works" in Romans 4:4-5, 11:6.

The first extreme at hand neglects the central role of active human faith in God in Paul's approach to righteousness. It thus misrepresents Paul's understanding of righteousness by grace through actively receptive faith. One result is a serious misunderstanding of the key role of human agency, and thus of human responsibility, in

---

[25] Ridderbos, *Paul*, p. 234. Benjamin Schliesser shares the extreme Reformed perspective of Ridderbos, including his exclusion of genuine human activity from faith. See Schliesser, *Abraham's Faith in Romans 4*, WUNT (Tübingen: Mohr Siebeck 2007), pp. 396-97. A similar neglect of the role of human activity in faith as understood by Paul can be found in Ernest Best, *The Letter of Paul to the Romans*, CBC (Cambridge: Cambridge University Press, 1967), p. 47; Stephen Westerholm, *Perspectives Old and New on Paul* (Grand Rapids: Eerdmans, 2004), pp. 311, 351, 384; and Douglas Campbell, *The Deliverance of God* (Grand Rapids: Eerdmans, 2009), pp. 78, 79, 829.

Paul's account of redemption by grace through faith in God. According to the first extreme, God's role in crediting righteousness replaces human activity and accountability in the active reception of divine righteousness.

The second extreme in interpreting Paul treats faith as a mere act reducible to an episode of human action. Ernst Käsemann offers an approach to Paul on faith that acknowledges a central role for human activity. He comments on Romans 4:1–8: "Faith is ... the 'condition' of salvation, not as a human achievement, but as receiving and keeping the word which separates us from all lords and all salvation outside Christ."[26] He adds: "We must insist strongly that faith in Paul ... is the act and decision of the individual person .... Faith is not in itself righteousness .... It is a condition as poverty is, or waiting for blessing."[27] Käsemann characterizes the active receptivity of faith to allow God's Word to be spoken to us: "God comes to us in his promise and makes us righteous – righteous in that we, as the receivers, allow him to come to us."[28] (Some of Käsemann's talk of righteousness suggests that the receivers could not have allowed otherwise, but we shall not digress.)

Rudolf Bultmann's perspective on Paul on faith figures in Käsemann's interpretation of Paul. Bultmann holds that Paul understands "work" in parts of Romans "in the fundamental sense – to earn claim to a reward" and that "faith, as decision, is even preeminently the deed of man."[29] Bultmann, we have noted, recognizes that "deeds" (or "actions") and "works" are not the same in Paul's thought. He interprets the deed of faith in Paul as a human act of self-surrender to the divine act of grace. It is the human means for receiving a new understanding of oneself that excludes human

---

[26] Käsemann, *Commentary on Romans*, pp. 109.
[27] Käsemann *Commentary on Romans*, p. 109, 111.
[28] Ernst Käsemann, *Perspectives on Paul*, trans. Margaret Kohl (Philadelphia: Fortress Press, 1971), p. 93.
[29] Bultmann, *Theology of the New Testament*, pp. 283–84.

boasting before God.[30] So, Paul's good news, according to Bultmann, "is, by nature, personal address which accosts each individual, throwing the person himself into question by rendering his self-understanding problematic, and demanding a decision of him."[31] The decision of faith, then, "is a deed in the true sense: In a true deed the doer himself is inseparable from it, while in a 'work' he stands side by side with what he does."[32] Bultmann contrasts the deed of faith with human "accomplishment" by characterizing the former as obedient submission to God's way of salvation.

Bultmann and Käsemann correctly acknowledge in Paul's thinking a central role for human activity in the reception of divine righteousness. Paul, as they see, understands God's crediting of righteousness to depend on human receptive activity. They thus notice that Paul considers Abraham to respond to God with an active faith that is a condition of God's crediting righteousness to him (Rom. 4:22). So, they acknowledge an active human contribution to the reception of divinely credited righteousness among humans. As a result, they should deny that only divine power figures in the redemption of humans.

While pointing in the right direction about Paul on faith, Bultmann and Käsemann misrepresent faith as a mere human deed or action. They neglect that a state of faith, in Paul's thought, is not merely episodic in the way that a deed or an action is. A deed or an action exists only while it is being performed; in that regard, it is episodic and differs from a state. Faith in God is not episodic in that way. It exists even when believers are not performing any actions, including, as suggested, when they are asleep. So, Paul does not limit faith in God to occurrent trusting as an action. Faith in God requires action in trusting God (at a time), but this action need not continue as a constant episode for faith to endure.

---

[30] Bultmann, *Theology of the New Testament*, pp. 300–301.
[31] Bultmann, *Theology of the New Testament*, p. 307.
[32] Bultmann, *Theology of the New Testament*, p. 316.

Faith in God is an action-based dispositional state that includes a person's having acted in trusting God. It also includes, on that basis, that the person would exercise (as an action) trust in God again in suitable circumstances. (We need not digress now to the exact suitable circumstances; some disagreement is allowable.) This factor figures in faith as something that can endure in a life over time, without being hostage to sporadic episodes in a life. So, action-based faith in God is not reducible to an episodic deed or to a series of such deeds. This general approach agrees with Paul's understanding of faith as enduring through life, despite its ups and downs. It also enables us to avoid the previous two extremes in understanding faith in God.

A voluntary approach to crediting righteousness through faith, that is, voluntary faith, fits well with Paul's view of divine election. It is an egregious mistake to read into Paul the view that God excludes certain people from redemption by causing them to distrust or otherwise reject either God or God's redemptive plan. Making this mistake by invoking Romans 9 typically twists the meaning of Paul's remarks by ignoring its illuminating context of Romans 10 and 11. If we keep that context in mind, we can preserve the voluntary nature of faith that receives divine credit for righteousness. We then can disavow the double predestination some commentators assign to Paul's view of divine redemption.[33]

Paul asks the urgent question for us, and he answers it: "I ask, then, has God rejected his people? By no means!" (Rom. 11:1). He continues: "Again I ask: Did they stumble so as to fall beyond recovery? Not at all! Rather, because of their transgression, salvation has come to the Gentiles to make Israel envious" (Rom. 11:11, NIV). Paul invokes a straightforward explanation: The people of Israel stumbled

---

[33] See, for instance, John Piper, *The Justification of God*, 2nd ed. (Grand Rapids, MI: Baker Academic, 1993), pp. 160–78; Douglas J. Moo, *The Epistle to the Romans*, NICNT (Grand Rapids, MI: Eerdmans, 1996), pp. 585–87; and Schreiner, *Romans*, BECNT (Grand Rapids, MI: Baker Academic, 1998), pp. 501–3. For dissent from double predestination in reading Romans 8–11, see Cranfield, *A Critical and Exegetical Commentary on the Epistle to the Romans*, vol. 2, pp. 488–89; Dunn, *Romans 9–16*, pp. 566–68; and Fitzmyer, *Romans*, pp. 524–25.

"because of their transgression" (τῷ αὐτῶν παραπτώματι), not because God caused them to distrust or otherwise to reject either God or God's redemptive plan.

In case someone misses his point about much of Israel, Paul adds: "They were broken off because of their unbelief, but you stand only through faith. So do not become proud, but stand in awe…. And even those of Israel, if they do not persist in unbelief, will be grafted in, for God has the power to graft them in again" (Rom. 11:20, 23). Paul speaks of being broken off "because of their unbelief" (τῇ ἀπιστίᾳ). He does not suggest that God caused this unbelief or otherwise caused people to be excluded from divine redemption. He easily could have suggested that, but he attributes the relevant human failure to humans, and not to God. It is thus misleading for David G. Peterson to claim of Paul in Romans 11: "Human stubbornness is emphasized, but God is portrayed as the ultimate cause."[34] Paul suggests that the dissenters in question need not "persist in unbelief" (ἐπιμένωσι τῇ ἀπιστίᾳ), thus confirming a voluntary approach to faith in God, contrary to a typical claim of double predestination.

Paul represents God as striving *for* the redemption of people distrusting or otherwise rejecting God. He cites, as mentioned, the book of Isaiah in characterizing God's attitude toward Israel: "Of Israel he says, 'All day long I have held out my hands to a disobedient and contrary people'" (Rom. 10:21; cf. Isa. 65:2). Paul gives no indication of God's causing people to distrust or otherwise to reject God; on the contrary, he portrays God as eagerly welcoming such people. This attitude of God does not fit with a claim of double predestination.

Paul gives a helpful indication of God's role in divine election with talk of divine foreknowledge. He writes regarding God's predestination of the elect: "Those whom he foreknew he also predestined to be conformed to the image of his Son, in order that he might be the firstborn within a large family. And those whom he predestined he

---

[34] David G. Peterson, *Commentary on Romans*, BTCP (Nashville, TN: Holman Reference, 2017), p. 405.

also called; and those whom he called he also justified; and those whom he justified he also glorified" (Rom. 8:29–30). God, according to Paul, predestines some people to redemption, but the pressing issue is the basis of that predestination.

Paul, as just indicated, invokes divine foreknowledge: "Those whom he foreknew he also predestined to be conformed to the image of his Son." Paul's perspective will be coherent only if we understand such foreknowledge to allow for voluntary human trust or distrust toward God. We have noted evidence for Paul's commitment to a voluntary and responsible human role in this area. The best interpretation of Paul's talk of divine foreknowledge in this context is that it enables God to know which people will respond positively to God's call to redemption. Such foreknowledge is no threat to genuine human agency in faith and in the human reception of redemption in divine–human reconciliation.

Paul thinks of God as causally sovereign in the final *standard* for redemption in mercy and judgment. He does not portray God, however, as the causal determinant of how *people* ultimately respond to that standard. He characterizes God as leaving causal room for genuine human agency in responding to God's call to redemption through mercy and judgment. God seeks to leave the whole world accountable to God (Rom. 3:19), and that goal calls for responsible human agency, including a voluntary human role in trusting or distrusting God.

We have noted that, according to Romans 11:2-8, God has not rejected his people. Instead, God has set a *standard* of grace through faith, and people voluntarily respond to it, with trust or distrust. That standard sets the mark for the divide, as God holds out his hands, with sincere welcome, to people who distrust God. Sam K. Williams points us in the right direction: "Romans 9:18 ('He hardens whom he will') is to be read in light of the decisive 'until' of [Romans] 11:25. Even more damaging [would be] a failure to consider the weighty import of [Romans] 11:32… To be sure, Paul stresses God's absolute freedom to bestow his mercy on whom he will, but at Romans 11:32 he affirms his conviction that God wills to bestow his mercy on all his human creatures: 'He imprisoned all in disobedience so that he might have mercy upon all.'"[35] Double predestination thus misrepresents Paul's view of the voluntary and responsible human role in trust or distrust toward God and his view of God's universal aim for human redemption (even if the aim is not ultimately fulfilled).

SPIRITED LIFE FOR CO-SACRIFICE

In Paul's perspective, it is important to maintain an active role for human faith in God as a basis for credited righteousness. What, however, gives such faith redemptive value, in Paul's thinking? The answer involves the Spirit of God as the way to receive and to share God's life of righteousness.

Paul relates voluntary faith in God to voluntarily receiving the Spirit of God. He asks the Galatian Christians: "Did you receive [ἐλάβετε] the Spirit by doing the works of the law or by believing what you heard? ... Does God supply you with the Spirit ... by your doing the works of the law, or by your believing what you heard?" (Gal. 3:2, 5). God's Spirit is Paul's concern, because he thinks of divine righteousness as delivering divinely inspired life to humans.

Paul draws a contrast between righteous life with God and the deliverance of the Mosaic law: "If a law had been given that could make alive [ζωοποιῆσαι], then righteousness would indeed come through the law" (Gal. 3:21). God's Spirit, however, can "make [humans] alive" with divine power and thereby empower divine righteousness for human lives. So, Paul claims that "in Christ Jesus the blessing of Abraham might come to the Gentiles, so that we might receive [λάβωμεν] the promise of the Spirit through faith" (Gal. 3:14). God supplies the promise and the Spirit, but they are to be received, rather than rejected, by humans, through faith in God.

---

[35] Sam K. Williams, "Review of John Piper, *The Justification of God*," *Journal of Biblical Literature* 104 (1985), 548.

The redemptive power of God's Spirit, according to Paul, is interpersonal and filial, represented and defined by God's unique Son, Jesus. Paul remarks: "God sent his Son, born of a woman, born under the law, in order to redeem those who were under the law, so that we might receive [ἀπολάβωμεν] adoption as children. And because you are children, God has sent the Spirit of his Son into our hearts, crying, 'Abba! Father! So, you are no longer a slave but a child, and if a child then also an heir, through God" (Gal. 4:4–7). The filial relation of adoption as children of God is to be "received" by humans. So, it is not a merely causal process brought about by God; it is not coercive of human wills toward God's will. Instead, the reception of such adoption depends on a voluntary human response of faith in God.

Paul stresses the importance of faith as including a voluntary resolve to "live to God" after the model of Christ:

> For through the law I died to the law, so that I might live to God. I have been crucified with Christ; and it is no longer I who live, but it is Christ who lives in me. And the life I now live in the flesh I live by faith in the Son of God, who loved me and gave himself for me. I do not nullify the grace of God; for if justification [righteousness = δικαιοσύνη] comes through the law, then Christ died for nothing.
> *(Gal. 2:19–21; cf. Rom. 7:4)*

Paul brings together here the key ideas of Christ's self-sacrificial love, voluntary faith in Christ, dying with Christ, living to God, and divine righteousness. This is a remarkable synthesis of the central components of Paul's perspective on redemption through the gospel of divine self-sacrifice.

Paul's conceptions of "living to God" and of "the Spirit of God" are defined by Christ as God's Son who "gave himself" for God's people. The Spirit of God is "the Spirit of his Son" (Gal. 4:6), in Paul's thought, and that Spirit seeks human reciprocity with God's and Christ's self-sacrificial love. Such reciprocity is co-sacrificial in the power of divine love, involving obedient humans in Christ's self-sacrifice for God. Paul thinks of it as a human partnership with God and Christ in redemptive self-sacrifice, in dying with Christ. His proposed reciprocity thus includes human participation, or sharing, in such self-sacrifice

Luke T. Johnson has observed the kind of reciprocal exchange at work in Paul's understanding in 2 Corinthians of living to God.

> Paul sees God's work of reconciliation in Christ as an exchange. Christ died so that others might live (4:13–15). He became sin so that others might become righteous (5:21). He became poor so that others might become rich (8:9). Paul therefore sees the ministry of reconciliation as involving the same self-emptying for the sake of others. The apostle carries about the death of Jesus so that others might live (4:7–12). He makes himself foolish so that others might become wise with the mind of Christ (11:16–12:13). Paul and the Corinthians are called ... to share in God's work of reconciliation in the world.[36]

Prior to Johnson, Morna Hooker had referred to this kind of exchange in Paul's thought as "interchange," as Chapter 1 indicated. I have recommended, however, talk of "reciprocal self-sacrifice" between God in Christ, at the origin, and the followers of Christ, in the aftermath.

My proposed talk of self-sacrifice follows Paul's own characterization in terms of sacrificing oneself to God in response to God's redemptive mercy in Christ (Rom. 12:1, 15:16, Phil. 2:17). This kind of reciprocity, in attitude and in action, is at the center of Paul's understanding of "living to God," rather than to the Mosaic law, or to any other alternative. Faith in God as including dying with Christ, according to Paul, cannot be separated from such reciprocal self-sacrifice. It is God's approved means for receiving a life of divine righteousness, the kind of righteousness that "makes alive," or "gives life," with divine power. This is the same interpersonal power that

---

[36] Luke T. Johnson, "Reconciliation in the New Testament," in Johnson, *The Living Gospel* (London: Continuum, 2004), p. 81.

Paul sees in his good news as "the power of God for salvation to everyone who has faith, to the Jew first and also to the Greek" (Rom. 1:16). In this good news, Paul finds, "the righteousness of God is revealed through faith for faith" (Rom. 1:17). It follows that Christlike self-sacrifice for the good of others represents God's distinctive moral character of righteousness. It is, in Paul's thinking, God's redemptive signature.

Divine righteousness, according to Paul, is not produced, constituted, or earned by human power or merit. God alone produces, constitutes, and supplies it, just as only God supplies God's Spirit for humans. Even so, human power (apart from merit) can and does figure in a person's receiving righteousness, or having righteousness credited to that person. So, God's crediting of righteousness to humans can and does depend on human actions, such as human trust of the kind central to faith in God, without corrupting divine righteousness. The human reception of divine righteousness is not to be confused with the divine righteousness on offer. Even so, how are we to test Paul's bold message of divine redemption in righteous self-sacrifice? How are we to assess for its truth or falsity? We turn, finally, to that urgent matter.

6 Assessing God's Gambit in Self-Sacrifice

> Test everything; hold fast to what is good.
>
> 1 Thessalonians 5:21

Paul's gospel of divine self-sacrifice may seem promising to some people, but it also may seem too good to be true, even a fairy tale, to other people. So, we need a reality check for it, and Paul's injunction to "test everything," including ourselves (2 Cor. 13:5), lends support to this important cause. We shall identify Paul's approach to the needed testing and thereby clarify the foundations of his perspective on human knowledge of God. His perspective shows remarkable insight regarding a complex topic, but it has not received the attention it merits. This chapter aims to correct that deficiency.

We shall see that Paul's message of divine self-sacrifice rests on resources needed to commend that message as not just helpful but also true. According to this chapter, Paul's message of self-sacrifice in Romans 12:1–2 itself holds the key to suitable assessment of his good news. A key consideration is that suitably apprehending divine righteousness in self-sacrifice will confirm God's reality and redemptive will. Such apprehending enables one to experience firsthand the divine self-sacrifice in one's own life, with its distinctive power to obey God. There is no circularity here, because the relevant experience is not the same as a message of divine self-sacrifice, but it can be a truth indicator, and thus evidence, for such a message.

GOD'S GAMBIT IN REDEMPTION

Paul's gospel of divine self-sacrifice assumes that God takes a risk for something good: the righteous redemption of humans. A gambit often includes, as in chess, a sacrifice for the sake of something good, and God's self-sacrifice in Christ for redemption fits this model. The risk for God is human rejection of the redemptive self-sacrifice, including God's plan for divine–human reconciliation. This is a risk of harm, including self-harm, done voluntarily by hearers of Paul's message, resulting in frustration and suffering for God. God undertakes that risk to allow for people to receive the good news voluntarily and thereby to enter into righteous life with God. The results of the good news are, of course, mixed among humans, and Paul was painfully aware of this, especially in relation to many fellow Jews.

Paul acknowledges, as Chapter 5 showed, the voluntary role for humans in responding to his message of redemption. One lesson was that God sets the standard for divine approval, without causing the way humans respond to that standard. They are responsible agents in this area, and they can frustrate God's redemptive plan for all people to be reconciled to God. Humans can say no to the divine offer of redemption by opposing or ignoring God, according to Paul, and they sometimes do, leaving God frustrated. So, God's ideal for the outcome of redemption is not always satisfied. The success of some divine plans is thus at the mercy of humans. This is part of the price paid, including by God, for having responsible humans with voluntary decisions.

Some people object that the price paid for God's gambit is too high. It leaves us with a world terribly mixed with bad and good, including in human response to divine redemption. Humans pay a price too high, and so does God, according to the objection. If God did not have the gambit, however, many people would doubt that God is good. God could eliminate the gambit either by doing nothing for the sake of human redemption or by replacing human agency in redemption with a dominating divine will that causes human responses. The former option would invite an understandable charge of moral failure in divine indifference. The latter option would attract the claim that God has undermined human agency with the overwhelming divine will, thereby blocking responsible humans as candidates for redemption. God, in that option, takes on a monopoly in the domain of volitional power and responsibility, and humans lose their voluntary agency regarding their response to God. So, the two alternatives to God's gambit seem not to be improvements for God's moral standing in redemption.

God's gambit in redemption is not the source for a theodicy that fully explains God's allowing terrible evil in response to divine redemption. Paul is forthright about this, stressing human inability now to give a full explanation of God's ways in redemption. He proclaims, in response to God's redemptive plan: "O the depth of the riches and wisdom and knowledge of God! How unsearchable are his judgments and how inscrutable his ways!" (Rom. 11:33).

Paul affirms of God's ways of relating to humans that we "know only in part," as if "seeing in a mirror, dimly" (1 Cor. 13:12). He does not expect humans to be able to explain fully God's purposes in allowing evil, even terrifying evil. In this regard, Paul concurs with the main lesson of the book of Job. This lesson includes the view that human knowledge of God does not depend on our having a full explanatory theodicy for God's ways.[1] We shall consider the latter view in Paul's thought.

REDEMPTIVE INTERPERSONAL KNOWING

Paul favors a pneumatic epistemology that gives a central role to the Spirit of God in human knowledge of God. It is a pneumatic wisdom epistemology, because it gives a key role to a special kind of wisdom, linked to Jesus Christ, in human knowledge of God. The Spirit and the wisdom in question are, in Paul's perspective, the Spirit and the wisdom of Jesus Christ. So, Paul's approach to knowing God is centrally Christological, owing to its role for Jesus Christ. In addition, it is grace-based, because it portrays God as relating to humans in terms of an undeserved gift, in a manner contrary to human earning of divine

---

[1] For a different approach to theodicy, independent of an intended full explanation, see Paul K. Moser, "Theodicy Incarnate: Divine Self-Justification," *Expository Times* 133, no. 5 (2022), 192–200.

favor. Cognitive grace, we shall see, thus figures in Paul's account of knowing God.

Paul acknowledges the God of Isaiah in the area of human knowing. That God brings judgment on humans, even in their knowing, for the sake of their redemption. Paul draws from the book of Isaiah in his following statement about knowing God:

> It is written, "I will destroy the wisdom of the wise, and the discernment of the discerning I will thwart." Where is the one who is wise? Where is the scribe? Where is the debater of this age? Has not God made foolish the wisdom of the world? For since, in the wisdom of God, the world did not know God through [its] wisdom, God decided, through the foolishness of our proclamation, to save those who believe.
>
> *(1 Cor. 1:19–21; cf. Isa. 29:14)*

This quotation represents Paul's view that "in the wisdom of God, the world did not know God through [its] wisdom." We may take this view to imply that humans do not come to know God just by their own resources, including their own thinking, reasoning, and explaining. Human knowers, according to Paul, are not impartial inquirers, at least relative to God's reality. They are alienated from God in their thinking and in their willing, and they often suppress the truth on offer from and about God (Rom. 1:18, 3:9–19; cf. 1 Cor. 2:14). As a result, they are not well-positioned to know God on their own, contrary to a common human attitude.

How are humans able to know God, if not on their own? Paul's answer: "No one comprehends what is truly God's except the Spirit of God. Now we have received not the spirit of the world, but the Spirit that is from God, so that we may [know (εἰδῶμεν) the things] bestowed on us by God" (1 Cor. 2:11–12; cf. 1 Cor. 2:14). Knowing God comes courtesy of God's self-revealing Spirit, not from self-sufficient human resources. With this theme, Paul goes against the grain of much traditional epistemology. Evidence of God, according to Paul, is one of the things "bestowed on us by God," so long as we are suitably cooperative toward God.

We can distinguish knowing that God exists and knowing God. The latter personal knowledge has causal, interactive directness relative to God that is logically unnecessary for the former merely factual knowledge. Such personal knowledge arises from person-to-person knowing where personal acquaintance or encounter occurs. It includes the acquaintance of one personal will with another personal will. Knowing God may entail knowing that God exists, but it does not follow that God values or supplies factual knowledge alone (e.g., knowledge that God exists). The latter knowledge is not necessarily redemptive, or salvific, for humans, because we can have it while hating God and deliberately opposing God and redemption by God. For instance, in the New Testament Gospels, demons manifest knowledge that Jesus is the Son of God but with opposition to him.

Paul focuses on knowledge of God that is redemptively valuable for human salvation by God. Such knowledge brings one into a filial relation of (deepening) reconciliation to God, whereby one becomes volitionally cooperative with God. Paul expresses such knowing in terms of "being known by God," and he links it directly to "loving God" (1 Cor. 8:3; cf. Gal. 4:9). He contrasts such knowing with the ordinary kind of factual knowing, of which he says: "Knowledge puffs up, but love builds up" (1 Cor. 8:1). So, knowing God redemptively does not promote harmful pride that sometimes accompanies human factual knowing.

Paul, as we noted, expresses a strategy for his ministry to the Corinthian Christians, as follows: "My speech and my proclamation were not with plausible words of wisdom, but with a demonstration of the Spirit and of power, so that your faith might rest not on human wisdom but on the power of God" (1 Cor. 2:4–5). Paul's idea of human faith in God "resting on the power of God" is evidential and not just psychological. The latter power is a truth indicator of what is believed. It concerns the kind of evidence, or truth indicator, that supports the content of such faith, and this evidence, according to

Paul, has its source in God's distinctive power. The latter source is no mere claim, belief, or argument; it includes features of God's moral character, such as divine righteous love, including self-sacrificial love.

Paul characterizes redemptive knowing in Christological terms, as being directed toward "the glory of God in the face of Jesus Christ." He writes: "It is the God who said, 'Let light shine out of darkness', who has shone in our hearts to give the light of the knowledge of the glory of God in the face of Jesus Christ" (2 Cor. 4:6). Paul has in mind an analogy between creation and re-creation: God the Creator re-creates cooperative persons by shining a life-giving light into their hearts through Christ. This lesson fits with Paul's view of knowing Christ: "Even though we once knew Christ from a human point of view, we know him no longer in that way. So if anyone is in Christ, there is a new creation: everything old has passed away; see, everything has become new!" (2 Cor. 5:16–17). Knowing Christ from a divine point of view includes becoming a "new creation," after the image of Christ, with due human cooperation.

Paul presents his epistemology of God from a divine re-creation point of view rather than a merely human point of view. This divine point of view gives a central evidential role to the unique divine power of self-sacrificial love exemplified in Jesus Christ. It does not rest with mundane evidence that omits the supernatural power manifested by God in Christ. Instead, it gives a central role to the kind of supernatural evidence in divine self-manifestation through Christ crucified and risen.

Paul characterizes "knowing Christ" for the Christians at Philippi:

> I regard everything as loss because of the surpassing value of knowing Christ Jesus my Lord. For his sake I have suffered the loss of all things, and I regard them as rubbish, in order that I may gain Christ and be found in him, not having a righteousness of my own that comes from the law, but one that comes through faith in Christ, the righteousness from God based on faith. I want to know

Christ and the power of his resurrection and the sharing of his
sufferings by becoming like him in his death.

(Phil. 3:8–10)

Paul is not thinking of mere knowledge that Christ exists. He is concerned instead with knowing Christ as Lord, even as *his* Lord, where such knowing bears authoritatively on the direction and the mode of everything in his life. It includes, at its center, knowledge of "the power" of the crucified Christ's resurrection.

Paul refuses to ignore the death of Christ that called for his resurrection by God in vindication. For the sake of knowing Christ, Paul desires "the sharing of his sufferings by becoming like him in his death." This is knowing Christ via *kenōsis*, the "loss" or letting go of all other things as a priority. It includes the emptying of one's own anti-God desires in order to obey God's will, after the example of the crucified Christ himself (Phil. 2:6–8; cf. Mk. 14:36). Redemptive filial knowledge of God is kenotic in just this cruciform, Christ-shaped manner, after the model set by Jesus in Gethsemane.

AGAPĒ IN KNOWING

What is the "light" of re-creation that God shines into the hearts of cooperative people to give them knowledge of the glory of God in the face of Christ and thereby to make them a new creation? To put the question in different terms from Paul: What is the "power of Christ's resurrection" that Paul is willingly dying (literally) to know? He offers his most straightforward answer as follows: "Hope [in God] does not disappoint us, because God's love has been poured into our hearts through the Holy Spirit that has been given to us" (Rom. 5:5; cf. 2 Cor. 1:22, 5:5; Rom. 8:23). Paul, I have suggested, would say the same of faith in God and of knowing God redemptively.

God, according to Paul, has done something cognitively important in relation to people cooperative toward God. God has supplied a ground, with distinctive evidence, for their hope and faith in God and their knowing God redemptively. This divine intervention in human experience includes God's self-presenting divine *agapē* in human hearts through the Spirit of God given to cooperative people. As a result, the humans in question are not disappointed, evidentially or psychologically, in their hoping and trusting in God. This is, in Paul's thinking, an important feature of the "light" of re-creation and "the power of resurrection" as coming from God's Spirit who presents divine *agapē* to human hearts.

God's *agapē* presented to human hearts is God's self-sacrificial righteous will to bring about what is morally and spiritually best for cooperative humans. Humans can refuse to cooperate with God and thereby block the transforming power of this *agapē* for themselves, because God does not coerce human wills regarding divine redemption (Rom. 10:21). Alternatively, when humans cooperatively receive divine *agapē*, in Paul's epistemology, they are transformed toward the moral and spiritual character of God in Christ (Rom. 12:1–2; cf. Eph. 4:21–23). They then undergo a change that reciprocates divine self-sacrificial love.

The Epistle to the Colossians, perhaps written by a close associate of Paul, suggests that sharing in divine *agapē* can lead to deepening knowledge of Christ: "I want their hearts to be encouraged and united in love, so that they may have all the riches of assured understanding and have the knowledge [ἐπίγνωσιν] of God's mystery, that is, Christ himself, in whom are hidden all the treasures of wisdom and knowledge [γνώσεως]" (Col. 2:2–3). He then adds that "I am saying this so that no one may deceive you with plausible arguments [πιθανολογίᾳ]" (Col. 2:4). He thus suggests that *agapē*-based redemptive knowledge of Christ is more basic and secure than plausible arguments or claims. This is an important feature of Paul's view of the foundational role of experienced divine *agapē* in knowing Christ and God.

Agapē-based redemptive knowledge of Christ, according to Paul, requires cooperatively responding to the intervention of God's *agapē*-bearing Spirit. Such responding can result in one's finding God's self-sacrificial will experienced within oneself, however imperfectly. This will includes God's will to love others sacrificially, even enemies of oneself and God (Rom. 12:14–21). We can be surprised by the new reality of divine *agapē* within ourselves, as it marks a noticeable change from our previous attitudes and inclinations toward others, particularly toward our enemies. This reality underwrites Paul's talk of "new creation" in one's coming to know Christ from a divine, Christlike point of view. Such redemptive knowing is not captured by factual knowledge that something is the case.

A unique, identifying feature of guided divine goodness and grounded assurance, in Paul's thinking, is God's self-presentation of enemy-love to humans. Paul taught that God's love for us was at work before we welcomed God, even while we were "ungodly" and "enemies" of God (Rom. 5:6, 10). God's guided goodness thus comes to enemies of God, who have no claim to merit it (cf. Rom. 4:2–4). Jesus worked with a similar assumption, and he regarded God's enemy-love as integral to God and being children of God: "You have heard that it was said, 'You shall love your neighbor and hate your enemy.' But I say to you, Love your enemies and pray for those who persecute you, so that you may be children of your Father in heaven; for he makes his sun rise on the evil and on the good, and sends rain on the righteous and on the unrighteous" (Matt. 5:43–45; cf. Luke 6:35–36). Enemy-love, according to Jesus, is God's unique signature or trademark, and Paul suggests a similar status for it (Rom. 12:9–10, 20–21; cf. Rom. 5:6, 10).

We have emphasized Paul's idea of divine love being poured by God's Spirit into the hearts of receptive people. This love includes enemy-love as the signature divine love, setting it apart from typical human love and grounding assurance of God's goodness for humans. As a matter of empirical fact, ordinary humans lack proficiency with enemy-love, even while endorsing it, and the same is true of many traditional claimants to the title "God." Jesus, however, portrayed God as distinctive in enemy-love, and we should be open to God's intervening Spirit to self-manifest divine love accordingly. When we have such love directed at us, at least at the start, it includes enemy-love, as suggested by Paul.

Divine enemy-love can prompt people to undergo change from being enemies of God to being faithful children of God. They must cooperate with God's moral character and will, but the basic motivating power is divine love of enemies. Paul thus remarks, as one who previously had opposed God's Messiah: "The life I now live in the flesh I live by faith in the Son of God, who loved me and gave himself for me" (Gal. 2:20). Such divine love reoriented, and guided, not only Paul's theology but also his life, particularly toward the Gentiles.

Applying his pneumatic epistemology, Paul writes to the Roman Christians: "You have received a spirit of adoption. When we cry 'Abba! Father!' it is that very Spirit bearing witness with our spirit that we are children of God" (Rom. 8:15–16; cf. Gal. 4:6–7; 2 Cor. 1:21–2). Paul's mention of adoption and of God's fatherhood suggests that he has filial knowledge in mind, whereby one comes to know God as one's authoritative and caring Father. So, the Spirit's witness to cooperative people indicates their being beloved children of God. As a result, God's Spirit prompts cooperative people to "cry 'Abba! Father!'" Paul's use of the Aramaic word "Abba" in a Greek epistle recalls the Aramaic reference by Jesus to God as Father, including in Gethsemane. Jesus serves as the perfect model for the desired filial relationship to God.

We have noted that the witness of God's Spirit, in Paul's perspective, calls for a response of reciprocal *kenōsis* from God's children. The response is to reflect the self-sacrificial obedience to God manifested by Jesus in Gethsemane and in his crucifixion (Phil. 2:5–8). Paul's pneumatic epistemology, then, comes with a robust moral and spiritual challenge to be conformed to the self-sacrificial character of Jesus. The *agapē* that underwrites redemptive filial knowledge of God in Christ mirrors, and emerges from, the self-sacrificial character of Jesus, which images the spiritual and moral character of God.

Romans 8:15–16 suggests a role for filial prayer in receiving divine assurance, including evidence of God, directly from God. So, even young children and others with little education can enter God's kingdom with well-grounded conviction, owing to their receiving the undeserved gift of God's intervening Spirit. Paul does not assume, however, that either educated or uneducated people can supply evidence on their own that will silence skeptics regarding God. God's intervening Spirit, in Paul's epistemology, provides the ultimate evidence of God's reality and moral character, and that Spirit does so with an inward challenge to the human will to yield to God's self-sacrificial righteous will. This evidence must be received from a first-person perspective on that evidence, and therefore it does not operate just by proxy.

As self-authenticating, Paul's God supplies the needed evidence for humans via divine self-manifestation, and God does this at the opportune divine time for cooperative people. In this vein, Paul attributes the following statement to God: "I have shown myself to those who did not ask for me" (Rom. 10:20). God's distinctive self-manifestation with righteous *agapē* toward humans has a central place in Paul's epistemology, but it need not be discursive or propositional. It can be nondiscursively experiential, akin, for instance, to one's being presented *de re* with an experienced quality of human caring toward oneself. Paul follows a Hebraic tradition of God's self-authentication via self-manifestation to humans (Isa. 45:22–23; Gen. 22:16–17; cf. Heb. 6:13–14). He thus differs from proponents of a largely discursive or rationalist approach to evidence of divine reality.

The evidence from divine self-manifestation, according to Paul, is not wedded to a public theophany or to any visible marker from God. The divine omission of visible markers is understandable if God is a Spirit (and not a visible body) set on morally robust interpersonal relations between God and humans. Such relations do not require visible markers for their existence or proliferation. John's Gospel has Jesus hint at this idea in his remark to Thomas: "Have you believed because you have seen [ἑωρακάς] me? Blessed are those who have not seen [ἰδόντες] and yet have come to believe" (John 20:29; cf. Matt. 16:17). As suggested previously, Paul remarks in a similar vein: "We look not at what can be seen [βλεπόμενα] but at what cannot be seen; for what can be seen is temporary, but what cannot be seen is eternal" (2 Cor. 4:16–18; cf. Rom. 8:24–25). Paul thus highlights the requirement of the things of God being "spiritually discerned [πνευματικῶς ἀνακρίνεται]" (1 Cor. 2:14), and this includes yielding, cooperatively, to God's Spirit in action. Visible markers may get our attention at times, but they also can distract us from the divine Spirit morally at work among us and within us. Their value is thus preliminary at best, including in public settings.

In his epistemology, Paul is an evidentialist and an experiential foundationalist about redemptive human knowledge of God. In his view, such knowledge requires evidence and is based ultimately on experiential foundations of divine intervention that are not beliefs but can be evidential support for some theological beliefs. These foundations include God's self-manifesting God's character to humans, such as divine righteous love. As self-authenticating for humans, God is no mere idea or theory, in Paul's thinking. Instead, God is a powerful intentional agent who can and does produce evidence for cooperative humans by intervening, with self-manifestation of divine goodness, in their experiences and lives. The latter goodness is goal-directed in aiming to guide people to (deeper) reconciliation with God, for the ultimate good of all concerned.

The central role for a personal divine Spirit in Paul's epistemology cannot be reduced to a role for a psychological faculty or process. Paul's epistemology is thus foreign to secular epistemology and even to any philosophy of religion or philosophical theology that neglects the cognitive or evidential role of God's Spirit. In addition to being pneumatic, it is an incarnational epistemology, because it assigns a central cognitive role to God's Spirit dwelling in humans, in such a way that they become a temple of God's Spirit. So, Paul asks the Corinthian Christians: "Do you not know that your body is a temple of the Holy Spirit within you, which you have from God, and that you are not your own?" (1 Cor. 6:19). God's Spirit thus works within people who are cooperative toward God, thus providing an indwelling, incarnational witness to God's reality and character. (See Chapter 3 on the larger context of this position.)

In Paul's incarnational epistemology, humans themselves can become personifying evidence of God's reality, owing to their receiving and manifesting the divine features of the inward Spirit of God. Such evidence stems from cooperative human acquaintance with God that enables humans to become agents who receive and reflect, if imperfectly, God's presence and moral character for others. The characteristic evidence of God's reality and moral character becomes increasingly available and salient to a person as that person becomes increasingly willing to be personifying evidence of God's reality. Such willingness allows God's power of *agapē* to come to its intended fruition in divine–human cooperation.

Paul's good news from God entails that followers of Jesus are privileged to reflect the glory and thus the reality of God as perfectly imaged in Jesus. Paul remarks: "All of us, with unveiled faces, seeing the glory of the Lord as though reflected in a mirror, are being transformed into the same image from one degree of glory to another; for this comes from the Lord, the Spirit" (2 Cor. 3:18). Humans thus become a "letter of Christ" (2 Cor. 3:3). The idea of the "image of God" discernible in humans cooperative toward God plays an important role in Paul's incarnational epistemology.

Paul's epistemology, as suggested, is grace-based, in that firsthand knowledge of God is a direct undeserved gift of God's Spirit that cannot be separated from the gift-giver. This is cognitive grace, because it includes a powerful cognitive gift and a personal evidential ground that displace any human need for intellectual earning or meriting from God. Paul acknowledges an offer of a freely given presence of God's transforming Spirit, who seeks cooperative fellowship with humans.

Humans must appropriate the cognitive gift and its evidential ground in personal struggles, given the human condition of selfishness, including selfish fear and pride. We may think of these as Gethsemane struggles, after the model of Jesus in Gethsemane, because human wills undergo challenges from God's Spirit to conform to God's righteous self-sacrificial will. The cognitive grace of God's intervening Spirit does not depend on philosophical sophistication, in Paul's approach; instead, it is an undeserved gift extended to all cooperative people. This gift can be an object of philosophical theory, but its reality and its value do not rely on such theory.

Offering lasting new life and fellowship with God, the gift under consideration is directly challenging toward selfish and willful human ways that resist God. This undeserved gift includes God as the (objective) cognitive ground of foundational beliefs that God is real and good. The divine aim of cognitive grace is twofold: that human faith in God have its ultimate cognitive ground not in human wisdom but rather in the power of God (1 Cor. 2:4–5) and that this ground provide what humans vitally need: lasting new life and fellowship in God's presence. Cognitive grace, then, aims to be redemptive for humans, not merely cognitive. It thus differs from typical secular understandings of cognition.

RIGHTEOUSNESS IN SPIRITUAL WISDOM

We should note a widely neglected parallel between Paul's view of knowing God and his understanding of righteousness or justification as a redemptive gift. Paul's theological epistemology owes its main features to the divine redemption of humans by grace that proceeds "through righteousness" (Rom. 5:21). The redemption of humans, according to Paul, entails their being reconciled to God via a self-manifestation of God's spiritual and moral character in Jesus Christ. Paul remarks, as noted: "In Christ God was reconciling the world to himself, not counting their trespasses against them, and entrusting the message of reconciliation to us" (2 Cor. 5:19).

Jesus is God's representative victim of human opposition who offers divine forgiveness and fellowship, instead of condemnation, to wayward humans. We may call this the divine manifest-offering approach to redemption, in line with Romans 3:21–26 (mentioning divine "manifestation" repeatedly). God's moral character of righteous and forgiving love is made manifest in Jesus Christ, and life-giving fellowship with God is offered self-sacrificially in Jesus Christ as an undeserved gift, in keeping with God's gracious character. As a result, divine love is also enacted toward humans.

The divine redemptive gift for humans is anchored in the forgiveness offered and manifested via God's self-giving sacrifice in Jesus Christ and God's resurrection vindication of Jesus as Lord and giver of God's Spirit. The manifestation of God's character in Jesus reveals a God who, in self-sacrifice, offers forgiveness and lasting fellowship to humans for their redemption as reconciled righteous life with God. That manifestation does not depend on human merit or approval.

The sacrificial death of Jesus by itself cannot bring about divine–human reconciliation, but it does aim to provide God's means of implementing redemption via divine manifestation and offering. Actual divine–human reconciliation requires that humans receive, or appropriate, the manifest offering of forgiveness and fellowship by means of grounded faith, including trust, in God. The latter faith includes dying with Christ, in reciprocity toward God's sacrifice of atonement in Christ. This kind of cooperative human response to God figures centrally in the divine redemptive plan outlined by Paul.

Jesus Christ, according to Paul, came from God to identify with humans in their weakness and despair, in order to offer them reconciled life with God (1 Thess. 5:9–10). Jesus represents God in righteous and merciful *agapē*, for the sake of reconciling humans to God (Rom. 5:6–8). He also represents humans to God in his obedience to God on their behalf (Rom. 5:17–19). As representative for God and humans, Jesus offers a personal bridge between them. He seeks to reconcile humans to God with the undeserved gift of lasting life of fellowship anchored in sacrificial righteous *agapē* as the power of God's Spirit. This good news announced by Paul is inherently theological and Christological and hence cannot be reduced to principles of morality. So, Paul is no mere moralist, and his gospel of divine self-sacrifice is no mere moralism.

Jesus Christ's yielding to death on the cross, according to Paul, was commanded of him by God. It manifests how far he and God will go to offer redemption to wayward humans (Rom. 3:25; 1 Cor. 5:7; Phil. 2:8; cf. Mark 14:23–24). In keeping with God's plan, Jesus sacrifices his life, out of God's self-sacrificial *agapē*, to manifest that God mercifully and righteously loves humans to the fullest extent. Jesus thereby offers humans redemption as the gift of unearned forgiveness, fellowship, and membership in God's family via reception of God's Spirit (Rom. 5:8, 8:38–39). This is the center of the good news of divine redemption for humans that Paul announces on the basis of supporting evidence from God's Spirit.

The cross of Jesus Christ, in Paul's message, is the definitive representative place where God mercifully judges and forgives human resistance to God (without condemning or judging Jesus). So, Paul reports to the Corinthian Christians: "When I came to you, brothers and sisters, I did not come proclaiming the mystery of God to you in lofty words or wisdom. For I decided to know nothing among you except Jesus Christ, and him crucified" (1 Cor. 2:1–2; cf. 1 Cor. 1:23; Gal. 6:14). We have noted that Paul has the risen Christ in mind and that he refrains from claiming that God punished Jesus on the cross (Gal. 3:13, citing a version of Deut. 21:23).

According to Paul, God sent Jesus into the world to undergo suffering and death from oppositional humans, and God mercifully deems his full obedience adequate for dealing righteously with human resistance to God. In this respect, Jesus as representative of God and humans enables God to be "just and the justifier" in the divine reconciliation of humans (Rom. 3:26). In manifesting and offering divine forgiveness and fellowship, Jesus offers an alternative to selfish fear, condemnation, shame, and guilt among humans toward God (Rom. 8:1).

The central divine motive behind the crucifixion of Jesus is (the enactment and manifestation of) God's righteous *agapē* for humans. Paul links God's righteousness as justification with God's *agapē*, as follows: "God manifests his own *agapē* for us in that while we were yet sinners, Christ died for us .... Since we have now been justified by his blood, how much more shall we be saved by him from the wrath [of God] . . . . [W]hile we were enemies [of God], we were reconciled to God through the death of his Son" (Rom. 5:8–10, my trans.). God thus takes the initiative and the means through Jesus Christ in offering an undeserved gift of divine–human reconciliation for human redemption. The self-sacrificial death of Jesus, as noted, enacts and manifests forgiving *agapē* and righteousness from God, and such divine *agapē* is morally significant in divine righteousness. Paul has this kind of morally robust *agapē* in mind when he makes his significant claim in Romans 5:5 about the evidential basis of hope and faith in God.

Mere forgiveness of humans by God would not adequately counter the wrongdoing that calls for forgiveness. Human neglect or opposition toward the divine authority needed for a lasting good life underlies the wrongdoing that produces alienation from God (Rom. 1:21, 28). In identifying and judging the basis of human wrongdoing, God upholds divine moral integrity in the redemption of humans and does not condone evil. Through the self-sacrifice of Jesus, God meets the standard of righteous *agapē* for humans, when they could not and would not. God then offers this gift of righteousness in Jesus to humans, as God's sacrificial Passover lamb for them (1 Cor. 5:7). On this basis, Paul announces to the Corinthian Christians: "You were bought with a price; therefore glorify God in your body" (1 Cor. 6:20; cf. 1 Cor. 7:23).

By God's standard, the redemptive gift on offer is to be received by faith in God and Jesus, which includes an attitude of obedience toward them. By divine prerogative, God credits such faith as righteousness. Otherwise, the human prospect for meeting the standard of divine righteous *agapē*, and for redemption by that standard, would be bleak at best. So, it is crucial that God take a gracious initiative.

In explaining and proclaiming the divine redemption of humans, Paul offers a crucial distinction between gift-righteousness from God for cooperative humans and humanly earned righteousness by means of, for instance, the Mosaic law (Phil. 3:9; Rom. 3:21–26; 9:30–32, 10:3–4; Gal. 3:11–12). Given their failure by the divine standard of righteous *agapē*, humans are not in a position to earn a right relationship with God (Rom. 3:10–20, 4:2–4). So, if this right relationship is to become actual, it must come from something other than human earning. The needed alternative is the divine gift of righteous redemption by grace offered to undeserving humans through faith in God and Christ.

Wayward humans need to struggle to receive or appropriate the divine gift through the rigors of faith (including trust) and obedience toward God. This struggle, in Paul's thought, does not include the human earning or meriting of God's approval. Human acts of obedience to God, as Chapter 3 noted, are not identical with "works" of earning before God, despite widespread confusions in this area. We have noted that in Romans Paul connects "works" with the paying of a debt of approval by God, as follows: "To one who works, wages are not reckoned as a gift but as something due" (Rom 4:4). Such "works" are incompatible with a divine gift and hence with God's redemptive grace (Rom. 11:6). They should not be confused with acts of obedience to God that can lead, in Paul's perspective, to righteousness (Rom. 6:16). Even many in national Israel, according to Paul, mistakenly pursued God's righteousness by works rather than as a gift (Rom. 9:30–32, 10:1–4). They thus fell short of the maturity of God's distinctive wisdom (Phil. 3:8–15).

Facing moral problems in the church at Corinth, Paul contrasts "human" wisdom with "God's wisdom, secret and hidden, which God decreed before the ages for our glory" (1 Cor. 2:5, 7). A key difference between the two is that God's wisdom has the divine power, including the power of self-sacrificial *agapē*, to give a lasting good life with God to cooperative humans, whereas human wisdom does not. Only God's wisdom can empower human redemption as a lasting good life with God and others. Such wisdom includes the kind of redemptive filial knowledge of God that is central to Paul's theological epistemology.

Paul emphasizes to the Corinthian Christians the role of their weakness and even impotence in relation to God's power: "We have this treasure [of redemption from God] in clay jars, so that it may be made clear that this extraordinary power belongs to God and does not come from us" (2 Cor. 4:7). The power and wisdom needed by humans for a lasting good life must come from God, because God alone has such power and wisdom. The Epistle to the Colossians describes the relevant power and wisdom: "We have not ceased praying for you and asking that you may be filled with the knowledge of God's will in all spiritual wisdom and understanding, so that you may lead lives worthy of the Lord, fully pleasing to him, as you bear fruit in every good work and as you grow in the knowledge of God. May you be made strong [=empowered] with all the strength [=power] that comes from his glorious power, and may you be prepared to endure everything with patience, while joyfully giving thanks to the Father" (Col. 1:9–12).

The Epistle to the Colossians represents Paul as praying for the Christians at Colossae that they have "knowledge of God's will in all spiritual wisdom." Such knowledge goes beyond mere knowledge that God exists; it figures in redemptive filial knowledge of God. Similarly, the relevant "spiritual wisdom" is not mere knowledge that a claim is true. Instead, it is spirited in its being empowered and guided by God's Spirit. It is directed toward "lead[ing] lives worthy of the Lord, fully pleasing to him," thus involving a mode of living and not just a mode of thinking, believing, or factual knowing. It welcomes God's power for the sake of joyfully and gratefully enduring the difficulties of human life with patience. This is the power to endure life while honoring and thanking God, come what may, even in the face of life's temptation to give up in its hardships (2 Cor. 1:8–11). Paul's Corinthian correspondence indicates that he would agree with the present theme from the Epistle to the Colossians.

We now have an important contrast between redemptive filial knowledge and spiritual wisdom regarding God, on the one hand, and mere factual knowledge and any kind of human wisdom, on the other hand. Redemptive filial knowledge and spiritual wisdom regarding God welcome God's power, including the power of righteous *agapē*, for the sake of living a lasting good life, pleasing to God (or "worthy of the Lord"). Mere factual knowledge that I cannot save myself by God's standard of righteous *agapē* does not amount to redemptive filial knowledge of God. Such factual knowledge can be accompanied by an oppositional volitional attitude toward God. I still could hate God and hate that I cannot save myself by God's standard, perhaps because I desire full autonomy and an option of redeeming myself, without any divine help.

The reality that I cannot save myself by God's perfectly righteous standard is not hateworthy, according to Paul, but is actually good. By this standard, in hating my inadequacy, I would hate something good for my redemption, and this would oppose the kind of redemptive knowledge and spiritual wisdom under consideration. Even a grudging or indifferent reception of something redemptively good would be a deficiency in redemptive knowledge and spiritual wisdom.

Redemptive knowledge and spiritual wisdom, unlike mere factual knowledge, must be volitionally attuned to what is redemptively good and welcoming of it when the opportunity arises. Such an involvement of the will indicates that we are not dealing with something merely intellectual. Redemptive knowledge and spiritual wisdom, then, are sensitive to human volition, and if human volition is distorted, human reception of such knowledge and wisdom can be difficult and even blocked. The volitional attitudes of a potential human recipient can resist redemptive knowledge and spiritual wisdom regarding God (Rom. 1:18, 21, 25).

Paul anchors redemptive knowledge and spiritual wisdom regarding God, not in an abstract principle or a Platonic Form, but in a personal agent who manifests God's power without defect. He refers to "Christ the power of God and the wisdom of God" (1 Cor. 1:24) and to "Christ Jesus who became for us wisdom from God ... and redemption" (1 Cor. 1:30). Paul identifies some features of Jesus Christ that constitute his being the power and the wisdom of God: "Christ Jesus, who, though he was in the form of God, did not regard equality with God as something to be exploited, but emptied himself, taking the form of a slave, being born in human likeness. And being found in human form, he humbled himself and became obedient to the point of death – even death on a cross" (Phil. 2:5–8).

A key feature is the willing conformity of Jesus to God's will, even when the result is self-sacrificial death (cf. Gal. 1:3–4, 2:20; Rom. 3:24–25, 4:24–25). The idea of Jesus's humble obedience to God captures this feature and differs from grudging obedience and even mere obedience. It ultimately welcomes God's perfect will, even if one is initially ambivalent and faces difficult consequences. This is the same obedience Jesus exemplified in Gethsemane (Mark 14:36). In his conformity to God's will, Jesus exemplified the power and wisdom of God as a human agent humbly and reverently cooperating with God on the basis of God's distinctive wisdom and power, including the power of self-sacrificial *agapē*. The attitude of Gethsemane and Calvary, then, becomes the attitude for properly receiving the gift of redemptive knowledge and spiritual wisdom from God. Such knowledge and wisdom stand in sharp contrast to the kind of natural theology some interpreters mistakenly assign to Paul.

TRADITIONAL NATURAL THEOLOGY OMITTED

Some interpreters read Romans 1 to suggest that Paul advances traditional natural theology. Paul's theological epistemology, however, contrasts sharply with traditional natural theology as a proposed avenue to knowledge of God. Unlike Paul's epistemology of redemptive knowledge, the arguments of traditional natural theology typically obscure the serious human need for divine cognitive grace. They usually cloud the importance for Paul's epistemology of God's personal Spirit taking the initiative to intervene in human experience, and of human turning, in volitional repentance, to cooperate with that intervention, in new life and fellowship with God.

The obscuring of relevant evidence arises from the focus of traditional natural theology on merely *de dicto* (propositional) arguments rather than on an experienced divine intervention *de re* in a human life. When we shift the focus from such speculative arguments to the personal intervention of God's Spirit, we consider a distinctive kind of personal, incarnational experience and evidence of God's reality. We then attend to a distinctive kind of intervening and goal-directed volitional pressure in human experience, such as in moral conscience, that can indicate the reality and presence of God's righteous Spirit.

Traditional natural theology suffers from undue attention to what we may call spectator evidence. Such evidence is volitionally neutral. It does not offer, for instance, a powerful volitional challenge to inquirers, on the basis of presented righteous *agapē*, to cooperate with God and thereby to become personifying evidence of God's reality. Traditional natural theology neglects authoritative evidence of God's reality that invites a human to cooperate with God's will and thereby to incarnate and reciprocate God's righteous *agapē* on offer. Given the prospect of such authoritative evidence from God in moral experience, one's commitment to remain volitionally neutral toward God's existence and will can hinder one from appropriating available evidence of God's existence through trust and obedience toward God.

Paul does not show any support for the arguments of traditional natural theology. Instead, he remarks as follows: "God ... has put his seal upon us and given us his Spirit in our hearts as a guarantee" (2 Cor. 1:21–22, RSV). Paul refers to the "God, who has given us the Spirit as a guarantee" (2 Cor. 5:5, RSV; cf. Eph. 1:13–14). The relevant notion of "guarantee" has an evidential component, signifying that God's Spirit indicates to us the reality and faithfulness of God. God's Spirit, in Paul's epistemology, does what no argument can. That Spirit, being intentional, leads cooperative inquirers to God and corresponding evidence of God's reality and redemptive presence (Rom. 8:14–16). Such intentional action is central to divine personhood but is not part of the natural world by itself.

One might *imagine* Paul saying that our guarantee of God's reality arises from arguments of natural theology involving: (a) the first cause or the ground of all contingent events; (b) the designer of order in the universe; (c) the fine-tuner of the physical universe; (d) the ground of agency, consciousness, or morality; or (e) the simplest explanatory postulate for a specified range of data. Paul nowhere says this, however, because he holds that God is self-authenticating via the self-manifestation of God's perfect moral character of righteous *agapē*.

We have noted that divine self-authentication, including the accompanying self-manifestation, comes from God's intervening Spirit, by whom God presents transforming divine *agapē* to the volitional centers of cooperative recipients. Paul thus has no need for the arguments of traditional natural theology. They are, in addition, dubious and impotent in ways that the intervening Spirit of God is not, as they fall short of indicating a God worthy of worship and trust.[2] They do not fit with Paul's understanding of redemptive knowledge or spiritual wisdom regarding God.

Many people have misunderstood Paul's remarks about God and creation in Romans 1. Nowhere does Paul say or imply that the created world by itself is evidence for a personal God worthy of worship. He does not claim or otherwise assume this in Romans 1. Paul claims that "God showed them" about God's reality via creation, but not via creation alone. His key remark is: "What can be known about God is plain to them, because God has shown it to them" (Rom. 1:19). We do not find a natural theological argument here or elsewhere in Paul. He is not giving an argument from design in Romans 1; he is simply reporting that God can and does self-manifest through nature (alone). It would be a different view, and an implausible one at that, to suggest that nature in itself reveals a personal God worthy of worship.

God must show people God's reality, if they are to know God redemptively. The elaborate natural universe does not do this by itself, as a "natural" source, even if God sometimes uses it as a medium for divine self-manifestation. That universe does not

---

[2] For elaboration, see Paul K. Moser, "Natural Theology: A Deflationary Approach," in *Natural Theology: Five Views*, eds. James K. Dew and R. P. Campbell (Grand Rapids, MI: Baker Academic, forthcoming).

exemplify God's morally unique character. So, natural theological arguments from nature alone will not deliver a personal God worthy of worship and trust. An analogy illustrates the point: When I call you on my cell phone, my phone by itself fails to give you evidence of me, as a personal agent. I myself, however, can use my phone (as a medium) to give you such evidence. Chapter 1 of Romans invites this distinction, in connection with Romans 1:19, even though most interpreters of Paul miss it.

The First Cause or the Designer of natural theology could be evil or nonpersonal, but Paul's God is not a genuine candidate for being evil or nonpersonal. So, Paul offers no inference from the imagined lesser god of natural theology to the God and Father of Jesus Christ. Careful reflection favors Paul's position here: It is highly doubtful that one can get to a personal God worthy of worship and trust from the merely natural premises of the traditional empirical arguments of natural theology. The problem is that one cannot thereby get to God's perfect personal and intentional moral character and thus to a God worthy of worship and trust, even if one can get to a lesser being, such as a mere causal source of a perceived effect or a design.[3] We would need to learn that God is the creator by God's *de re* testimony, after we learn of God's moral character in Gethsemane struggle with the intervening Spirit of God. We should understand Paul's theological epistemology, accordingly, as omitting traditional natural theology but being firmly evidentialist.

Paul's theological epistemology finds an evidential base for knowing God in human moral experience rather than in abstract theology. The relevant experience is marked by divine power, given the intervention of God's redemptive Spirit who manifests self-sacrificial righteousness. It does not depend, however, on human theological sophistication, and it therefore fits with the scope of

---

[3] Even if one could reason to a lesser being, the insurmountable problem would be how to reason from the existence of such a being to the existence of a God worthy of worship and trust. We have no basis for assuming success here.

Paul's gospel in extending to all people and not just to intellectuals. His gospel is, as suggested, available to anyone who is cooperative toward God's intervening Spirit.

SCANDAL OF SELF-SACRIFICE

Paul, we have noted, refers to "Christ the power of God and the wisdom of God" (1 Cor. 1:24) and to "Christ Jesus, who became for us wisdom from God" (1 Cor. 1:30). His view about divine power and wisdom entails personalism: the view they are inherently a personal, intentional agent and not just a body of information, rules, or guidelines. (1 Cor. 1:30). What does Paul mean in calling a person, the person Jesus Christ, "the wisdom of God"?

Marcus Dods has commented on Paul's view of wisdom from God in Christ:

> The very fact that it was a Person, not a system of philosophy, that Paul proclaimed was sufficient proof that he was not anxious to become the founder of a school or the head of a party. It was to another Person, not to himself, he directed the attention and faith of his hearers. And that which permanently distinguishes Christianity from all philosophies is that it presents to men, not a system of truth to be understood, but a Person to be relied upon. Christianity is not the bringing of new truth to us so much as the bringing of a new Person to us. The manifestation of God in Christ is in harmony with all truth; but we are not required to perceive and understand that harmony, but to believe in Christ.[4]

Paul's message of good news focuses on a person from God, God's unique Son, an intentional agent with intentional power from God aimed at human redemption.

In identifying the person of Christ with wisdom from God, Paul assigns intentional power to divine wisdom. He thereby contrasts it

---

[4] Marcus Dods, *The First Epistle to the Corinthians*, Expositor's Bible (London: Hodder and Stoughton, 1891), p. 53.

with the wisdom offered by humans, including the wisdom of philosophers (1 Cor. 1:20). The latter wisdom, with its focus on ideas and principles, is typically more convenient and less challenging for humans than wisdom anchored in a self-sacrificial intentional agent. Such an agent can probe more deeply in human experience and conscience than any mere idea or principle. This consideration may figure in the widespread avoidance of distinctly Christian wisdom among philosophers and others. It also may fit with Paul's idea of a human tendency to "suppress the truth" from God (Rom. 1:18).

Paul thinks of the person of Christ as God's wisdom for humans, because Christ, as an intentional agent, gives humans lasting good life from and with God. He exemplifies and offers the kind of life sought, at least in the abstract, by Socrates and Plato: life worth living and dying for. It is worth living and dying for, because it is life from and with God, the one who alone supplies and sustains lasting good life. No mere principle or idea could give humans lasting good life with God, because neither a principle nor an idea can give actual life to humans, even if it gives a notion or a theory of life.

Christ crucified, in Paul's understanding, links God with a stumbling block or scandal (σκάνδαλον) of "foolishness" and even "weakness" (1 Cor. 1:23, 25, 18). An underlying issue is this: What kind of God would allow and even have God's appointed and approved representative to undergo torture and death by crucifixion at the hands of humans? In that scenario, human power defeats divine power, and this evidently entails a God who is foolish and weak. God's approved agent, in typical human thinking, should not suffer and die under human power, because God is more powerful than any power from humans. Such thinking runs afoul of Paul's good news.

The Christian scandal of foolishness and weakness emerges not just from an event but primarily from a scandalous person, the person of Christ crucified. He is a scandalous intentional power-center, owing to the divine intentional power characteristic of him. Dods comments on this offensive power:

> The Cross [of Jesus] seemed to [the people around him] a confession of weakness. They sought a demonstration that the power of God was in Christ, and they were pointed to the Cross. But to them the Cross was a stumbling block they could not get over. And yet in it was the whole power of God for the salvation of the world. All the power that dwells in God to draw men out of sin to holiness and to himself was actually in the Cross. For the power of God that is required to draw men to himself is not power to alter the course of rivers or change the site of mountains, but power to sympathize, to make men's sorrows His own, to sacrifice self, to give all for the needs of His creatures. To them that believe in the God there revealed, the Cross is the power of God. It is [the] love of God.[5]

God's righteous love, then, is an intentional power for redemptive action, but it is a scandalous power alien to the human power of dominating control. Its scandal comes from God and God's Son who enact, for human benefit, the power of self-sacrificial love instead of domination toward wayward humans. That power is no mere supplement to characteristic human power; it is an alternative to it. As a result, it is scandalous for humans set on their own characteristic power.

The divine scandal in Christ is not just the surprise that God is self-sacrificial in righteous love toward undeserving humans. It goes deeper. We humans do not fully, or even adequately, understand the self-sacrificial love of God in Christ crucified, particularly with regard to the severity of what Christ experienced. H. R. Mackintosh explains:

> The great reason why we fail to understand Calvary is not merely that we are not profound enough; it is that we are not good enough. It is because we are such strangers to sacrifice that God's sacrifice leaves us bewildered. It is because we love so little that his love is mysterious. We have never forgiven anybody at such a cost as his. We have never taken the initiative in putting a quarrel right with

---

[5] Dods, *The First Epistle to the Corinthians*, pp. 55–56.

his kind of unreserved willingness to suffer. It is our unlikeness to God that hangs as an obscuring screen impeding our view, and we see the Atonement [in Christ crucified] so often through the frosted glass of our own lovelessness.[6]

Our inadequate understanding of Christ crucified stems from our being strangers to lived self-sacrifice out of righteous *agapē*. Even if we have a sketchy intellectual understanding, we lack a felt, or experienced, understanding that bears on our will and affections.

We can focus the redemptive scandal in Christ crucified. Why would God appear to add insult to injury in allowing for Jesus's tortured cry of dereliction on the cross? According to Mark's Gospel: "At three o'clock Jesus cried out with a loud voice, 'Eloi, Eloi, lema sabachthani?' which means, 'My God, my God, why have you forsaken me?'" (Mark 15:34; cf. Matt. 27:46). Why is God's redemptive high point so severe for Christ, leading to what looks like (at least felt) child abandonment, if only for a time? One might invoke a need for divine self-identification with humans in their suffering, but this is not a full explanation.

Why would God allow in the first place for the severity of human experience that calls for a needed divine response to felt abandonment? We lack not only a full but also a satisfactory answer to this question. As a result, our best explanation of the suffering of the crucified Christ, and of many other humans, is at best fragmentary and less than satisfactory.[7] Paul, we have seen, was not surprised or discouraged by this kind of cognitive limitation and deficiency (1 Cor. 13:9–12).

The explanatory value of the Christian message is not just incomplete but notably unsatisfactory in various areas. The area of

---

[6] H. R. Mackintosh, "An Indisputable Argument," in Mackintosh, *Sermons* (Edinburgh: T&T Clark, 1938), pp. 176–77. Cf. T. R. Glover, *The Jesus of History* (London: Association Press, 1917), p. 182.

[7] For discussion of this matter in relation to the absence of a full theodicy, see Moser, *Understanding Religious Experience*, ch. 8; and Moser, "Theodicy Incarnate."

extreme unjust suffering is particularly difficult for any quest for a satisfactory explanation. One thus will be offended, or scandalized, in expecting God to supply a worldview with impeccable explanatory value. This consideration bears on evidence and epistemology regarding God. It suggests that the Christian message is not ultimately an impeccable explanation, at least for now; nor does this message figure in a larger worldview that now yields an impeccable explanation of relevant data.

Dods comments on Paul's approach: "If we believe in Christianity because it approves itself to our judgment as the best solution of the problems of life, that is well; but still, if that be all that draws us to Christ, our faith stands in the wisdom of men rather than in the power of God .... Have we allowed the Cross of Christ to make its peculiar impression upon us?"[8] From Paul's perspective, we diminish the power of Christ crucified when we put its focus on its intellectual payoff for us. Instead, its focus is on an interpersonal place for our meeting a scandalous personal God of righteous self-sacrificial *agapē* even for ungodly enemies.

Paul's message of good news is more about God's meeting us self-sacrificially, aimed at our reciprocal self-sacrifice, than about our impeccably or even unsurpassably explaining the world with a claim to God's reality. A perspective that neglects this fact distorts the character of Paul's Christian message of good news. Such a perspective, even under the name of "Christian theology" or "Christian philosophy," can get in the way of one's meeting and knowing God. It can obstruct with arguments and principles a direct self-manifestation of God in moral experience, such as conscience, thereby creating human distance from God's unique power and thus from God. In the end, God's interpersonal power of righteousness does the convicting and converting of receptive people; arguments and principles lack the needed intentional power. Uses of Paul's thought

---

[8] Dods, *The First Epistle to the Corinthians*, p. 60.

in Christian apologetics, however well-intentioned, sometimes neglect this important consideration.

Paul saw a crucial role for power from Christ crucified in the evidential basis of faith in God, that is, the basis in the redemptive power of God. Given that Paul understands the redemptive power of God in terms of Christ crucified, he has in mind faith resting on (the evidence from) the power of Christ crucified, that is, the power of a scandalous intentional agent who is self-sacrificial for others. The key foundational evidence and power are in a person and not in an idea or a principle; they thus are irreducible to the ideas and principles of a human theology or philosophy. As a result, Paul contrasts this evidence and power with "human wisdom," including the wisdom from human philosophy. According to Paul, God seeks to be known, and to have divine reality known, on the basis of God's unique personal power, and not mainly by divine theoretical (e.g., explanatory) effects or benefits. This stems from the fact that God's unique power, in Paul's thinking, is inherently personal and redemptive toward humans.

Paul offers a key reason for his personalist approach to evidence for God as follows: "Since, in the wisdom of God, the world did not know God through [its] wisdom, God decided, through the foolishness of our proclamation, to save those who believe" (1 Cor. 1:21). Paul notes that the world did not "know God" through its wisdom, including the wisdom of the world's philosophers. His understanding of "knowing God," we have noted, goes beyond mere factual knowledge that God exists, the latter knowledge being compatible with hating God. Paul has in mind something more directly interpersonal, along the lines of what has come to be called "I–Thou" knowledge of God. Such knowledge requires direct acquaintance or encounter with the person known, even if the knowledge is partial rather than comprehensive.

The direct acquaintance with God stems from what Paul, following the book of Isaiah, considers to be God's "self-manifestation" to humans (Rom. 10:20). God sets distinctive epistemic standards for humans on the basis of God's unique righteous character of self-sacrificial love. Seeking redemptive self-manifestation to humans, God self-reveals the divine moral character to receptive humans in their moral experience, including conscience. Paul finds this self-manifestation in two areas, one public and the other inward. The public area is the historical episode of the crucified Christ (1 Cor. 1:18, 24, 2:2); the inward area is a person's current moral experience, in a person's "heart," or volitional center (Rom 5:5; cf. Rom. 8:14–16).

Divine self-manifestation, in Paul's understanding, fits with the biblical theme of God as sui generis and thus as swearing by God alone instead of by some lesser figure or reality. This kind of self-evidencing and self-authenticating on God's part would invite people to adjust to divine evidence rather than to have God conform to human expectations for divine evidence. This order of priority is offensive for many inquirers, particularly those who put human expectations first. It is, however, God's cognitive reversal, according to Paul, and it aims to meet real human needs.

P. T. Forsyth has commented on the inward divine experience as irreducibly interpersonal:

> Our experience of Christ is quite different from our experience of an objective world. Our moral sense of an agent, and that agent a Redeemer, is a different thing from the inference or postulate of an objective world behind sense to account for our impressions. That may be a cause but this is a Creator. When the objective announces itself as a heart and will, which not only chooses, or influences, me, but saves me, then the response of my active will, of myself as a person, is a different thing from the common sense that instinctively places an object behind passive sensation. The relation of a cause to a sensation is not analogous to the relation of a person to a person.[9]

---

[9] P. T. Forsyth, *Positive Preaching and the Modern Mind*, 2nd ed. (London: Independent Press, 1909), pp. 47–48.

As an intentional agent seeking human redemption, God seeks uncoerced, voluntary conviction of humans toward cooperation with God's self-manifested will.

The experienced content of the divine redemptive effort is not presented as passive or static. Instead, it is presented as active and goal-directed in human moral experience, including conscience, at least if humans do not ignore or suppress their conscience. It indicates an active intentional agent at work in conscience, aiming to convict humans in the direction of God's character and will and away from anti-God ways. It thus includes intentional leading toward God's moral character, as Paul says: "All who are led by the Spirit of God are children of God" (Rom. 8:14; cf. Rom. 9:1; 2 Cor. 1:12).[10]

Forsyth remarks on a typical depersonalizing approach to human knowledge of God: "The common vice of [many] imperfect forms of religion is that they treat God as an *object* of knowledge more or less theoretic, instead of treating him as the *subject* of a knowledge, which is inceptive and creative [and] searching."[11] The same vice applies to many forms of philosophy, including Christian philosophy. It is serious because it neglects God's inherently intentional, and thus personal, character, as self-manifested and actively goal-directed toward humans. A correction would acknowledge that divine evidence and wisdom for humans are ultimately self-revealed by God and not argued to by humans (1 Cor. 2:9–10, 12–13). A correction also would include a distinctive interpersonal and active role for God in human moral experience, such as the experience of conscience.

In divine self-revelation, according to Paul, we have a basis for a sharp contrast between an undeserved gift and a source of human self-boasting. So, he asks: "What do you have that you did not receive?

---

[10] For more on the inward experience of divine conviction, see Moser, *The God Relationship*, ch. 5; Moser, *Understanding Religious Experience*, chs. 7–8; and Moser, "Responsive Phenomenology of God," *Expository Times* 132 (2021), 426–35. See also Thomas Erskine, "The Purpose of God," in Erskine, *The Spiritual Order*, 2nd ed. (Edinburgh: Edmonton and Douglas, 1876), pp. 47–75.

[11] P. T. Forsyth, *The Principle of Authority* (London: Hodder and Stoughton, 1913), p. 151.

And if you received it, why do you boast as if it were not a gift?" (1 Cor. 4:7). His questions concern a range of gifts from God, including an evidential gift of the experienced power of righteous *agapē* in divine self-manifestation. This is cognitive grace at work in human experience.

Much philosophy diminishes the primary role of divine self-revelation and personal power in God's relating to humans. It does so by assuming a need for a human contribution to evidence that leads to human boasting in something other than God and God's self-revelation (1 Cor 1:28–29, 31, 3:21). Such boasting yields factions of the kind seen widely in religion, theology, and philosophy. Many theorists, however, favor such a human contribution over the offense of a redemptive gift from God that removes human self-credit and boasting. God, according to Paul, prefers to offer a gift of self-revelation in order to shame the wise and powerful among humans (1 Cor. 1:27). The shaming is a redemptive challenge to acknowledge the inferiority of human wisdom and moral standing to God's wisdom and moral standing (1 Cor. 1:25, 31).

The epistemological scandal is that God's ultimate evidence for self-revelation to humans does not rely on human arguments or any other source of human self-boasting or self-credit. The relevant evidence from God's self-revelation removes the basis for human self-credit and thus offends humans who tend to self-boast. This is not a ground for the monergism of Calvinism, because it allows for the role of a voluntary and responsible human will in receiving God's gift. (See Chapter 5 on the voluntary human role in this connection.) The latter role concerns the reception of a gift, and it does not entail earning or meriting the gift. As a result, one cannot take credit for the gift's being offered to one, and it would be perverse indeed to take credit for merely receiving an undeserved gift that is offered without human merit. A divine gift of self-revelation thus can leave humans responsible for receiving the gift in the gracious manner intended by God.

C. K. Barrett has commented on the scandal posed by divine self-revelation: "Religious egocentricity will inevitably find *Christ crucified... a scandal* (something that trips people up), for in the cross God does precisely the opposite of what he is expected to do; the intellectual egocentricity of wisdom-seeking Gentiles finds the same theme *folly*, because incarnation, crystallized in crucifixion, means not that man has speculated his way up to God but that God has come down to man where man is."[12] Speculating "our way up to God" might include our arguing our way up to God, as some philosophers and theologians have been known to try. Paul offers a contrary approach on the ground that God takes the initiative and draws near in self-manifestation to receptive humans (Rom. 10:6–8). Even so, the relevant evidence from God does not aim to coerce human wills; it is rejectable by humans. This feature is typical of a gift offered to humans, and the presence of an undeserved divine gift removes a basis for human self-credit. Such countering of human pride creates an opportunity for yielding to God with due humility and teachableness. It opposes the "intellectual egocentricity" that easily takes credit where human credit is not due.

A relevant problem stems from an observation of Cicero on the arguments used by Stoic philosophers: "Their meagre little syllogisms are mere pin-pricks; they may convince the intellect, but they cannot convert the heart, and the hearer goes away no better than he came."[13] In contrast, interpersonal evidence from an intentional agent's self-manifestation can convict and convert a person, without coercion. It can be thus effective in manifesting a moral character that sets a contrasting standard in a person's felt experience, thereby challenging that person at a level of moral depth. This can occur in conscience, where the power of moral conviction is widely experienced by humans. Divine character-manifestation, then, can be more effective than arguments for conviction and conversion.

---

[12] C. K. Barrett, *A Commentary on the First Epistle to the Corinthians* (New York: Harper and Row, 1968), p. 55.

[13] Cicero, *De Finibus Bonorum et Malorum*, trans. H. Rackham, Loeb Classical Library (Cambridge, MA: Harvard University Press, 1914), iv. 31.

We have noted Paul's suggestion that the interpersonal evidence from God is to be appropriated by dying to one's own selfish will in order to live for God. Paul's suggestion focuses on received and embraced lordship, offering a way of knowing God beyond "a human point of view" (2 Cor. 5:14–17). The appropriation of the scandalous evidence of Christ crucified is indicated in this remark: "The love of Christ urges us on, because we are convinced that one has died for all; therefore all have died. And he died for all, so that those who live might live no longer for themselves, but him who died." (2 Cor. 5:14–15).

The appropriation in reciprocity is Gethsemane-style obedience to God. It is the kind of obedience Paul cites as the motivation for Jesus himself in yielding to crucifixion by humans (Phil. 2:8; cf. Mark 14:36). Such appropriation fits with Jesus's injunction to "take up one's cross" (Matt. 16:24; Luke 9:23) and Paul's injunction to "put on the Lord Jesus Christ" (Rom. 13:14). In thus obeying, one shares and reflects the divine self-sacrificial power of the crucified Christ, where divine "power is made perfect in [human] weakness" (2 Cor 12:9). Paul thus thinks of Christians as co-crucified with Christ (see Gal 2:20, 6:14; 2 Cor 4:10). So, the appropriation of the scandalous evidence is itself Christ-shaped in relying on *imitatio Christi*, which in turn is *imitatio Dei*. This sacrificial appropriation makes the cross of Christ contemporaneous with the life of a disciple, rather than a mere historical artifact. Christ then becomes contemporaneous rather than just an artifact of history.

Faith in God as self-sacrificial appropriation of divine evidence fits with the interpersonal nature of that evidence on offer. Forsyth remarks: "As Revelation is God disposing of his personality to us in grace, faith, if we are to answer in kind, can only answer by disposing of our personality to God. We do not respond according to an irresistible law of our nature, but according to a free choice of our will."[14] So, the process, as noted, is not coercive. It does demand, however, a full

---

[14] Forsyth, *The Principle of Authority*, p. 163.

personal commitment as a life-priority, and that commitment, according to Paul, includes self-sacrificial reciprocity with God. So, it does not allow for mere intellectual acceptance, as it calls for sincere volitional resolve in sharing in divine redemptive goodness, including in dying and rising with Christ. In this regard, it is irreducibly interpersonal, in response to irreducible personal evidence. The process is person-forming and character-defining in a manner more challenging than a mere intellectual commitment.

The evidence in question does not leave a recipient with wishful thinking. Leander Keck explains Paul's position: "Those who believe the word of the cross know it as both the power of God and the wisdom of God. How will they know this? In a word, they have experienced the rectitude of God as rectification, the holiness of God as sanctification and the power of God as redemption because in believing the word of the cross they know that God made Christ 'our wisdom, our righteousness and sanctification and redemption', as 1 Corinthians 1:30 puts it."[15] It would be more accurate to speak of those who believe in the God of the word of the cross, because merely believing a word can be just intellectual and not receptive of divine power.

A person's actual experience of divine rectitude (or goodness) would include the experience of God's righteous *agapē*, as noted in connection with Romans 5:5, and this includes divine forgiveness. This experience, when it attracts human cooperation, is interpersonal in a way that undermines the parading of it as a mere commodity for human exploitation. H. Wheeler Robinson has characterized the relevant experience of God's Spirit as aiming to "reinforce the voice of conscience, to awaken the slumbering spark of higher aspiration into a clear flame, to bear with us the shame of our broken vow and frequent fall."[16] He sees in this "fellowship" the *kenōsis* of God's

---

[15] Leander Keck, "Biblical Preaching as Divine Wisdom," in *A New Look at Preaching*, ed. John Burke (Wilmington, DE: Michael Glazier, 1983), p. 153.

[16] H. Wheeler Robinson, *Redemption and Revelation* (New York: Harper, 1942), p. 294; cf. p. 292.

Spirit. That feature fits well with Paul's theme of the self-sacrifice of God in righteous redemption.

RESURRECTION THROUGH SELF-SACRIFICE

We should consider, in conclusion, why the previous perspective from Paul on distinctively Christian evidence and wisdom in terms of reciprocal self-sacrifice lacks prominence in much writing on Paul and redemption. The answer is that a certain theological distortion characterizes much Christian theology, including much interpretation of Paul. We may call it "resurrectionitis." It values resurrection results without the due valuing of the moral character and power of the crucified, self-sacrificial Christ who was resurrected in vindication by God.

Resurrectionitis focuses on triumphal power, including triumphal intellectual power, without due focus on the self-sacrificial power of the crucified Christ. It neglects the cruciform one who was raised by God in approval and vindication of his self-sacrificial moral character before God. So, Paul's main problem at Corinth is still with us. The antidote has its source in the scandalous but impeccable moral character of Christ, including Gethsemane obedience to God's command to show self-sacrificial righteous *agapē* to God's enemies, including typical humans. It counters the boasting and pride characteristic of triumphal human power, including intellectual power, while it manifests, in reciprocity, God's self-sacrificial righteous power instead.

The resurrection of Jesus is the divine vindication or approval of the crucified self-sacrificial Christ. It cannot be properly understood without the Christ whose Gethsemane obedience to God led to his crucifixion and death. Resurrection then, as noted by Georges Casalis, "is not a victory over the cross; it is the victory of the cross.... The reason why the cross is a victory is that it has opened a breach, once for all, in the prison wall of the selfish will to power."[17] This cross-

---

[17] Georges Casalis, "Jesus: Neither Abject Lord nor Heavenly Monarch," in *Faces of Jesus*, ed. Jose Bonino (Maryknoll, NY: Orbis Books, 1984), pp. 75, 74.

centered, self-sacrificial understanding of resurrection counters what Douglas John Hall calls "resurrectionism," that is, "a blend of cultic-folkloric heroism, New World optimism, and religious triumphalism."[18] Resurrectionitis as just characterized can be motivated by such resurrectionism, to the detriment of Paul's gospel of divine self-sacrifice.

Paul's gospel, by his own understanding, ceases to be authentic if it omits the central role of Christ crucified. Keck observes: "For Paul, the gospel does not merely have its origin in the event which the cross epitomizes, but has its permanent criterion and center in the cross, so that the word of the cross is the means by which that event reaches hearers as a revelation [from God] which redeems."[19] If, for explicit clarification, we replace "the cross" here with "Christ crucified," we have an important lesson that guards against the corrosive effects of resurrectionitis. It counsels against removing Christ crucified from our thinking as we talk of divine resurrection. It thereby keeps the self-sacrificial Gethsemane obedience of Christ, and in turn of his disciples, front and center in understanding and responding to Paul's gospel of divine self-sacrifice. In doing so, it safeguards the divine power available to humans from its many counterfeits, including intellectual triumphalism in theology, philosophy, and elsewhere.

Resurrectionitis is an old problem among Christians, including Christian intellectuals. We find it in the earliest church at Corinth, founded by Paul himself. It led to Paul's clear reminder to the Corinthian Christians: "I decided to know nothing among you except Jesus Christ, and him crucified" (1 Cor. 2:2). Paul, we have noted, had in mind the Christ raised from the dead by God, but his point is that this Christ is inextricably the crucified Christ. Omitting the crucified Christ leaves no one worthy of vindication in resurrection by God, and it thus drains resurrection of its moral power and glory.

---

[18] Douglas John Hall, *Professing the Faith* (Minneapolis, MN: Fortress Press, 1993), p. 96.
[19] Keck, "Biblical Preaching as Divine Wisdom," p. 147.

Resurrection then becomes something morally deficient, and it invites the infamous moral problems haunting the earliest church at Corinth, complete with intellectual and religious factions and corrosive sexual immorality.

Ernst Käsemann gets Paul right: "By declaring that he had 'decided to know nothing among you except Jesus Christ and him crucified' (1 Cor. 2:2), Paul emphasizes that the core of his doctrine of resurrection remains the cross. The point is that the resurrection is one aspect of the message of the cross, not that the cross is simply one chapter in a book of resurrection dogmatics."[20] Käsemann adds: "Christian existence thrives only under the cross. If it breaks away from that place, even by a very little, if it is wearing a halo that keeps the shadow from being seen, then that life is not Christian.... We can remain under the power of the resurrection, and in the real hope of being ourselves raised again, only when the crucified Christ rules over us and is glorified through us."[21] The issue, then, is really about which of the many alleged christs in circulation is actually one's Lord.

Paul invokes the relevance of lordship in announcing: "We do not proclaim ourselves; we proclaim Jesus Christ as Lord and ourselves as your slaves for Jesus's sake" (2 Cor. 4:5).[22] Of course, Paul has in mind the crucified Jesus Christ as Lord, the same Lord raised by God from death. So, a choice remains to be made about lordship, by each person able to inquire, inside or outside theology and philosophy. This choice rarely emerges clearly in theology and philosophy as commonly practiced, but its role is central in Paul's ministry and gospel.

---

[20] Ernst Käsemann, "For and Against a Theology of Resurrection," in Käsemann, *Jesus Means Freedom*, trans. Frank Clarke (London: SCM Press, 1969), pp. 67–68. For a defense of the "priority" of the cross relative to resurrection in Paul's thought, see Michael J. Gorman, "Cruciform or Resurrectiform?," in Gorman, *Participating in Christ* (Grand Rapids, MI: Baker Academic, 2019), pp. 53–76. I prefer talk of "mutual cruciality" to talk of "priority," regarding the relation of the cross and the resurrection.

[21] Käsemann, "For and Against a Theology of Resurrection," pp. 71–72.

[22] On the relevance of lordship, see Timothy Savage, *Power through Weakness*, SNTSMS (Cambridge: Cambridge University Press, 1996), pp. 154–57.

If our preferred Christ is not the crucified Christ of divine righteous self-sacrifice, according to Paul, we do not have God's approved Christ or God's corresponding resurrection power. We do not then have the genuine Christian article. The reason is clear: Divine power for humans is not in human triumph but in human self-surrender to and cooperation with God's redemptive power in the crucified, self-sacrificial Christ. Resurrectionitis, then, is a counterfeit of Christian truth. Its god is not the God and Father of the crucified Christ. It rests on misplaced human self-assertion over divine redemptive power. Its antidote, according to Paul's message, is in conforming, through reciprocity, to the divine redemptive power it diminishes for the sake of misplaced human self-assertion. Humans are themselves responsible for discerning and embracing the curative power needed, to the exclusion of contrary powers.

Divine power is not adequately captured or appropriated by our intellectual abilities to explain, question, and solve problems. These abilities are, at their very best, fragmentary, as our limits in accounting for unjust suffering, including that of the crucified Christ, show clearly. These limits undermine any boasting in Christian theology or philosophy as offering a satisfactory account of the overall human predicament. We lack such an account if the latter requires a satisfactory account of the unjust suffering among us. At best, as Paul observes, we "know in part" and "see through a lens dimly." Candor in the face of unjust suffering makes this lesson indisputable.

Where do our obvious intellectual and explanatory limits leave Christian theology and philosophy? In fragments, in our best scenario. Even so, those fragments do not block or undermine our meeting God in scandalous, self-sacrificial divine power, the signature power of Christ crucified. They do not defeat the unique evidence from divine self-manifestation in human moral experience, including conscience. God's salient power and self-authentication can emerge in our experience without our having a satisfactory explanation of our world at large. So, God can work in and around our intellectual fragments, even redemptively. Paul acknowledges as much, with candor.

In our fragments, we lack an adequate base to approach God (or humans) with human triumph, whether intellectual or otherwise. Instead, we should approach with due modesty and submission, as modeled by Christ in Gethsemane. We should approach God after and with the crucified Christ, the one who first approached God with Gethsemane submission to please God for our sake. In his Gethsemane mode and power, we approach God and appropriate God's unique power in an interpersonal, I–Thou meeting, not with our satisfactory theories. Christian theology and philosophy should make room for this vital meeting, and they should embrace without shame the redemptive significance of this meeting for humans, including theologians and philosophers. Paul's message suggests as much.

We now can see the bearing of Christ crucified on any Christian theology or philosophy worthy of the name. People can use the terms "Christian theology" and "Christian philosophy" however they wish (and their uses are wildly diverse), but if we want to accommodate the historic Christ, as Paul did, we face definite limits. We then face the scandalous limit of the crucified, self-sacrificial Christ in his supreme revelation of God. Christian theology and philosophy should not proceed without a defining anchor in the crucified Christ who reflects God. Otherwise, they fail to be Christian in their core message, at least by Paul's lights.

As an intentional agent, the crucified Christ manifests a moral character, distinctive actions, and teaching content. These set the core personal standard, a normative framework, for the central content and mode of Paul's theology, including his gospel of divine self-sacrifice. This is a standard for the lordship of the crucified Christ over all people, including Christian theologians and philosophers.

The standard of lordship includes two priorities for Christian theology and philosophy and their proponents. First, the personal standard in Christ gives priority to the divine redemptive wisdom that seeks the reconciliation of all humans to God in the crucified Christ, including their Gethsemane-based fellowship with God. Second, the personal standard in Christ gives priority to a mode of interpersonal exchange that manifests his self-sacrificial moral character for others. This should remove boasting and arrogance from the practice of Christian theology and philosophy.

We should say of philosophy what Käsemann has said of theology: "No theology that does not lead us to [the crucified] Jesus deserves the term 'Christian,' however interesting it may otherwise be. A theology ... that does not become a theology of the cross is bound to lead, as the Corinthian example shows, to wrong-headed enthusiasm."[23] No theology or philosophy, then, that does not point to the crucified Jesus Christ deserves the term "Christian." We can make this point without collapsing Christian philosophy into Christian theology, given the wider scope of philosophy.

Paul's antidote to counterfeits of the true God, we have suggested, is not a mere principle or idea but a person who seeks interpersonal meeting: the risen Christ crucified. This person, God's supreme representative and Son, offers humans a needed focus, guide, and Lord. His moral character offers needed moral character to the proponents of Christian theology and philosophy, courtesy of *imitatio Christi*.

Christian theology and philosophy under Christ's lordship will become Christ-shaped, in content and in mode. They thereby will lead to their Lord and thus to their God, if indirectly at times. As a result, they will be irreducible to any alternative not under Christ crucified. This lesson holds even if we lack a recipe that yields all of the ingredients of a Christian theology or philosophy. We can focus on the center, the risen Christ crucified under God, and allow his lordship, in an interpersonal I–Thou meeting, to lead any inquiry in matters of detail. This will sound foolish from the standpoint of much theology and philosophy, but Paul has prepared us for that scandalous result.

Paul's good news of divine self-sacrifice admits of adequate assessment only in the thick of human life with its moral challenges. It should be assessed for what it intends to be: good news of a divine

---

[23] Käsemann, "For and Against a Theology of Resurrection," p. 82.

self-sacrificial intervention to be received as life-giving through the reciprocity of human self-sacrifice to God. This would save us from wielding standards of assessment inhospitable to relevant available evidence for Paul's gospel. Much theology and much philosophy suffer from such an inhospitable approach to Paul's gospel, and we are now in a position to correct that defect.

A rough analogy helps our understanding. A lifeguard can open the swimming pool to me and present me with refreshing pool water. My swimming or learning to swim in the water, however, depends on my actively cooperative response. If I ignore or oppose the opportunity to get wet, I will not swim, leaving the lifeguard frustrated with me. The lifeguard's intention will come to fruition in my swimming only if I welcome the water and swim in it.

My actively cooperating with the lifeguard calls for my denying my own will to stay dry and comfortable at poolside as just a spectator. The lifeguard would self-sacrifice the comfort of the poolside to attract or teach me to swim, but that sacrifice could go unrequited by me. I could resolve to keep myself dry, despite the effort of the lifeguard. With some reconsideration and nudging, however, I could enter the water and follow the lifeguard's lead. I then could swim and even learn to prevent myself from drowning. My cooperation would enable me to reap the benefits of the lifeguard's sacrificial offer to guide my swimming.

Paul's gospel of divine self-sacrifice is no swimming pool, but he does take it to promise the "spiritual water" of life, to be drunk from Christ as God's supreme representative and Son (1 Cor. 10:4). If Christ is God's approved "lifeguard," our analogy is straightforward. God's redemptive self-sacrifice in Christ can be for my benefit, but it calls for my cooperative response in the reciprocity of self-sacrifice to God.

I can ignore or oppose Christ's example of sacrifice to God, choosing instead the apparent easiness of a selfish life, complete with excess wealth and worldly comforts. Upon serious moral reflection and the nudging of conscience, however, I could pivot toward the example of Christ crucified and risen. Paul calls it "turning to the

Lord" (2 Cor. 3:16), and he says that something then happens to a person. A "veil is removed," and "all of us, with unveiled faces, seeing the glory of the Lord as though reflected in a mirror, are being transformed into the same image from one degree of glory to another; for this comes from the Lord, the Spirit" (2 Cor. 3:18). We are then learning to swim in God's water, with a due learning curve, complete with struggles, doubts, and setbacks (2 Cor. 4:8–10).

The transformative evidence of God is present, according to Paul, as we cooperate with it in reciprocal self-sacrifice. We then experience the power of divine righteous *agapē* in our own lives, guiding our own actions suited to the divine sacrifice on offer. We then "walk in newness of life" now, "presenting ourselves to God as those who have been brought from death to life, and presenting our members to God as instruments of righteousness" (Rom. 6:4, 13). The power of divine inward resurrection arises in the midst of human suffering and dying, even now.

The veil mentioned by Paul blocks or obscures human apprehension of divine self-revelation, the basic evidence for divine reality and presence. It arises from a human intention, if implicit, to avoid or to reject divine evidence, including divine self-manifestation in self-sacrifice. Paul says that "only in Christ is it set aside" (2 Cor. 3:14). The veil results in what Paul calls the "veiled" or "hidden" character of his gospel for some people. He remarks: "Even if our gospel is veiled [κεκαλυμμένον], it is veiled to those who are perishing. In their case the god of this world has blinded the minds of the unbelievers, to keep them from seeing the light of the gospel of the glory of Christ, who is the image of God" (2 Cor. 4:3–4; cf. 1 Cor. 2:6–13). Paul has in mind a will at odds with God's will to redeem people through Christ's self-sacrificial love that seeks reciprocity in human self-sacrifice. God seeks redemption for all people, but some people dissent, if only through indifference.

Paul remarks that the good things given by God to humans are often not recognized by them as coming from God, because those things are to be spiritually discerned (πνευματικῶς ἀνακρίνεται,

1 Cor. 2:14; cf. Col. 1:9). This position suggests that the value of God's self-manifestation in human perception can be hidden from some humans owing to their failure to engage in spiritual discernment of a particular kind. Proper spiritual discernment relative to divine self-manifestation would include a careful response that allows its value to emerge for what it is: a divine intervention of primary value for one's life. Such discernment would become cooperative when joined with a sympathetic or agreeable human attitude. It thus would enable human experience of God to be what God intends it to be: redemptive in righteousness for humans. It would become redemptive as part of a cooperative human relationship with the God one encounters.

Paul links his idea of spiritual discernment to a notion of one's having the mind of Christ (νοῦν Χριστοῦ, 1 Cor. 2:16). The latter notion arises in a context concerned with redemptive self-sacrifice, both from God and in human response to God. Such sacrifice is at the heart of what Paul, among various New Testament writers, takes to be righteous *agapē*, and it separates divine love from various popular conceptions. We have seen that it is at the center of Paul's gospel of righteous redemption because it is at the center of God's character that is worthy of worship and trust.

We may wonder why the divine evidence in question is found in redemptive self-sacrifice modeled on Jesus Christ, given the difficulty of it all. Paul's understanding of God is that this is where God lives. In other words, this is who God is as inherently righteous in self-giving love for others, as seen in Christ. When God is in the temple, it is a temple of righteous self-sacrifice, because that characterizes God's spiritual and moral character and power. The evidence in question, then, reveals this distinctive divine character and power, climactically in Christ, and it does so better than any alternative. This is where Paul's explanation comes to an end: with who God in Christ is, spiritually, morally, and as worthy of worship and trust.

Paul leaves his audience with a definite, if discomforting, choice: sink or swim (2 Cor. 2:14–17). God's swim stroke is righteous self-sacrifice, as perfected in Christ and calling for human reciprocity.

This stroke is Paul's guide to life with God and that is resurrection life, life from death. Our own wills die into that life, or they do not enter at all (Phil. 3:10–11; on bodily resurrection, see 1 Cor. 15:36–37). On their own, our wills get in the way, blocking the stroke we need to receive divine power for righteous life with God. Jesus models this lesson, particularly in Gethsemane and at Calvary. Paul's gospel thus leaves us with a question: Are we willing to die in righteous self-sacrifice for the sake of life with God?

As an invitation to God's moral life, Paul leaves us with a portrait of the unmatched self-sacrificial love from Christ crucified, as portrayed in 1 Corinthians 13:

> If I understand all mysteries and all knowledge, and if I have all faith, so as to remove mountains, but do not have love, I am nothing. Love is patient; love is kind; love is not envious or boastful or arrogant or rude. It does not insist on its own way ... it does not rejoice in wrongdoing, but rejoices in the truth. We know only in part ... but when the complete comes, the partial will come to an end. Now we see in a mirror, dimly, but then we will see face to face. Now I know only in part; then I will know fully, even as I have been fully known. And now faith, hope, and love abide, these three; and the greatest of these is love.

Select Bibliography

Banks, Robert J. *Paul's Idea of Community*, 3rd ed. Grand Rapids, MI: Baker Academic, 2020.

Barclay, John M. G. *Obeying the Truth: Paul's Ethics in Galatians*. Edinburgh: T&T Clark, 1988.

Barclay, John M. G. *Paul and the Gift*. Grand Rapids, MI: Eerdmans, 2015.

Barrett, C. K. *Paul*. London: Continuum, 1994.

Barth, Markus, *Justification*, trans. A. M. Woodruff. Grand Rapids, MI: Eerdmans, 1971.

Beker, J. Christiaan. *The Triumph of God: The Essence of Paul's Thought*. Minneapolis, MN: Fortress Press, 1990.

Betz, Hans Dieter. *Galatians*, Hermeneia. Minneapolis, MN: Fortress Press, 1979.

Bird, Michael F. *The Saving Righteousness of God: Studies on Paul, Justification, and the New Perspective*. Milton Keynes: Paternoster, 2006.

Bird, Michael F. *An Anomalous Jew: Paul among Jews, Greeks, and Romans*. Grand Rapids, MI: Eerdmans, 2016.

Brown, Raymond E. *The Death of the Messiah*, ABRL, 2 vols. New York: Doubleday, 1994.

Bruce, F. F. *Commentary on Galatians*, NIGNTC. Grand Rapids, MI: Eerdmans, 1982.

Bultmann, Rudolf. *Theology of the New Testament*, trans. Kendrick Grobel, 2 vols. New York: Charles Scribner's Sons, 1955.

Burton, Ernest De Witt. *A Critical and Exegetical Commentary on the Epistle to the Galatians*, ICC. New York: Charles Scribner's Sons, 1920.

Campbell, Douglas. *The Deliverance of God: An Apocalyptic Rereading of Justification in Paul*. Grand Rapids, MI: Eerdmans, 2009.

Cousar, Charles B. *Galatians*, Interpretation. Louisville, KY: John Knox, 1982.

Cranfield, C. E. B. *A Critical and Exegetical Commentary on the Epistle to the Romans*, ICC, 2 vols. Edinburgh: T&T Clark, 1975.

Cranfield, C. E. B. "'The Works of the Law' in the Epistle to the Romans." *Journal for the Study of the New Testament* 43 (1991), 89–101.

Davies, W. D. *Paul and Rabbinic Judaism*, 2nd ed. London: SPCK, 1955.

Denney, James. *The Christian Doctrine of Reconciliation*. London: Hodder and Stoughton, 1917.

Duncan, George. *Epistle of Paul to the Galatians*, MNTC. New York: Harper, 1934.
Dunn, James D. G. *Jesus and the Spirit*. London: SCM Press, 1975.
Dunn, James D. G. *Romans*, WBC, 2 vols. Dallas, TX: Word Books, 1988.
Dunn, James D. G. *Commentary on the Epistle to the Galatians*. London: Black, 1993.
Dunn, James D. G. *The Theology of Paul the Apostle*. Grand Rapids, MI: Eerdmans, 1998.
Dunn, James D. G. "When Did the Understanding of Jesus' Death as an Atoning Sacrifice First Emerge?" In *Israel's God and Rebecca's Children*, eds. D. B. Capes et al., pp. 169–81. Waco, TX: Baylor University Press, 2007.
Dunn, James D. G. *The New Perspective on Paul*, rev. ed. Grand Rapids, MI: Eerdmans, 2008.
Dunn, James D. G. *Jesus, Paul, and the Gospels*. Grand Rapids, MI: Eerdmans, 2011.
Fee, Gordon D. *God's Empowering Presence: The Holy Spirit in the Letters of Paul*. Peabody, MA: Hendrickson, 1994.
Fee, Gordon D. *Paul's Letter to the Philippians*, NICNT. Grand Rapids, MI: Eerdmans, 1995.
Ferguson, Everett. "Spiritual Sacrifice in Early Christianity and its Environment." In *Aufstieg und Niedergang der römischen Welt*, II 23:2 (1979), pp. 1152–89.
Fitzmyer, Joseph A. *Romans*, AB. New York: Doubleday, 1993.
Fitzmyer, Joseph A. *First Corinthians*, AYB. New Haven, CT: Yale University Press, 2008.
Forsyth, Peter T. *The Work of Christ*. London: Hodder and Stoughton, 1910.
Forsyth, Peter T. *The Justification of God*. London: Duckworth, 1916.
Fredriksen, Paula. *Paul: The Pagans' Apostle*. New Haven, CT: Yale University Press, 2017.
Furnish, Victor Paul. *Theology and Ethics in Paul*. Nashville, TN: Abingdon Press, 1968.
Furnish, Victor Paul. *The Love Command in the New Testament*. Nashville, TN: Abingdon Press, 1972.
Furnish, Victor Paul. *II Corinthians*, AB. New York: Doubleday, 1984.
Gager, John G. *Reinventing Paul*. New York: Oxford University Press, 2000.
Garlington, Don. *Faith, Obedience, and Perseverance*, WUNT. Tübingen: Mohr Siebeck, 1994.
Gathercole, Simon. *Defending Substitution: An Essay on Atonement in Paul*, ASBT. Grand Rapids, MI: Baker Academic, 2015.
Gorman, Michael J. *Cruciformity: Paul's Narrative Spirituality of the Cross*. Grand Rapids, MI: Eerdmans, 2001.

Hafemann, Scott J. *Paul, Moses, and the History of Israel*, WUNT. Tübingen: Mohr Siebeck, 2005.

Hays, Richard. "Christology and Ethics in Galatians: The Law of Christ." *Catholic Biblical Quarterly* 49 (1987), 268–90.

Hooker, Morna D. "Interchange and Atonement." In *From Adam to Christ: Essays on Paul*, ed Morna D. Hooker, pp. 26–41. Cambridge: Cambridge University Press, 1990 [1978].

Hooker, Morna D. *Not Ashamed of the Gospel*. Carlisle: Paternoster, 1994.

Hooker, Morna D. "On Becoming the Righteousness of God: Another Look at 2 Cor. 5:21." *Novum Testamentum* 50 (2008), 358–75.

Hultgren, Arland J. *Paul's Letter to the Romans*. Grand Rapids, MI: Eerdmans, 2011.

Johnson, Luke T. *The Canonical Paul*, 2 vols. Grand Rapids, MI: Eerdmans, 2021.

Käsemann. Ernst. "Worship in Everyday Life: A Note on Romans 12." In *New Testament Questions of Today*, ed. Ernst Käsemann, trans. W. J. Montague, pp. 188–95. London: SCM Press, 1969 [1960].

Käsemann, Ernst. "'The Righteousness of God' in Paul." In *New Testament Questions of Today*, trans. W. J. Montague, pp. 168–82. London: SCM Press, 1969 [1961].

Käsemann, Ernst. *Commentary on Romans*, trans. G. W. Bromiley. Grand Rapids, MI: Eerdmans, 1980.

Keck, Leander. *Romans*, ANTC. Nashville, TN: Abingdon Press, 2005.

Keck, Leander. *Christ's First Theologian: The Shape of Paul's Thought*. Waco, TX: Baylor University Press, 2015.

Kim, Seyoon. *Paul and the New Perspective*. Grand Rapids, MI: Eerdmans, 2002.

Kirk, J. R. Daniel. *Unlocking Romans: Resurrection and the Justification of God*. Grand Rapids, MI: Eerdmans, 2008.

Levenson, Jon D. *The Death and Resurrection of the Beloved Son*. New Haven, CT: Yale University Press, 1993.

Longenecker, Richard. *Galatians*, WBC. Waco, TX: Word, 1990.

Lull, David John. *The Spirit in Galatia: Paul's Interpretation of Pneuma as Divine Power*. Chico, CA: Scholars Press, 1980.

Marshall, I. Howard. *Aspects of Atonement*. Milton Keynes: Paternoster, 2007.

Martin, Ralph P. *Reconciliation: A Study of Paul's Theology*. Atlanta, GA: John Knox Press, 1981.

Martin, Ralph P. *2 Corinthians*, WBC. Waco, TX: Word Books, 1986.

Martyn, J. Louis. *Galatians*, AB. New York: Doubleday, 1997.

Martyn, J. Louis. "*Nomos* plus Genitive Noun in Paul." In *Early Christianity and Classical Culture: Comparative Studies in Honor of Abraham J. Malherbe*, ed. John T. Fitzgerald, pp. 575–87. Leiden: Brill, 2003.

Meyer, Paul W. "Romans 10:4 and the 'End' of the Law." In *The Divine Helmsman*, eds. J. L. Crenshaw and Samuel Sandmel, pp. 59–78. New York: KTAV, 1980.

Moule, C. F. D. "Sanctuary and Sacrifice in the Church of the New Testament." *Journal of Theological Studies* 1 (1950), 29–41.

Moule, C. F. D. "The Sacrifice of Christ." In Moule, *Forgiveness and Reconciliation*, pp. 135–76. London: SPCK, 1998 [1956].

Moule, C. F. D. "The Sacrifice of the People of God." In Moule, *Essays in New Testament Interpretation*, pp. 287–97. Cambridge: Cambridge University Press, 1982 [1962].

Moule, C. F. D. "Jesus, Judaism, and Paul." In *Tradition and Interpretation in the New Testament*, eds. Gerald Hawthorne and Otto Betz, pp. 43–52. Tübingen: Mohr Siebeck, 1987.

Peterson, David. "Worship and Ethics in Romans 12." *Tyndale Bulletin* 44 (1993), 271–88.

Rabens, Volker. *The Holy Spirit and Ethics in Paul*, 2nd ed. Minneapolis, MN: Fortress Press, 2014.

Räisänen, Heikki. *Paul and the Law*, WUNT. Tübingen: Mohr Siebeck, 1983.

Ridderbos, Herman. *Paul: An Outline of his Theology*, trans. J. R. De Witt. Grand Rapids, MI: Eerdmans, 1975.

Sampley, J. Paul. *Pauline Partnership in Christ*. Philadelphia: Fortress Press, 1980.

Sanders, E. P. *Paul and Palestinian Judaism*. Philadelphia, PA: Fortress Press, 1977.

Sanders, E. P. *Paul, the Law, and the Jewish People*. Minneapolis, MN: Fortress Press, 1983.

Sanders, E. P. *Paul*. Oxford: Oxford University Press, 1991.

Schnabel, Eckhard J. "Repentance in Paul's Letters." *Novum Testamentum* 57 (2015), 159–86.

Schreiner, Thomas. *Romans*, BECNT. Grand Rapids, MI: Baker Academic, 1998.

Segal, Alan F. *Paul the Convert*. New Haven, CT: Yale University Press, 1990.

Stanton, Graham. "The Law of Moses and the Law of Christ." In *Paul and the Mosaic Law*, ed. James D. G. Dunn, WUNT, pp 99–116. Tübingen: Mohr Siebeck, 1996.

Tannehill, Robert C. *Dying and Rising with Christ*, BZNW. Berlin: Töpelmann, 1966.

Tannehill, Robert C. "Participation in Christ." In Tannehill, *The Shape of the Gospel*, pp. 223–37. Eugene, OR: Cascade Books, 2007.

Taylor, Vincent. "A Great Text Reconsidered [Romans 3:25]." In Taylor, *New Testament Essays*, pp. 127–39. London: Epworth Press, 1970 [1939].

Taylor, Vincent. *The Cross of Christ*. London: Macmillan, 1956.

Taylor, Vincent. *The Atonement in New Testament Teaching*, 3rd ed. London: Epworth Press, 1958.

Thompson, Michael B. *Clothed with Christ: The Example and Teaching of Jesus in Romans 12–15*, JSNTSS. London: Sheffield Academic Press, 1991.

Thrall, Margaret E. "Christ Crucified or Second Adam? A Christological Debate between Paul and the Corinthians." In *Christ and Spirit in the New Testament*, eds. Barnabas Lindars and Stephen S. Smalley, pp. 143–56. Cambridge: Cambridge University Press, 1973.

Thrall, Margaret E. "Salvation Proclaimed: 2 Corinthians 5:18–21: Reconciliation with God." *Expository Times* 93 (1982), 227–32.

Thrall, Margaret E. *A Critical and Exegetical Commentary on the Second Epistle to the Corinthians*, ICC, 2 vols. London: T&T Clark, 1994.

Tobin, Thomas H. *Paul's Rhetoric in Contexts*. Peabody, MA: Hendrickson, 2004.

Travis, Stephen H. *Christ and the Judgement of God*. Peabody, MA: Hendrickson, 2008.

Wenham, David. *Paul: Follower of Jesus or Founder of Christianity?* Grand Rapids, MI: Eerdmans, 1995.

Westerholm, Stephen. *Perspectives Old and New on Paul*. Grand Rapids: Eerdmans, 2004.

Williams, Sam K. "The 'Righteousness of God' in Romans." *Journal of Biblical Literature* 99 (1980), 241–90.

Williams, Sam K. *Galatians*, ANTC. Nashville, TN: Abingdon Press, 1997.

Young, Frances. *Sacrifice and the Death of Christ*. Philadelphia: Westminster Press, 1975.

Young, Frances. *The Use of Sacrificial Ideas in Greek Christian Writers from the New Testament to John Chrysostom*, PM. Cambridge, MA: Philadelphia Patristic Foundation, 1979.

Index

Abba, 12, 76, 116, 181, 193
Abraham, 5, 9, 29, 34–37, 55–56, 64–65, 67, 95, 103, 123, 152, 156, 158, 163, 167–69, 171–72, 176, 180
agapē, 12, 35, 42–43, 45, 50–61, 63, 65–67, 79, 105, 111–13, 190–91, 193–94, 196, 198–202, 204–6, 211–12, 216, 219–20, 227–28. *See* love
Allison, Jr., Dale C., 133
antinomianism, 60
apostles, 3, 75, 98
Aquinas, Thomas, 131
atonement, 11, 13, 22, 29, 97, 145, 153, 169, 198
Aulén, Gustaf, 57
authority, 66–67, 87, 89, 91, 103, 108, 125, 127, 131–34, 147, 200

Banks, Robert J., 41
Barclay, John M. G., 44, 63, 92, 118, 163–64
Barrett, C. K., 216
Barth, Karl, 59
Barth, Markus, 16, 21, 147
Bauckham, Richard, 146
Becker, Jürgen, 1
Beker, Christiaan, 2
Berkouwer, G. C., 161
Betz, Hans Dieter, 49
Bird, Michael F., 9, 104, 168
blood, 11, 17, 143, 153, 199
Bradley, Ian, 21
Brown, Raymond E., 1, 144
Bruce, F. F., 44
Buber, Martin, 55
Bultmann, Rudolf, 84, 110, 164, 175–76
Burton, Ernest De Witt, 44–45

Campbell, Douglas, 174
Casalis, Georges, 220
Catchpole, David, 145
Cerfaux, Lucien, 71
Christ, 2–6, 11–12, 14–16, 18, 20, 22, 24, 27, 29–32, 42–43, 46, 49–55, 58–62, 65, 67–70, 72–80, 82, 84–85, 87–104, 110–12, 114, 116–17, 131, 137, 140, 148, 151–53, 155, 161, 168, 173, 175, 180–82, 185–86, 189–91, 193, 196–99, 201, 203, 207–14, 216, 218–28. *See* Jesus
crucified, 69–70, 75, 77, 181, 189–90, 199, 209–14, 217–18, 220–26, 229
church, 3, 5, 32, 54, 78, 81, 201, 221
Cicero, 217
Clark, Kenneth W., 96
conscience, 101, 114, 138, 143, 205, 209, 212, 214–15, 217, 219, 223, 226
conviction, 71, 180, 193, 215, 217
cooperation, 9, 18–19, 46, 51, 56, 71–72, 78, 85, 96, 114, 118, 120–21, 143, 149–50, 189, 196, 215, 219, 223, 226
Corinthians, 16–17, 30, 93, 95, 99, 148, 159, 182, 208, 219, 229
Cousar, Charles B., 43
covenant, 11, 80, 94, 99, 101, 103
Cranfield, C. E. B., 14, 57, 83–85, 87, 91, 111, 139, 143, 155–60, 164, 170, 177
creation, 17, 32, 48, 58, 74, 102, 114–15, 189–92, 206
Cross of Christ, 212. *See* Christ crucified
curse, 29, 31, 34

Davies, W. D., 31, 133
death, 6, 9–18, 20, 24–25, 30, 33, 40, 52, 69, 73–79, 81, 84, 88–90, 93–94, 97, 99, 109, 119, 129, 140, 143–44, 146–47, 155, 166, 169, 182, 190, 198–200, 204, 209, 220, 222, 227, 229
of Christ, 12–13, 15
Deines, Roland, 83
Denney, James, 89
Dods, Marcus, 208–9, 212
Duncan, George, 44–45, 96
Dunn, James D. G., 11, 17, 23, 28, 44–45, 49–50, 63–64, 70, 83, 86, 89, 92, 98, 114, 152, 166, 170, 177
dying and rising, 17, 219

235

Eichrodt, Walther, 126
epistemology, 101–2, 186–87, 189, 191, 193–97, 201, 204–5, 207, 212
eschatology, 105, 109
Evans, C. Stephen, 125
evidence for God, 41, 71, 213
experience, 26, 40, 49, 52–53, 56, 59, 71, 78, 105, 109–11, 113, 116–17, 119–20, 124, 138, 143–44, 146–50, 160, 184, 191, 204, 207, 209, 211–12, 214–15, 217, 219, 223, 227–28
of God, 113, 149, 219
moral, 52, 114, 138, 143, 205, 207, 212, 214–15, 223
religious, 123

faith, 1–2, 5, 7, 9–11, 19, 22–23, 25–26, 28–29, 33–35, 37, 40, 42–46, 48–67, 69, 73–75, 77, 79, 81–83, 85–86, 89, 91–96, 100–2, 104, 107–9, 116, 118, 124, 143, 151–53, 155–58, 161–63, 165, 167–81, 183, 188–90, 193, 197–98, 200–1, 208, 212–13, 218, 229. *See* trust
family, 1, 93, 178, 199
Father, as God, 193. *See* Abba
fear, x, 35, 72, 104–5, 116, 121–22, 124–37, 139–47, 149–50, 164–66, 196, 199
Fee, Gordon, 23, 52, 164
fellowship, 4, 117, 196–99, 204, 219, 224
Ferguson, Everett, 31
Fitzmyer, Joseph A., 11, 13, 17, 23, 44, 90–91, 115, 133, 144, 166, 170, 177
flesh, 2, 33, 46, 50, 60, 66, 73, 75, 82, 87, 96, 100, 102, 115, 118, 160, 181, 193
forgiveness, 9, 20, 28, 30, 58, 71, 93, 136–37, 197–200, 219
Forsyth, Peter T., 12, 15, 89, 214–15, 218
Fout, Jason A., 124–25
Frances M. Young, 31
Fredriksen, Paula, 89
freedom, 18, 33, 58, 77, 90, 94, 97, 108, 114–15, 119, 156, 162, 166, 174, 179
fruit, 40, 46, 49–50, 54, 150, 157, 202
frustration, 33, 151, 156, 164–65, 185
Furnish, Victor Paul, 30, 43–44, 51, 57, 61, 84, 95, 98, 136, 154, 157, 159, 164
future, 70, 101, 106–7, 109, 111–12, 114–15, 117, 141, 144–46

Gager, John G., 6
Garlington, Don, 86
Gathercole, Simon, 15
Gentiles, 2–5, 10, 21–22, 29, 34, 39, 56, 62–63, 65–68, 84, 86, 89, 96, 98, 103, 152, 177, 180, 193, 217
Gethsemane, 35, 40, 76, 78, 143–45, 190, 193, 196, 204, 207, 218, 220–21, 224, 229
gift, 11, 18, 20, 22, 51, 63–64, 68, 76, 83, 97, 139, 153–54, 157–59, 161–62, 167, 169–71, 173, 186, 194, 196–98, 200–1, 204, 215–16
goodness, xi, 24, 26–28, 52, 57, 59, 71, 81, 106, 111, 114, 118–21, 124, 126–30, 132, 134, 136–37, 139, 142, 149–50, 153–54, 166, 168, 192, 195, 219
Gorman, Michael J., 44, 222
gospel, 1–7, 11, 13, 20–23, 25, 27, 32, 34, 41–42, 56, 65, 67, 70–71, 74, 81, 103–4, 122, 151–52, 155–56, 167, 172–74, 181, 184, 198, 208, 221–22, 224, 226–29
grace, 2–3, 11, 18–20, 33, 42–43, 45, 51, 56–58, 61, 63–65, 68, 76, 83–84, 95, 97, 137, 151–56, 158–59, 161, 163–66, 169–70, 172–75, 179, 181, 186, 196–97, 201, 204, 216, 218
Greeks, 10
guilt, 199

Hafemann, Scott J., 95
Hall, Douglas John, 221
Hays, Richard, 91
heart, 26, 28, 39–40, 51–53, 56, 67, 72, 77, 86, 96–97, 100, 117–18, 150, 156, 174, 214, 217, 228
Hengel, Martin, 83
history, 12, 19, 32–33, 99, 109, 218
holy, x, 2, 20, 23, 32, 81, 84
Holy Spirit, 22, 40, 50–51, 101, 111, 113, 131, 190, 195
Hooker, Morna D., 13, 16, 89, 182
hope, 32, 40, 48–49, 51–54, 101, 104–17, 120–22, 126, 138, 146, 148, 150, 190, 200, 222, 229
Hultgren, Arland J., 13, 50, 141
humility, 217

idolatry, 39, 78
imitation of Christ, 76

in Christ, 11, 14–16, 27, 29, 51–53, 58, 62, 74, 87–89, 93, 95, 97, 99, 102–3, 131, 152–53, 181, 189, 198, 208, 210, 224, 226, 228
Israel, 4, 32, 36–37, 62–64, 84, 93–95, 109, 119, 140–41, 159, 165, 170, 172, 177–78, 201

Jesus, 1–2, 4–6, 11–12, 16–18, 22, 24, 27–29, 40–43, 45, 49, 51–52, 58–59, 61–62, 67–71, 73–80, 87, 89, 96, 98, 100–1, 103, 105, 109, 112, 120, 133–34, 136–37, 139–50, 153, 155, 161, 169, 180–82, 186, 188–90, 192–94, 196–200, 203–4, 207–8, 210–11, 218, 220–22, 225, 228–29. *See* Christ
Jews, 5, 10, 21, 29, 63, 65–68, 70, 83, 86, 96, 103, 134, 152, 172, 185
Jindo, Y. Job, 125
John the Baptist, 140
Johnson, Luke Timothy, 2, 50, 182
Judaism, 64–65, 83, 173
judgment, 28, 30, 36–37, 70, 72, 98, 101, 127–28, 136–43, 155–56, 179, 187, 212
justification, 6, 28, 69, 82, 84, 94, 152, 155, 161, 181, 197, 199

Käsemann, Ernst, 8, 23–24, 52, 57, 90–92, 114, 156, 175–76, 222, 225
Keck, Leander, 21, 23, 53, 58, 87, 114, 162, 164, 219, 221
Kierkegaard, Søren, 109–10, 132
Kim, Seyoon, 170
kingdom of God, 140–41, 145
Kirk, J. R. Daniel, 69
knowledge of God, 134, 184, 186, 188, 190, 193, 195–96, 201, 203–4, 213, 215

law, 10, 18, 27, 29, 42, 48–50, 59–66, 79–95, 97–104, 119, 134, 152, 155, 158, 167, 169, 172–73, 180–81, 189, 218
  incarnate, 86
  Mosaic, 65, 87, 89–90, 94–95, 97, 103, 167, 169–70, 180, 182, 200
  of God, 42, 59–61, 65, 67, 79–82, 86, 92–93, 95, 99, 102–4
legalism, 65
Levenson, Jon D., 19, 36
Longenecker, Richard, 44

Lord, 2–6, 11, 16, 18, 23, 28, 30, 34–38, 40, 43, 51, 58, 68–69, 74, 76, 94–95, 98–99, 104, 119, 122, 125, 137, 145, 159, 189–90, 196, 198, 202–3, 218, 222, 225, 227
love, 12, 16, 22, 24, 27–28, 30, 35, 38, 40–46, 48–54, 58–61, 63, 71, 74, 79, 88–89, 92, 96–99, 101–5, 111–13, 116–21, 124, 126, 131, 135–37, 139–40, 142, 145, 148–50, 161, 166, 181, 188–93, 195, 197, 210, 213, 218, 227–29. *See* agapē
Lull, David John, 50

Mackintosh, H. R., 211
Marshall, I. Howard, 14–15, 20
Martin, Ralph P., 89, 95, 138, 154
Martyn, J. Louis, 44, 46, 54, 91–92, 162
Meier, John, 136
Messiah, 1, 5, 193. *See* Christ
Meyer, Paul W., 92
miracles, 49
mission, 1, 4–5, 41, 70, 72, 98, 112
missionary, 1, 7
Moberly, R. W. L., 125
Moltmann, Jürgen, 105, 108–10, 112–13, 147
Morris, Leon, 14
Moses, 36–37, 86, 90, 93–94, 119, 123, 159
Moule, C. F. D., 20–21, 61, 64, 75, 86, 154
mystery, 133, 191, 199

natural theology, 204–7
new life, 87, 90, 197, 204
Nicholson, Ernest W., 9
nomism, 80, 95, 97–98, 103
Nygren, Anders, 59

obedience, 2, 9, 16, 21, 24–25, 31, 33, 35–39, 43, 56, 58, 66–67, 73, 75–79, 83–84, 86, 89, 91–92, 102, 106, 118, 124–27, 135, 143–45, 148, 157, 162, 164–65, 167, 169, 173–74, 193, 198–201, 204–5, 218, 220–21. *See* cooperation
Old Testament, 31

participation, 75, 114, 143, 182
passion, 90
Passover, 31, 200
peace, 5, 46, 51–52, 68, 70, 166
Peterson, David G., 24, 178
philosophy, 195, 208, 212–13, 215–16, 221–26

Piper, John, 177
power, 2, 7, 9–10, 12, 19, 27, 33, 36, 40, 44, 46, 49–52, 55, 57–58, 62, 70, 73, 75–79, 81, 88–89, 94, 97, 101, 113, 117, 119–21, 126, 133, 147, 149, 151, 154–56, 158, 160, 162, 164–65, 167, 169, 172–73, 176, 178, 180–82, 184, 186, 188–91, 193, 196–98, 201–4, 207–9, 212, 216–21, 223–24, 227–28
prayer, 55, 145, 193
preaching, 3, 6, 22, 34
presence, 41, 52, 71, 109–10, 114, 129, 132, 135, 147, 160, 164, 196–97, 205, 217, 227
present, 7, 15, 18, 20, 25
prophet, 7, 38, 68
propitiation, 14, 21
purpose, divine, 62–63, 66, 84, 88, 151

Rabens, Volker, 159
Räisänen, Heikki, 90
reason, 54, 56, 63, 95, 106, 132, 149, 152, 171, 210, 213, 220, 223
reciprocity, ix, xi, 19–23, 28, 74, 104, 154, 181–82, 198, 218–20, 223, 226–28
reconciliation, 22, 32, 38, 42, 58, 67–71, 80, 89, 93–94, 97–98, 101, 106, 114, 120, 135–37, 139, 142–43, 145, 149–50, 152, 154, 179, 182, 185, 188, 195, 197–200, 224
redemption, 11–14, 17–22, 25–27, 30, 32–33, 35, 37, 39, 41–42, 51, 56, 65, 68, 74, 78, 85, 88, 96, 101, 104–5, 115, 117, 119, 121, 138, 140, 142, 150–53, 155–56, 158–59, 165–66, 169, 171, 175–81, 183–85, 187–88, 191, 197, 199–201, 203, 208, 215, 219–20, 227–28
Reiser, Marius, 140–41
repentance, xi, 26, 28, 57, 118, 136, 140–41, 154, 204
representation, 16
representative, 15–16, 31, 65, 74, 197–99, 209, 225–26
resurrection, 2, 6, 29, 69–70, 76–77, 79, 90, 109, 115, 140, 147–48, 190, 198, 220–21, 223, 227, 229
resurrectionism, 221
resurrectionitis, 220–21
revelation, 3–5, 61, 160, 215–16, 221, 224, 227
Ridderbos, Herman, 161, 173

righteousness, 1, 7–14, 16, 18–19, 21–22, 24–26, 28–30, 32–40, 42, 49, 51, 56–57, 59, 62, 64, 67–69, 71–75, 77–79, 82–84, 92–93, 97, 100, 104, 113, 118, 123–24, 136, 142, 145, 153–55, 157, 161, 163–64, 166–77, 180–82, 184, 189, 197, 199–201, 207, 212, 219, 227–28
Robinson, H. Wheeler, 70, 219
Robinson, N. H. G., 59
Rossé, Gérard, 147

sacrifice, 1, 11–12, 16, 20–25, 27–31, 33, 35, 41, 47, 71, 73–74, 76, 79–80, 97, 101–2, 104–5, 122, 124, 151, 153–54, 166–67, 169, 181–84, 198, 200, 210–12, 220–21, 223–28
  self, 1, 11–12, 20, 22–25, 27, 31, 42, 73–74, 80, 97, 102, 105–6, 124, 151, 166, 182–84, 198, 226–28
salvation, 1, 5–7, 37, 58, 72, 122, 141, 156, 164, 175–77, 183, 188, 210
Sampley, Paul J, 41
sanctification, 68, 219
Sanders, E. P., 50, 60, 64, 66, 71, 81–83, 85, 164
Schnabel, Eckhard J., 154
Schrader, Dylan, 131
Schreiner, Thomas R., 14, 83
science, 109
scripture, 5, 34, 56, 67, 152, 167
Segal, Alan F., 4
sin, 9–12, 14–15, 18, 20, 22, 25, 28–30, 62, 75, 77, 81, 84, 87, 89–90, 94, 97, 99–100, 123, 155, 167, 169, 174, 182, 210
Son of God, 2, 49–50, 57, 69, 96, 181, 188, 193
sources, 107
Spirit, 6, 12, 18, 28–29, 33, 46, 48–49, 51–53, 60, 62, 66, 68–70, 75, 80, 85, 87, 89–91, 94–95, 97, 99–100, 103, 111, 113, 115–20, 157, 159–60, 162, 180–81, 183, 186–88, 191–96, 198, 202, 204–7, 215, 219, 227
Stanton, Graham, 92
substitution, 15–16, 74
suffering, x, 16, 40, 51, 75–76, 79, 146, 185, 199, 211–12, 223, 227

Tannehill, Robert C., 75, 89, 162
Taylor, Vincent, 14, 19, 25, 29, 31, 72, 77

temple, 33, 40, 70, 195, 228
testimony, 207
theology, 33, 39, 41, 55, 69, 81, 147, 151, 193, 195, 204–5, 207, 212–13, 216, 220–26
Thielicke, Helmut, 148
Thompson, Michael B., 76
Thrall, Margaret, 89, 102, 104, 154
Tobin, Thomas H., 50
tradition, 31, 194
Travis, Stephen H., 36, 136, 143
trust, x–xii, 9–10, 29, 35–40, 55, 62, 65, 68, 75, 77–78, 92, 95, 100, 104, 118, 124, 147, 161, 163, 165, 171, 177, 179, 183, 198, 201, 205–7, 228. *See* faith

Villiers, Pieter G. R., 132–33
von Rad, Gerhard, 106, 124–25

Wenham, David, 77, 98
Westerholm, Stephen, 174
Williams, Sam K., 8, 179
wisdom, 7, 53, 68, 126, 186–88, 191, 197, 199, 201–4, 206, 208–9, 212–13, 215–17, 219–20, 224
witness, 116, 193, 195
worship, 20, 24, 35, 39, 138, 206–7, 228
wrath, 14, 136, 199
Wright, G. Ernest, 32

For EU product safety concerns, contact us at Calle de José Abascal, 56–1°,
28003 Madrid, Spain or eugpsr@cambridge.org.

www.ingramcontent.com/pod-product-compliance
Ingram Content Group UK Ltd.
Pitfield, Milton Keynes, MK11 3LW, UK
UKHW042017180425
457535UK00010B/97